INTERGROUP CONTACT THEORY

Intergroup contact theory has been one of the most influential theories in social psychology since it was first formulated by Gordon Allport in 1954. This volume highlights, via a critical lens, the most notable recent developments in the field, demonstrating its vitality and its capacity for reinvention and integration with a variety of seemingly distinct research areas.

In the last two decades, the research focus has been on the variables that explain why contact improves intergroup attitudes and when the contact–prejudice relationship is stronger. Current research highlights that contact is not a panacea for prejudice, but it can represent a useful tool that can contribute to the improvement of intergroup relations. The book includes coverage of a number of previously under-researched fields, which extend the full potential of contact theory within the personality, acculturation and developmental domains. The chapters also examine the methodological advances in the field and the applied implications of current research.

The book offers a rich picture of the state of the field and future directions for research that will be invaluable to students and scholars working in social psychology and related disciplines. It aims to provide fertile ground for the development of new, exciting and dynamic research ideas in the field of intergroup relations.

Loris Vezzali is Associate Professor at the University of Modena and Reggio Emilia, Italy, where he teaches Social and Group Psychology. His main research interests concern intergroup relations and, in particular, strategies for the reduction of explicit and implicit prejudice.

Sofia Stathi is Senior Lecturer in Psychology at the University of Greenwich, UK, where she teaches Social and Cultural Psychology and Social Cognition. Her research focuses mainly on intergroup relations, categorization processes and multiculturalism.

Current Issues in Social Psychology

Series Editor: Arjan E. R. Bos

Current Issues in Social Psychology is a series of edited books that reflect the state of the art of current and emerging topics of interest in basic and applied social psychology.

Each volume is tightly focused on a particular topic and consists of seven to ten chapters contributed by international experts. The editors of individual volumes are leading figures in their areas and provide an introductory overview.

Example topics include: self-esteem, evolutionary social psychology, minority groups, social neuroscience, cyberbullying and social stigma.

Self-Esteem
Edited by Virgil Zeigler-Hill

Social Conflict within and between Groups
Edited by Carsten K.W. De Dreu

Power and Identity
Edited by Denis Sindic, Manuela Barret and Rui Costa-Lopes

Cyberbullying: From Theory to Intervention
Edited by Trijntje Völlink, Francine Dehue and Conor Mc Guckin

Coping with Lack of Control in a Social World
Edited by Marcin Bukowski, Immo Fritsche, Ana Guinote and Mirosław Kofta

Intergroup Contact Theory: Recent Developments and Future Directions
Edited by Loris Vezzali and Sofia Stathi

INTERGROUP CONTACT THEORY

Recent Developments and
Future Directions

Edited by
Loris Vezzali and
Sofia Stathi

Routledge
Taylor & Francis Group

LONDON AND NEW YORK

First published 2017
by Routledge
2 Park Square, Milton Park, Abingdon, Oxon OX14 4RN

and by Routledge
711 Third Avenue, New York, NY 10017

Routledge is an imprint of the Taylor & Francis Group, an informa business

British Library Cataloguing in Publication Data
A catalogue record for this book is available from the British Library

Library of Congress Cataloging in Publication Data
Names: Vezzali, Loris, editor. | Stathi, Sofia, editor.
Title: Intergroup contact theory: recent developments and future directions / edited by Loris Vezzali and Sofia Stathi.
Description: Abingdon, Oxon; New York, NY: Routledge, 2017. | Series: Current issues in social psychology | Includes bibliographical references and index.
Identifiers: LCCN 2016029582| ISBN 9781138182301 (hardback) | ISBN 9781138182318 (pbk.) | ISBN 9781315646510 (e-book)
Subjects: LCSH: Acculturation. | Intergroup relations. | Social interaction.
Classification: LCC HM841 .I5835 2017 | DDC 303.48/2--dc23
LC record available at https://lccn.loc.gov/2016029582

ISBN: 978-1-138-18230-1 (hbk)
ISBN: 978-1-138-18231-8 (pbk)
ISBN: 978-1-315-64651-0 (ebk)

Typeset in Bembo
by Florence Production Ltd, Stoodleigh, Devon, UK

CONTENTS

CONTRIBUTORS

Dominic Abrams, University of Kent, UK
Rupert Brown, University of Sussex, UK
Lindsey Cameron, University of Kent, UK
Becky L. Choma, Ryerson University, Canada
Richard J. Crisp, Aston University, UK
John Dixon, Open University, UK
John F. Dovidio, Yale University, USA
Anja Eller, National Autonomous University of Mexico (UNAM), Mexico
Roberto González, Universidad Católica de Chile, Chile
Sylvie Graf, Czech Academy of Sciences, Brno, Czech Republic
Siwar Hasan-Aslih, Interdisciplinary Center (IDC) Herzliya, Israel
Gordon Hodson, Brock University, Canada
Rose Meleady, University of East Anglia, UK
Stefania Paolini, University of Newcastle, Australia
Tamar Saguy, Interdisciplinary Center (IDC) Herzliya, Israel
Noa Shchori-Eyal, Interdisciplinary Center (IDC) Herzliya, Israel
Danit Sobol, Interdisciplinary Center (IDC) Herzliya, Israel
Sofia Stathi, University of Greenwich, UK
Rhiannon N. Turner, Queens University Belfast, UK
Loris Vezzali, University of Modena and Reggio Emilia, Italy

1

THE PRESENT AND THE FUTURE OF THE CONTACT HYPOTHESIS, AND THE NEED FOR INTEGRATING RESEARCH FIELDS

Loris Vezzali and Sofia Stathi

Key words: intergroup contact; contact hypothesis; integration of research fields; intergroup relations; prejudice reduction

There is no doubt that the contact hypothesis, proposed by Allport in his classic book *The Nature of Prejudice* (1954), has been remarkably influential in social psychology. The basic premise of the contact hypothesis is that contact between individuals who belong to different groups can foster the development of more positive out-group attitudes. Why is the issue of intergroup contact so popular in social psychology research? A possible answer is that prejudice and conflict remain intractable characteristics of the societies in which we live, despite attempts of politicians and policymakers to successfully implement social change. As such, contact and its effectiveness at improving out-group attitudes has been an appealing and enduring research topic for social scientists.

Probably, one of the reasons for the success of the contact hypothesis rests on its immediacy and simplicity. However, the actual finding that contact *can* reduce prejudice is not trivial. Before the formulation of the contact hypothesis, there was skepticism regarding the effectiveness of intergroup contact (Baker, 1934; Sumner, 1906), skepticism that some scholars still endorse (e.g. Dixon, Durrheim, & Tredoux, 2005).

Initial studies provided mixed evidence for the benefits of intergroup contact. In fact, while some studies found that contact improved attitudes towards the out-group (e.g. Smith, 1943; Zeligs & Hendrickson, 1933), others did not reveal any significant effects (e.g. Horowitz, 1936; Sims & Patrick, 1936). A possible explanation for these divergent findings is that some of these initial studies were conducted in contexts that were—structurally—unfavorable to the development of positive intergroup relations. Subsequent research, conducted under more favorable conditions, provided good foundation for the development of the contact hypothesis, by showing that contact could indeed represent a key variable in the development of positive intergroup relations (Brophy, 1946; Stouffer, 1949).

Strong evidence for the effectiveness of intergroup contact was provided, for instance, by the famous studies by Deutsch and Collins (1951), which showed that following non-race-based assignment of apartments, stereotyping of Black people (among White housewives) was reduced compared to when the assignment of apartments was based on race; and by Sherif (1966), who showed that intergroup relations improved when contact between different teams was characterized by cooperation and common goals.

Williams (1947) proposed an initial formulation of contact theory, noting that contact would be more effective when relations between groups were characterized by equal status, same interests, cooperation and potential to develop more intimate friendships. Within this theoretical framework, Allport (1954) proposed his formulation of the contact hypothesis. Importantly, Allport was clearly aware that intergroup contact could also increase intergroup tension and prejudice in some situations. Therefore, he suggested that prejudice reduction would only occur when "optimal" conditions were present, and this is in our view the greatest merit of the contact hypothesis. In particular, he proposed that contact should reduce prejudice when groups meet under conditions of equal status, cooperate in order to achieve superordinate goals and when intergroup contact is supported by institutions and norms (see also Hodson & Hewstone, 2013b; Pettigrew, 1998).

After more than six decades of research, we now have consistent evidence that contact "works". The meta-analysis by Pettigrew and Tropp (2006), including 713 independent samples from 515 studies, revealed that contact is negatively associated with prejudice, and more so when optimal conditions are present. According to the meta-analysis, contact has positive effects on out-group attitudes across several types of out-group targets (including racial groups, disabled individuals, older people, homosexual people) and is effective both among children and adults, irrespective of gender and geographical area. Notably, these effects extend beyond the contact situation and generalize to the out-group as a whole—and even to uninvolved out-groups (secondary transfer effect; see also Lolliot et al., 2013; Pettigrew, 2009).

Research on intergroup contact, especially over the last two decades, identified the mediators of contact effects, which are primarily represented by affective variables, thus showing *why* contact works (Brown & Hewstone, 2005; Pettigrew & Tropp, 2008). Research also uncovered several moderators, providing this way indications regarding *when* contact effects should be expected or likely to be stronger (Brown & Hewstone, 2005). Research culminated in various influential reviews of contact theory (e.g. Al Ramiah & Hewstone, 2013; Hewstone, 2009; Hewstone & Swart, 2011; Pettigrew, Tropp, Wagner, & Christ, 2011) and in prominent books that summarized an extremely wide corpus of studies (Dovidio, Glick, & Rudman, 2005; Hodson & Hewstone, 2013a; Pettigrew & Tropp, 2011; Wagner, Tropp, Finchilescu, & Tredoux, 2008). Based on this wealth of knowledge on intergroup contact, it is highlighted that contact is not a panacea for prejudice, but it can represent a useful tool that, under some conditions, can contribute to the improvement of intergroup relations (Dixon et al., 2005; Hewstone, 2003; Hodson, Hewstone, & Swart, 2013).

From this very brief overview of the contact hypothesis, one may wonder if there is actually anything that remains to be studied in the field. Could it be that after more than 60 years of fruitful research on intergroup contact, there is nothing interesting left to explore? In other words, can research on intergroup contact still provide exciting avenues for researchers? We believe that it can, and this book aims to highlight some of the most exciting current directions in the field of intergroup contact. In fact, an analysis of research trends points to an increased interest in the field; after an initial surge of studies investigating intergroup contact, which peaked between the 1950s and 1960s, the interest of researchers declined up until the 1990s, before resurging in the 2000s and rapidly expanding in more recent years, from 2010 to present. We believe that one reason behind this renewed interest in contact is its recent developments, which uncover new theoretical as well as practical implications, and its integration with other research fields in psychology.

With these recent developments in mind, we were truly excited to have the opportunity to work on this book. Our aim has been to focus on intergroup contact theory and highlight, through a critical lens, its noteworthy recent developments, which build on theoretical, applied and methodological advances in social psychology, and are likely to shape significant future research avenues. In particular, the book takes into account recent developments in contact research by focusing on its integration with research areas that were often considered as separate fields. Integration between contact theory and other fields (outlined below), as well as an applied focus and methodological advances, can allow a more precise understanding of the complex current social reality. We wish to believe that with this book we will provide fertile ground for the development of new, dynamic and topical research ideas based on intergroup contact.

In the second chapter, Hodson, Turner and Choma discuss the integration of research on individual difference variables with intergroup contact literature, by considering the role that these individual difference variables have in shaping the effects of contact. Individual differences have generally been neglected when considering the literature on intergroup contact; however, there is a current trend of research that argues for their importance. The authors recognize this and consider a broad range of individual differences, from personality factors to social ideologies and cognitive abilities, and examine if and how they interact with contact to predict attitude improvement. Moreover, the authors take into account various populations, contexts and underlying processes before addressing the limitations of existing literature and proposing avenues for future research.

In the third chapter, González and Brown provide an integrated account of research that considers concepts from contact and acculturation literature, which have generally been detached. The authors offer a theoretical rationale as to why the contact and acculturation fields should be integrated and focus on their research program to support their arguments. Notably, they consider the relation between acculturation preferences and both direct and indirect contact experiences, by also examining with longitudinal methodologies the processes underlying the effects.

Their conclusions are not limited to theoretical considerations, but also extend to policy implications that take into account both contact and acculturation findings.

In the fourth chapter, Saguy, Shchori-Eyal, Hasan-Aslih, Sobol and Dovidio review a current line of research that suggests that intergroup contact reinforces existing social inequalities and prevents social change. Their analysis reveals that, although this effect is especially likely among disadvantaged group members, it can extend to the advantaged group. In this latter case, evidence is more mixed and the authors aim to address the sometimes conflicting literature. They then present two new lines of relevant work, the first linking harmonious emotions, such as hope, to lower support for collective action, the second centering on the role of romantic relationships on feeding system justifying beliefs. By focusing on the complexity and consequences of intergroup harmony, this chapter provides important indications regarding the ironic consequences of positive contact and how they could be overcome.

In the fifth chapter, Abrams and Eller propose a new theoretical model that aims to integrate intergroup contact theory and intergroup threat theory. Although several studies have investigated the reciprocal associations between contact and threat, the two research domains have in fact been separate. The authors offer a highly innovative theoretical framework, which exposes the oversimplification of existing approaches that assume linear causal paths. They provide a more realistic account of how various types of positive and negative contact relate over time with different types of threat, by also considering the temporal frame for both contact and threats. After presenting their theoretical model and providing initial empirical evidence, the authors indicate possible avenues for future research.

In the sixth chapter, Graf and Paolini look into the effects of negative in addition to positive contact. The chapter begins by identifying reasons as to why the examination of negative contact has generally been neglected by research, while also presenting research on positivity and negativity in other psychology domains. The authors then discuss a model that advances the differential effects that contact—both positive and negative—has on category salience and out-group attitudes. The authors also present recent evidence supporting the basic tenets of the proposed model, using a wide variety of methodologies and designs, that demonstrate the prominence of negative over positive contact.

In the seventh chapter, Vezzali and Stathi provide an overview and a discussion of recent developments of the extended contact hypothesis, one of the most prominent indirect contact strategies for the reduction of prejudice. In the first part of the chapter, the authors review the original extended contact hypothesis by Wright, Aron, McLaughlin-Volpe and Ropp (1997), the theoretical accounts explaining it, the main mediating processes and evidence of its effectiveness. In the second part, the focus is on the most recent developments and, in particular, on the distinction between extended and vicarious contact, and on the importance of considering a social network perspective in the analysis of extended contact effects. Both these developments can constitute bases for more informed future research on prejudice reduction.

In the eigth chapter, Meleady and Crisp present evidence for imagined inter-group contact, a recently developed prejudice reduction indirect contact technique. After reviewing research showing that imagined contact impacts a range of intergroup outcomes, the authors consider the importance of taking research from the laboratory to the field, along with the related questions that need to be addressed. The chapter further identifies several new areas of investigation beyond intergroup relations, including applications to behavioral domains (from economics to innovation), in which imagined contact can provide a useful and effective tool.

In the ninth chapter, Cameron and Turner consider the integration of social and developmental research on intergroup contact, by reviewing evidence of the effectiveness of contact strategies among children. The chapter begins by summarizing research on the effects of contact on out-group attitudes, cross-group friendships, prosocial behavior and intergroup exclusion. The authors then discuss research on cross-group friendships among children before providing a review of interventions applying contact principles to educational settings. Finally, in addition to proposing the novel concept of "confidence in contact", several indications of areas neglected by research are discussed, including the need for considering minority group members' perspectives.

In the conclusion chapter, Dixon presents an analysis on the past, present and future of the contact hypothesis. In the first part of the chapter, he discusses the historical emergence and political significance of research on the contact hypothesis. He takes into account the context in which the contact hypothesis was first proposed and its role in providing scientific justification to institutional attempts to promote social change, for instance in the form of desegregation policies. The chapter then continues by highlighting how new research presented in this book has contributed to the development in the field. Finally, Dixon critically reflects on the state of contact research, also in light of recent developments, and proposes promising avenues for future research.

Importantly, all chapters include a section on future directions in the relevant area, which aims to stimulate the development of future research by discussing ideas about how contact theory can be developed further. This way, the chapters can provide a dynamic tool for scholars who are interested in not only seeing intergroup contact through traditional frameworks, but also seeking to understand how the field may shape in the future.

As we noted above, we now know that intergroup contact, as a prejudice reduction method, *works*, as well as when and why its effects occur. Nonetheless, the research field of intergroup contact continues to develop actively and excitingly. It finds new ways to reinvent itself and expand by integrating with other research areas. This book precisely aims to present recent developments that are likely to stimulate future research, by integrating contact with apparently distinct (although connected) research fields, and by using novel theoretical frameworks and rigorous methodologies.

We worked with enthusiasm and passion on this book, and we were very fortunate to be supported by highly esteemed authors from around the world. The chapters of this book, in fact, were written by colleagues in Australia, Canada, Chile, Czech Republic, Israel, Italy, Mexico, United Kingdom and United States of America, which provides a showcase of how thriving the field is. Our hope is that this book will help highlight the versatility of intergroup contact and inspire both new and established scholars to continue to work towards a tolerant global society.

Loris Vezzali and Sofia Stathi

References

Al Ramiah, A., & Hewstone, M. (2013). Intergroup contact as a tool for reducing, resolving, and preventing intergroup conflict. *American Psychologist*, *68*, 527–42. doi: 10.1037/a0032603

Allport, G.W. (1954). *The nature of prejudice*. New York, NY: Addison-Wesley.

Baker, P.E. (1934). Negro-White adjustment in America. *Journal of Negro Education*, *3*, 194–204.

Brophy, I.N. (1946). The luxury of anti-Negro prejudice. *Public Opinion Quarterly*, *9*, 456–66.

Brown, R., & Hewstone, M. (2005). An integrative theory of intergroup contact. *Advances in Experimental Social Psychology*, *37*, 255–343. doi: 10.1016/S0065-2601(05)37005-5

Deutsch, M., & Collins, M.E. (1951). *Interracial housing: A psychological evaluation of a social experiment*. Minneapolis, MN: University of Minnesota Press.

Dixon, J., Durrheim, K., & Tredoux, C. (2005). Beyond the optimal contact strategy: A reality check for the contact hypothesis. *American Psychologist*, *60*, 697–711. doi: 10.1037/0003-066X.60.7.697

Dovidio, J.F., Glick, P., & Rudman, L.A. (Eds.) (2005). *On the nature of prejudice: Fifty years after Allport*. Malde, MA: Blackwell.

Hewstone, M. (2003). Intergroup contact: Panacea for prejudice? *Psychologist*, *16*, 352–5.

Hewstone, M. (2009). Living apart, living together? The role of intergroup contact in social integration. *Proceedings of the British Academy*, *162*, 243–300.

Hewstone, M., & Swart, H. (2011). Fifty-odd years of inter-group contact: From hypothesis to integrated theory. *British Journal of Social Psychology*, *50*, 374–86. doi: 10.1111/j.2044-8309.2011.02047.x

Hodson, G., & Hewstone, M. (Eds.) (2013a). *Advances in intergroup contact*. New York, NY: Psychology Press.

Hodson, G., & Hewstone, M. (2013b). Introduction. Advances in intergroup contact. In G. Hodson & M. Hewstone (Eds.), *Advances in intergroup contact* (pp. 3–20). New York, NY: Psychology Press.

Hodson, G., Hewstone, M., & Swart, H. (2013). Advances in intergroup contact. Epilogue and future directions. In G. Hodson & M. Hewstone. (Eds.), *Advances in intergroup contact* (pp. 262–305). New York, NY: Psychology Press.

Horowitz, E.L. (1936). The development of attitude toward the Negro. *Archives of Psychology* (Columbia University), No. 194, 47.

Lolliot, S., Schmid, K., Hewstone, M., Al Ramiah, A., Tausch, N., & Swart, H. (2013). Generalized effects of intergroup contact: The secondary transfer effect. In G. Hodson & M. Hewstone. (Eds.), *Advances in intergroup contact* (pp. 81–112). London, UK: Psychology Press.

Pettigrew, T.F. (1998). Intergroup contact theory. *Annual Review of Psychology*, *49*, 65–85. doi: 10.1146/annurev.psych.49.1.65

Pettigrew, T.F. (2009). Secondary transfer effect of contact: Do intergroup contact effects spread to noncontacted outgroups? *Social Psychology*, *40*, 55–65. doi: 10.1027/1864-9335.40.2.55

Pettigrew, T.F., & Tropp, L.R. (2006). A meta-analytic test of intergroup contact theory. *Journal of Personality and Social Psychology*, *90*, 751–83. doi: 10.1037/0022-3514.90.5.751

Pettigrew, T.F., & Tropp, L.R. (2008). How does intergroup contact reduce prejudice? Meta-analytic tests of three mediators. *European Journal of Social Psychology*, *38*, 922–34. doi: 10.1002/ejsp.504

Pettigrew, T.F., & Tropp, L.R. (2011). *When groups meet: The dynamics of intergroup contact.* New York, NY: Psychology Press.

Pettigrew, T.F., Tropp, L.R., Wagner, U., & Christ, O. (2011). Recent advances in intergroup contact theory. *International Journal of Intercultural Relations*, *35*, 271–80. doi: 10.1016/j.ijintrel.2011.03.001

Sherif, M. (1966). *In common predicament: Social psychology of intergroup conflict and cooperation.* Boston, MA: Houghton Mifflin.

Sims, V.M., & Patrick, J.R. (1936). Attitude toward the Negro of northern and southern college students. *Journal of Social Psychology*, *7*, 192–204.

Smith, F.T. (1943). *An experiment in modifying attitudes toward the Negro* (Vol. 887). New York, NY: Teachers College Contributions to Education.

Stouffer, S.A. (1949). *The American Soldier*, Princeton, NJ: Princeton University Press.

Sumner, W.G. (1906). *Folkways.* New York, NY: Ginn.

Wagner, U., Tropp, L., Finchilescu, G., & Tredoux, C. (Eds.) (2008). *Improving intergroup relations: Building on the legacy of Thomas F. Pettigrew.* Oxford, UK: Blackwell.

Williams, R.M. Jr. (1947). *The reduction of intergroup tensions.* New York, NY: Social Science Research Council.

Wright, S.C., Aron, A., McLaughlin-Volpe, T., & Ropp, S.A. (1997). The extended contact effect: Knowledge of cross-group friendships and prejudice. *Journal of Personality and Social Psychology*, *73*, 73–90. doi: 10.1037/0022-3514.73.1.73

Zeligs, R., & Hendrickson, G. (1933). Racial attitudes of 200 sixth grade children. *Sociology and Social Research*, *18*, 26–36.

2

INDIVIDUAL DIFFERENCES IN INTERGROUP CONTACT PROPENSITY AND PREJUDICE REDUCTION

Gordon Hodson, Rhiannon N. Turner and Becky L. Choma

Keywords: contact, cross-group friendship, personality, individual differences, prejudice

> I don't like that man. I must get to know him better.
> (Attributed to Abraham Lincoln)

The notion that contact with others leads to more favorable attitudes towards the target has considerable intuitive appeal. The so-called contact hypothesis (Allport, 1954; Pettigrew & Tropp, 2006) postulates the rather simple premise that contact with an out-group member can result in more favorable attitudes towards the contact partner that subsequently generalize to the out-group as a whole (see also Brown & Hewstone, 2005). Over 60 years of research on the topic provides clear evidence that contact serves this function (Pettigrew & Tropp, 2006; see also Hodson & Hewstone, 2013a). Until recently, however, it was much less clear who is drawn to (or pushed from) intergroup contact, and even more pressingly, who benefits from its potential effects (Hodson, 2011). We suspect that those well-schooled in the intergroup relations literature view Lincoln's statement with considerable bemusement if not skepticism.[1] Is human nature such that all people alike desire out-group contact and are amenable (or at least susceptible) to positive attitude change as a result of contact? This question, we argue, is fundamental for the contact field to address. If contact primarily works among low-prejudiced (LP) persons, or worse, is ineffective (or even backfires) among those highly prejudiced (HP), then contact has questionable utility as a strategy for prejudice reduction or social change. If, on the other hand, contact works well among prejudice-prone persons despite their dislike of out-group interaction, such evidence would provide a strong test of contact's potential. The present chapter reviews the latest advances in our understanding of this empirical yet often overlooked question, before addressing shortcomings in the field's knowledge and recommending future directions.

By *individual differences* we refer to between-person variability in the naturally occurring levels of psychological constructs relevant to personal and/or intergroup life. Much of the recent literature, for instance, has considered whether contact works among those higher (vs. lower) in ideological constructs such as right-wing authoritarianism (RWA; characterized by conventionality, traditionalism and willingness to aggress against norm violators; Altemeyer, 1996) or social dominance orientation (SDO; characterized by endorsement of intergroup hierarchies and group-based inequality; Sidanius & Pratto, 1999). Others have focused on variables that are psychologically more distal to prejudice and more cognitive in nature, such as the need for cognitive closure (NFC), which is the motivated desire for closure in thinking modes, the desire for "*an* answer on a given topic, *any* answer . . . compared to confusion and ambiguity" (Kruglanski, 1990, p. 337). Other more distal constructs involve broad personality factors, such as Agreeableness (being friendly and cooperative), Openness to Experience (being accepting of new situations, knowledge and change) and Extraversion (being sociable, talkative, etc.). We assume a certain degree of familiarity with these constructs in our reader. Therefore, in the interest of brevity and to cover as much of the new research on contact findings as a function of such individual differences, the interested reader can find descriptions and sample scale items in Table 2.1, along with information about different contact variables such as contact frequency or quantity (i.e. amount of contact), contact quality (i.e. pleasant vs. negative), friendship and so on. For those wishing more detail, we refer the reader to longer texts (e.g. Altemeyer, 1996; Hodson & Dhont, 2015; Hodson, Choma, et al., 2013; Islam & Hewstone, 1993; McCrae & Costa, 1987; Roets & Van Hiel, 2011; Sidanius & Pratto, 1999; Turner, Dhont, Hewstone, Prestwich, & Vonofakou, 2014).

On the question of individual differences, the contact literature has historically been either moot or pessimistic, for a variety of reasons. For some theorists and researchers, individual differences were largely irrelevant to the contact question, in part due to strong interest in contact among social identity researchers, who by and large dismiss or downplay person-based factors (e.g. Reynolds, Turner, Haslam, & Ryan, 2001). Others have treated person factors as predictors alongside contact (e.g. Miller, Smith, & Mackie, 2004), or conceptually (and statistically) handled them as covariates to be eliminated as "noise" (e.g. Liebkind, Haaramo, & Jasinskaja-Lahti, 2000). Still others considered individual differences, such as authoritarianism, as obstacles or impediments to positive intergroup attitudes and relations. Allport (1954) himself doubted whether contact could work where the "inner strain" towards intolerance was strong. Indeed, reasons for pessimism and skepticism are warranted given that many (if not most) prejudice interventions have proven resistant to prejudice reduction among HP, or even backfired, making intergroup relations worse (see Hodson, 2011, for a more detailed discussion; see Hodson, Costello, & MacInnis, 2013). Such concerns are certainly valid, mostly as we know of no studies suggesting that HPs particularly enjoy or approach contact. Rather, HPs bristle at the idea. Nonetheless, there is reason for considerable optimism given that intergroup contact improves intergroup attitudes by reducing

TABLE 2.1 Summary of key terms and concepts

Construct	Description	Sample scale item(s)
Contact Variables		
Quantity/ Amount	Having a little to a lot of contact with an out-group and/or its representative	How frequently do you have contact with [out-group]? In an average week, how many hours do you spend interacting with [out-group]? [Voci & Hewstone, 2003]
Quality	Having poor quality (or negative) to high quality (or positive) contact with an out-group and/or its representative	When you meet [out-group], do you find the contact "pleasant"/"cooperative"/"superficial" or "insincere"? [Voci & Hewstone, 2003]
Institutional Support	Degree to which an institution is seen to reject or support intergroup contact	This [institution] does little to promote friendly interactions between inmates from different racial groups [reversed] [Hodson, 2008]
Direct Friendship	Having an out-group member as a personal friend; positive relations	Please indicate the number of [out-group members] that you consider to be a friend [Hodson, Harry, & Mitchell, 2009]
Indirect Friendship (extended contact)	Having an in-group member (who has an out-group friend) as a personal friend; positive relations	Please indicate the number of [in-group] friends that you have, who are friends with [out-group members] [Hodson, Harry, et al., 2009]
Person-based individual differences		
Agreeableness	Being relatively friendly, warm, cooperative	Likes to cooperate with others [John, Donahue, & Kentle, 1991]
Openness to Experience	Being imaginative, with broad interests, accepting of differences	Is curious about many different things [John et al., 1991]
Extraversion	Being talkative, fun-loving, desiring social contact	Is talkative; is outgoing, sociable [John et al., 1991]

Social Dominance Orientation (SDO)	Support for unequal group relations and intergroup hierarchies	Superior groups should dominate inferior groups [Sidanius & Pratto, 1999]
Right-Wing Authoritarianism (RWA)	Support for conventions, traditions, and aggression against norm violators	What our country really needs, instead of more "civil rights" is a good, stiff dose of law and order [Altemeyer, 1996]
Need for Closure (NFC)	Cognitive preference for answers and solutions (vs. lack of structure and uncertainty)	I don't like to go into a situation without knowing what I can expect from it; I dislike questions which could be answered in many different ways [Roets & Van Hiel, 2011]
Intergroup Disgust Sensitivity (ITG-DS)	Affect-laden revulsion towards out-groups; belief in stigma transfer and social superiority	I feel disgusted when people from other ethnic groups invade my personal space; After interacting with another ethnic group, I typically desire more contact with my own ethnic group to "undo" any ill effects from intergroup contact [Hodson, Choma, et al., 2013]
In-group Identification	Strong bond with, and identity importance of, a social category or group	To what extent is the membership of this group an important part of your identity? [Hodson, Harry, et al., 2009]

threat and anxiety and increasing trust and empathy (Pettigrew & Tropp, 2008; see also Hodson, Hewstone, & Swart, 2013; Table 2.1). These psychological constructs have the most potential to "move" among HPs, given that such persons are characterized by anxiety and fearfulness, making intergroup contact a strong contender to reduce bias among such people.

A question of mediation: individual differences predicting prejudice via contact

It has long been recognized that prejudice-prone persons are reluctant if not hostile participants in intergroup contact settings (e.g. Allport, 1954). More recently, researchers have asked whether individual differences make some persons more or less likely to engage in contact or consider contact positive, and whether this in turn predicts out-group attitudes. That is, might contact *mediate* the impact of individual differences on prejudice, such that Person → Contact → Prejudice? To address this question, Jackson and Poulsen (2005) examined the relation between basic/broad personality factors and prejudice, in particular whether contact mediates theoretically plausible pathways. In several American university samples, the authors assessed contact and attitudes towards Blacks (Study 1) and Asians (Study 2). As expected, higher Openness or Agreeableness predicted more positive contact experiences with the relevant out-group, which in turn predicted more favorable attitudes towards the target out-group. In other words, individuals who are more open or more cooperative engage in more contact, which (in part) explains their more positive attitudes towards those contacted groups. This investigation, however, considered the effects of each personality factor (Openness, Agreeableness) and each contact variable (quantity, quality) separately across various regression analyzes, and employed Sobel tests for mediation (which are increasingly criticized as tests of indirect effects; see Hayes, 2009). Utilizing their correlation matrices, we conducted a secondary analysis of their data (see Kline, 2011, pp. 47–49; see Hodson & Busseri, 2012; Hodson & Skorska, 2015, for examples). We employed MPlus 7 software to simultaneously test the effects of Openness and Agreeableness on attitudes through contact quantity and quality simultaneously. As illustrated in Figure 2.1, this reanalysis confirms the importance of Openness and Agreeableness in predicting prejudice, through positive contact quality (not quantity), with significant indirect effects observed. This reanalysis clarifies the relative importance of contact *quality* in particular; Openness predicts greater and more positive contact, but Agreeableness predicts only better *quality* contact. In predicting attitudes towards Blacks, the effects of Agreeableness were completely explained through positive contact; in predicting Asian attitudes, the effects of Openness were in part explained through both types of contact.

The question of whether personality predicts out-group attitudes through contact, and in particular cross-group friendships, an intimate and special form of contact that represents the ideals of contact, was recently undertaken by Turner and colleagues (2014). In addition to examining Agreeableness and Openness,

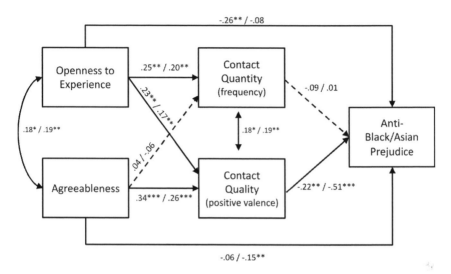

FIGURE 2.1 Indirect effect of Openness via contact quality (IE = −.05, p = .042/
IE = −.08, p = .008); indirect effect of Agreeableness via contact quality
(IE = −.07, p = .019/IE = −.13, p = .005). Standardized estimates shown.
★ p < .05; ★★ p < .01; ★★★ p < .001. Reanalyzed data from Jackson and
Poulsen (2005); Study 1 on left of slash, Study 2 on right of slash. Dotted
lines were non-significant paths in each study.

Turner and colleagues considered the potential role of Extraversion (i.e. sociability).
Study 1 (White UK university students) confirmed that both Openness and Agreeableness were associated with more favorable attitudes towards Asians (which in
the UK largely refers to people from India, Pakistan and Bangladesh). Although
greater Extraversion predicted more favorable attitudes, this effect was fully indirect,
channelled through greater cross-group friendships. In this instance, being sociable
was a better predictor of cross-group friendship than either Openness or
Agreeableness, shedding new light on new pathways that personality and contact
reduce prejudice. In a follow-up study, the same questions were posed in another
White UK sample. However, the authors also measured the number of White
friends, to rule out whether "friendship" in general was explaining the previous
findings, and intergroup anxiety (feelings of discomfort, awkwardness and unease
about interacting with Asians). The results confirmed the first study and furthered
our understanding of these structural relations. Agreeableness and Openness exerted
effects on positive attitudes towards Asians through lower intergroup anxiety (with
Openness also exerting a direct path). In contrast, greater Extraversion predicted
more cross-group friendships, which in turn predicted more favorable attitudes
through lower levels of intergroup anxiety. These patterns held after controlling
for in-group friendships, a potential confound. Relevant to our upcoming discussion,
both studies found that cross-group friendship was a stronger predictor of improved
attitudes among those lower in Agreeableness or Extraversion. Indeed moderated

mediation tests revealed that the contact effects on prejudice through lowered anxiety were significant among those low (not high) in Agreeableness.

Thus far in our review, the evidence suggests that Openness and Agreeableness[2] predict less prejudice (in part) through greater positive out-group contact (Jackson & Poulsen, 2005; see also our Figure 2.1 reanalysis), and that Extraversion predicts less prejudice through more cross-group friendships (Turner et al., 2014). Related research enquires about individual differences in ability rather than character. For instance, individuals lower in abstract reasoning abilities are more prejudiced towards gay people, in part through lower contact with gay people, even when controlling for authoritarianism (Hodson & Busseri, 2012). This is in keeping with the hypothesis that intergroup interactions are cognitively draining and avoided by those with fewer mental resources at hand. Each of the studies reviewed in this section share the overall notion that more distal individual differences (e.g. broad personality factors, cognitive abilities) predict intergroup attitudes, in part, through out-group contact (Hodson & Dhont, 2015).

A question of moderation: efficacy of contact among HPs

Prior to outlining how contact and individual differences might jointly impact intergroup attitudes in a Person (P) × Situation (S) manner, an important conceptual distinction is worth noting. Most of the research in this review (and indeed our own research) emphasizes contact as the focal variable (i.e. on the x-axis) as a predictor of prejudice (along the y-axis), with individual differences (LP vs. HP) as the moderator. Such a pattern is illustrated in the top portion of Figure 2.2. This framing addresses the extent to which contact predicts lower prejudice, but additionally asks this question within subpopulations characterized by lesser or greater proclivities towards prejudice. Alternatively, of course, with the same data researchers can emphasize the individual difference as the focal variable (i.e. along the x-axis) as a predictor of prejudice, asking whether this relation varies as a function of contact conditions (see lower portion of Figure 2.2). This approach was recently adopted by Hodson, Dube and Choma (2015) to better understand the nature of a relatively new individual difference predictor, intergroup disgust sensitivity (Hodson, Choma, et al., 2013), previously shown to be relatively impervious to non-contact intervention (Choma, Hodson, & Costello, 2012). Statistically these two approaches are identical (i.e. P × S = S × P), differing only conceptually, but with implications for interpretation, such as when testing simple slopes. With the contact field primarily interested in contact as the focal variable, much of the analysis asks the former question (i.e. Does the benefit of contact on prejudice vary as a function of individual differences?) and will form the basis of our review.[3]

With this in mind, there are several basic patterns that might emerge from asking whether contact is effective among HPs and LPs (Hodson, Costello, et al., 2013, Figure 3.1). First, contact might be effective among both LP and HP individuals equivalently, largely the assumption in the field, as evidenced by ignoring individual differences. Of course, the aforementioned skepticism about

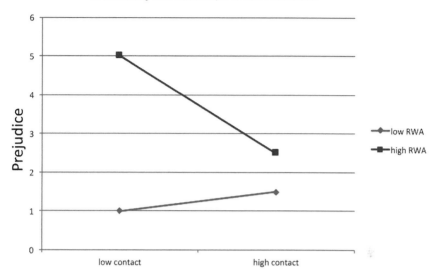

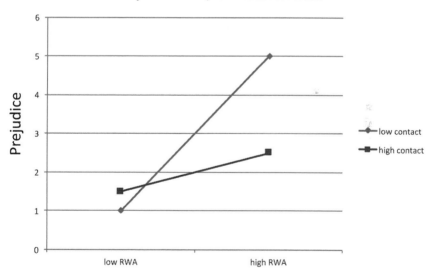

FIGURE 2.2 Conceptualization of Person x Situation interactions, with individual difference (e.g. right-wing authoritarianism [RWA]) as moderator of contact effects (top panel) or as focal variable (bottom panel). These fictitious patterns employ the same data points to stress different questions.

the benefits of contact among HPs (outlined in our introduction) might prove correct, meaning that contact might only reduce prejudice among those not predisposed towards bias in the first place (LPs), failing to impact or even exacerbate bias among HPs. Given our contemporary understanding that contact reduces anxiety and threat and increases empathy and trust, this pattern is theoretically the least likely of the potential patterns, at least over the longer term. Alternatively, contact might work very well among HPs and less well among LPs (who may even show little benefit, being relatively low in prejudice in the first place). This position is supported by the many studies finding that contact operates on prejudice by lowering threat and anxiety and raising empathy and trust (e.g. Hodson et al., 2015; Turner et al., 2014; Turner, Hewstone, & Voci, 2007; for review, see Hodson, Hewstone, et al., 2013).

In perhaps the first direct test of differential contact efficacy between LPs and HPs, Maoz (2003) examined the impact of a 2-day dialog exercise, whereby Israeli and Palestinian 15- to 16-year-old adolescents engaged in structured programs designed to "promote coexistence and peace building" (p. 704) between the groups. In keeping with the field's earlier skepticism (e.g. Allport, 1954), Maoz predicted that "doves" (people preferring negotiation and cooperation) would approach contact more, and benefit more from contact, relative to "hawks" (people characterized by tough-minded defense of in-group interests). Whereas Jewish-Israeli doves (LPs) were indeed more open to contact, they benefitted very little from intergroup contact, contrary to the author's predictions. In contrast, Jewish-Israeli hawks (or HPs) showed significantly more favorable attitudes following contact. Unfortunately data were not provided regarding Palestinians' attitudes; nonetheless, this early study provided relatively clear evidence that, contrary to historic concerns, contact works well on HPs.

Given that contact exerts stronger effects in more (vs. less) confined and structured (i.e. low choice) contexts, such as workplaces or schools (Pettigrew & Tropp, 2006, Table 2), Hodson (2008) decided to examine contact in several prisons. This provides a strong (and conservative) test of the benefits of contact. That is, if contact is associated with more positive out-group attitudes in such tense and power-defined contexts, where out-group avoidance is limited (if not impossible), this would certainly not represent contact tested under idealized or optimized settings (Dixon, Durrheim, & Tredoux, 2005). Moreover, if contact is shown to have beneficial effects among HPs in prison, this would offer considerable promise for contact as a prejudice intervention more generally. Across two studies in different UK prisons, contact frequency was assessed among White inmates, along with attitudes towards Black inmates. Perceptions of institutional support for interracial contact (Study 1) or quality (positivity) of contact (Study 2) were also assessed. In this investigation, individual differences in SDO were assessed, where those scoring higher (vs. lower) endorse intergroup inequalities and hierarchies, and generally score higher in prejudice. Overall, the results supported the benefits of contact among those higher in SDO (i.e. HPs); more favorable attitudes towards Black inmates were expressed by those: (a) with more frequent out-group contact

(Studies 1 and 2); (b) who perceived institutional support for contact (Study 1); or (c) who experienced positive quality of contact (Study 2). Among those higher in SDO, contact predicted lower in-group bias through elevated empathy for Black inmates (Study 2). Importantly, HPs in prison contexts with more contact (or more favorable contact conditions or experiences) expressed significantly less prejudice, whereas those similarly HP in nature but without contact expressed more prejudice. Contact, in contrast, had much less influence among those lower in SDO, akin to the general interaction pattern shown in Figure 2.2 (top portion).

An important question, however, is whether contact is similarly associated with less prejudice among HPs in less structured, day-to-day settings. Several studies subsequently tested this possibility. For instance, Hodson, Harry and Mitchell (2009) assessed contact (quality and quantity) and cross-group friendships (direct and indirect [an in-group friend with an out-group friend]) in a sample of UK heterosexual undergraduates. Specifically, contact and attitudes towards gay people were assessed. Two types of prejudice-prone individual differences were tapped: (a) RWA and (b) heterosexual identification, where those scoring higher consider their in-group membership (heterosexual) an important aspect of their identity. Authoritarianism has long been studied within the individual differences literature (e.g. Allport, 1954; Hodson & Dhont, 2015), whereas in-group identification has long been studied within the social identity approach (e.g. Tajfel & Turner, 1979), and both are linked with greater prejudice (e.g. Hodson, Harry, et al., 2009). Overall, the results supported the predictions, such that those higher in RWA or in-group identification expressed less anti-gay attitudes to the extent that they experienced more gay contact, better quality gay contact, more gay friendships, or had more straight friends with gay friends. These effects were generally larger for HPs than LPs (who experienced little benefit from contact, expressing little prejudice overall). Of note, in statistical tests of a contact variable (e.g. quantity), the other forms of contact (e.g. quality; direct friendship; indirect friendship) were statistically controlled, highlighting the unique importance of each type of contact for HPs. This investigation shed light also into mediating mechanisms, with many of the positive contact/friendship effects among HPs being explained by perceptions that gay people promote (vs. threaten) societal values, and by a sense of mental overlap between self and gay friends (or straight friends with gay friends). Another subsequent study confirmed the benefits of contact with gay people on reducing homophobia, revealing that religious fundamentalists with greater (vs. lesser) gay contact expressed less anti-gay bias (Cunningham & Melton, 2013).[4] A subsequent study on identification in Northern Ireland (i.e. Protestant–Catholic contact) demonstrated stronger contact effects on increased forgiveness among those higher (vs. lower) in religious identification (although no such pattern emerged for attitudes; Voci, Hewstone, Swart, & Veneziani, 2015).

In several Belgian community samples, Dhont and Van Hiel (2009) examined RWA and SDO as potential moderators of contact effects on attitudes, with regard to contact quantity (Study 1) or quality (Study 2). In each study, contact and attitudes towards immigrants were considered. In Study 1, those higher (vs. lower) in RWA expressed more favorable attitudes towards immigrants to the extent that they experienced more contact with immigrants. Similar patterns were observed for SDO, with high SDOs benefitting from contact but low SDOs not (although the benefit for highs was not significantly greater than for lows). Their second study tapped positive and negative contact experiences separately. Among those higher in RWA or SDO, more positive contact or less negative contact experiences with immigrants were associated with more favorable immigrant attitudes. Overall the benefits of contact were stronger for HPs than LPs (and non-significant among the latter). These findings, in conjunction with those of Hodson (2008) and Hodson, Harry et al. (2009), provide consistent evidence that more and better contact with out-groups is associated with less prejudice towards those groups among HPs, tested across population types (prison, university student, community), nations (UK and Belgium), targets (Black inmates, gay people, immigrants) and individual differences (SDO, RWA, identification).

It is important to keep in mind, however, that HPs (vs. LPs) engage in relatively little contact with out-groups. Theoretically, therefore, HPs should benefit from contact particularly if they have previously had relatively little out-group contact. Dhont and Van Hiel (2011) tested this possibility in a large, nationally representative sample of Dutch adults with regard to contact and attitudes towards immigrants. The individual difference of interest was RWA, and the researchers examined various types of contact, such as contact quantity and quality, but also indirect contact (i.e. in-group friends with out-group friends). This large sample size allowed Dhont and Van Hiel to test three-way interaction patterns, asking whether having indirect friendships with immigrants works well among high RWAs, particularly if they have experienced very little personal past contact with immigrants generally. The results confirmed this hypothesis, presumably suggesting that having in-group members engaging in intergroup friendships is particularly powerful among HPs in a compensatory manner, "making up" for little out-group experience personally. The reasons for this effect were again consistent with the theoretical and established benefits of contact; that is this pattern was explained by greater out-group trust and lower out-group threat perceptions among the high RWAs who reported greater levels of indirect friendship but lower levels of personal contact. Evidence such as this confirms that being prejudice-prone is not necessarily an obstacle to positive contact effects, but rather that contact operates to create more favorable attitudes by alleviating the precursors of prejudice (here, low trust, high threat). In a large longitudinal sample of Dutch middle-school students, others have found that indirect out-group friendships improved out-group stereotypes (over time), especially for those initially with more negative out-group stereotypes (i.e. HPs) (Munniksma, Stark, Verkuyten, Flache, & Veenstra, 2013).

Adopting a rather unique approach, Graham, Frame and Kenworthy (2014) tapped pre-existing attitudes towards gay people at Time 1, 1–2 months prior to an intervention, and again afterwards. This represents a relatively "pure" measure of HP or LP status, as opposed to tapping generalized or group non-specific ideologies (e.g. RWA, SDO) or tapping in-group identification. In the experimental phase, non-gay American undergraduates engaged in a role-playing exercise with a confederate trained to disclose, through the natural course of discussion, that he or she is gay (through the supposed sex of their romantic partner). The task was described as a "paired group problem-solving game" and involved an exercise to get to know each other, followed by a decision-making task about surviving a hypothetical crisis. As predicted, and in keeping with much of our present review, Time 2 attitudes were significantly more positive when the contact experience involved a supposedly gay (vs. straight) interaction partner, an effect significantly more enhanced among those who pretested with more negative anti-gay attitudes (i.e. HPs). In this study, participants were randomly assigned to contact with an out-group or not, with stronger contact benefits emerging among those predisposed towards bias.

Prejudice is also predicted by factors more distal than pre-existing out-group attitudes, ideology or in-group identification (Hodson & Dhont, 2015), begging the question of whether contact predicts more favorable out-group attitudes among those, for instance, characterized by a need for cognitive closure (NFC). With those higher in NFC desiring firm and conclusive answers and disliking ambiguity, it is not necessarily obvious whether contact, which risks exposure to different "truths", values and norms, reduces prejudice among such persons. To the extent that contact reduces intergroup anxiety, however, those higher in NFC might benefit from contact. This proposition was tested by Dhont, Roets and Van Hiel (2011) across a series of studies. Their first several studies adopted a correlational approach to contact and attitudes towards immigrants in Belgian samples, among university students (Study 1) or community adults (Study 2). The authors also tapped frequent positive contact (both studies), and indirect contact (Study 2), with regard to more subtle (Study 1) or more blatant (Study 2) prejudices. In both studies, the hypothesis that greater contact of each kind is associated with more positive attitudes towards immigrants among those higher in NFC (i.e. HPs) was supported, with effects somewhat weaker and/or non-significant among LPs. An impressive third study examined the effects of experimentally assigned intergroup contact, whereby Belgian high school students were randomly assigned to a week-long exchange program trip to Morocco or to stay in Belgium. In addition to a main effect of contact, whereby those experiencing the trip (relative to control) expressed less negative attitudes towards Moroccans, a predicted NFC × contact interaction effect was revealed, finding that contact (vs. control) led to more favorable attitudes among those high (not low) in NFC. This critical study, strengthened by random assignment to out-group contact, helps to establish that the theorized contact-to-attitudes path is causally plausible, with the benefits experienced primarily among those most in need of intervention. Finally, correlational findings in Studies 4 and 5 revealed that contact–attitude benefits (and, in Study 5, lowered hostile behavioral tendencies) among those higher in NFC operated through lower levels of intergroup anxiety. As predicted, contact was beneficial among HPs (here, those higher in NFC) as a result of lowered anxiousness and awkwardness around the out-group.

Challenges to a person-based understanding of contact benefits

Our review has documented an impressive range of studies that demonstrate, across a range of methods, individual differences, target groups and participant sample types, that increased and more positive contact and/or friendships (including indirect friendships through in-group members) is associated with more favorable out-group attitudes. Moreover, the review reveals that this relation is quite robust among HPs, who are those most in need of attitude change intervention. This is true not only in university-based or "idealized" contact settings, but also in areas rife with conflict (e.g. Israeli–Palestinian conflict; Maoz, 2003) or fierce power dynamics and tension (e.g. prison; Hodson, 2008). The theoretical and applied significance of these findings is best evaluated in comparison to a host of non-contact-based interventions that have historically failed or backfired among HPs (Hodson, 2011; Hodson, Costello, et al., 2013). Although contact researchers for decades were either conzvinced that contact would fail among the prejudice-prone, or that prejudice-proneness was not generally germane to the topic of contact, the evidence trail reviewed clearly supports the power of contact. In fact, failure to consider individual differences has arguably obscured the potential of contact as an intervention (Hodson, Costello, et al., 2013; Hodson, Harry, et al., 2009).

However, this line of inquiry, like all, is not without its critics.[5] Here, we outline some issues that have been raised by reviewers and authors over the years. First is the claim that these findings are not terribly valuable but rather represent floor or ceiling effects among LPs (e.g. Pettigrew & Tropp, 2011, p. 212), depending on which way the variables are coded. This criticism in many ways overlooks the key objectives of employing contact to reduce prejudicial attitudes. For one, it was not all that clear from the start that contact would even work among HPs given the skepticism in the field (for review, see Hodson, Costello, et al., 2013). Thus, isolating and replicating the finding that contact works well among HPs, after years of failing to directly address this most critical of questions, is an advance that advocates of any prejudice intervention ought to provide. The true challenge lies in addressing the attitudes of HPs. An emphasis on how LPs respond, and how they benefit less from contact, is akin to bemoaning that a literacy intervention only works among those with poor reading skills, or that a sleeping intervention only works among those with sleep problems (Hodson, 2011). In many ways, the P × S emphasis has proven to be a distraction, with some readers and critics focusing heavily on whether contact *works better among HPs than LPs* (i.e. a difference in the slopes in Figure 2.2, top panel). Although we ourselves have at times stressed that contact works even better among HPs (e.g. Hodson, 2008, 2011, in press; Hodson, Costello, et al., 2013; Hodson, Harry, et al., 2009), such statements merely described the data and were not intended to imply that a difference in slopes is necessary or is the point of interest. Instead, the prime focus concerns whether contact *works among HPs*, those most in need of intervention (Hodson, 2011), not the difference between LPs and HPs. The advantage of adopting a P × S conceptual framework and statistical approach is that it allows for statistical comparisons between groups (LP vs. HP), potentially of interest to some readers, that also speaks to how the historically observed effect sizes of contact on attitudes may have been under-estimated by not examining individual differences. At times finding positive contact effects among LPs (e.g. Hodson, Costello, et al., 2013) does not detract from the central question of whether contact works among HPs, any more than does the failure of a sleeping pill to improve the sleeping patterns of those without sleep problems.

A second issue concerns the heavy use of self-reported contact measures in many of the studies (but see also the experimental contact work reviewed, including Dhont et al., 2011; Graham et al., 2014). The relevance of this point is made with humour in the movie *Annie Hall*, where a therapist asks a married couple about their frequency of sexual intercourse. The wife replies "*Constantly*, I'd say three times a week", whereas Woody Allen's character chimes in "*Hardly ever*, maybe three times a week" (Hodson, Costello, et al., 2013). The point is that the same relatively objective activity, be it sexual intercourse or intergroup contact, might be differentially experienced subjectively by different parties. When asking people whether they experience *a little* or *a lot* of contact with the out-group, might LPs and HPs differentially construe reality? After all, a given amount of contact for an HP might feel like "a lot" but for an LP feel like "a little". This is a legitimate concern, one that has been addressed in several ways. For instance, some manipulated rather than measured contact (e.g. Dhont et al., 2011; Graham et al., 2014), side-stepping the issue methodologically. Others have relied less on subjective accounts (e.g. *a lot; a little*) but rather asked about one's specific numbers of friends, or hours of contact per unit of time, etc. (e.g. Hodson, 2008; Hodson, Harry, et al., 2009; Voci & Hewstone, 2003). These methods are presumably subject to less bias yet produce comparable results to the more subjective measures. A final approach examines this differential "calibration" problem head on. For instance, Hodson, Costello, et al. (2013) had participants rate their contact with multiple out-groups, and express their attitudes towards each group. Using this approach, one can then examine within-person contact–attitude correlations that largely side-step the issue of what an individual means by *a lot* or *a little*, as this is held constant within the respondent. These analyzes revealed that these within-person correlations were of similar direction and magnitude to the typical between-person correlations. Moreover, this within-person contact–attitude correlation posi-tively related to RWA, suggesting again that those higher (vs. lower) in RWA show stronger contact–attitude relations, even when controlling for idiosyncratic differences in responding to scale anchors. These within-person correlations were unrelated with SDO or conservatism, meaning that LPs and HPs (as operationalized by these constructs) did not differ in contact–attitude relations using this method. In other words, contact–attitude relations were positive, even among HPs, when individually calibrated within-person.

Others have accepted the general premise that contact can work among HPs but claim one exception—benefits among higher SDOs. Many of the studies reviewed above have observed positive contact benefits among higher SDOs (e.g. Dhont &

Van Hiel, 2009, Studies 1–2; Hodson, 2008, Studies 1–2; Hodson, Costello, et al., 2013), with the "hawk" versus "dove" findings (Maoz, 2003) presumably mapping most directly onto SDO as a construct. Yet Al Ramiah and Hewstone (2013) conclude that ". . . the moderating role of intergroup ideology variables, such as SDO, on the contact effect remains unclear" (p. 530). Others have also raised this qualification. For instance, Asbrock, Christ, Duckitt and Sibley (2012) examined RWA × contact and SDO × contact effects in large-scale adult German datasets. In Study 1, they found the typical finding, whereby those higher in RWA particularly benefit from contact in both cross-sectional and longitudinal data. But they found contact benefits among lower SDOs (and no effects among higher SDOs). In Study 2, increased contact worked among those higher in RWA or SDO (in keeping with our central premise). Overall, contact among higher SDOs was ineffective (but did not backfire) (Study 1), or was associated with lower levels of prejudice (Study 2). These impressive studies use large-scale datasets and simultaneously tested the RWA × contact and SDO × contact interaction patterns to isolate unique effects. Yet in this large sample, RWA and SDO were only tapped by two or three items each, resulting in low reliability (also in the contact items), most at or below .60.[6] Moreover, the specific RWA items chosen tapped the aggression aspects of authoritarianism, not traditionalism or conventionality. Given that authoritarian aggression most overlaps conceptually with SDO, we recommend some caution in interpreting efforts that pit this aggression-only version of RWA against SDO.

In follow-up studies, Asbrock, Gutenbrunner and Wagner (2013) examined whether RWA and SDO moderated the effects of imagined contact—that is, mentally simulating positive out-group contact (Crisp & Turner, 2009). These studies used longer, more complete measures of RWA and SDO, with greater reliability. Across two studies, those higher (vs. lower) in RWA benefitted from imagined contact by reporting less negative emotions towards Turks (Study 1), and were more willing to engage in contact with Romani people (Study 2). In Study 1, lower SDOs showed positive outcomes from imagined contact, but higher SDOs showed no effects of contact. Study 2 showed no SDO × imagined contact effects and the authors did not examine simple slopes among low or high SDOs. These studies offer food for thought, and perhaps cause for reflection, but it is important to keep in mind that these studies involve mentally simulated contact (hypothetical future contact), not contact experiences per se. Moreover, others caution that past contact experiences interact with imagined contact for some targets (gay people) but not others (Muslims; see Hoffarth & Hodson, 2016). Moreover, in neither of the Asbrock et al. (2013) studies did SDO itself predict the criteria (negative emotions towards Turks in Study 1; contact intentions with Romani people in Study 2). In these samples, therefore, higher SDOs were not strong or clear exemplars of HP character. So what to take from these studies? First, they support the notion that contact can reduce prejudice among prejudice-prone persons, extending this finding to German samples. And they demonstrate that contact among higher SDOs did not demonstrably worsen prejudice. Future research can draw on the clear strengths of these projects (i.e. large samples, simultaneous testing of individual differences) and include full(er) measures of the key individual differences, particularly those that demonstrably predict the outcome (e.g. prejudice).

Future directions

The contact field has expanded rapidly since the turn of the century (Hodson & Hewstone, 2013b; Figure 1.1). Intergroup contact is not only an effective prejudice reduction strategy (see meta-analysis by Pettigrew & Tropp, 2006), effective outside of lab settings (see meta-analysis by Lemmer & Wagner, 2015), but is also particularly effective relative to other prejudice interventions (see meta-analysis by Beelman & Heinemann, 2014). And, as this review highlights, contact works very well among HPs (those most in need of intervention). Indeed, contact effect sizes may have been underestimated in reviews and meta-analyzes that have not accounted for individual differences (Hodson, Costello, et al., 2013; Hodson, Harry, et al., 2009). One of the key developments over the past decade, we argue, has been the integration of individual differences into this important domain. This change has opened up a range of future directions for researchers, some of which we outline below.

Effects of contact on individual differences

The field (and our review) has largely focused on how individual differences predict whether contact occurs, and whether HPs in particular can benefit from contact in terms of prejudice reduction. But can contact exert an effect on the prejudice-prone individual differences themselves? This is not generally the goal of contact researchers, given that individual differences tend to be relatively stable and most researchers consider prejudice (not ideology) a social problem in need of attention. Instead, emphasis is typically devoted to changing aspects of the context (e.g. threat, trust or anxiety cues) to ensure that HPs reduce prejudice following contact (Hodson, in press). Nonetheless, future research is needed to determine if and when contact alters ideological orientations such as RWA and SDO, cognitive variables such as NFC, or affective-laden variables such as intergroup disgust sensitivity and intergroup anxiety. Indeed, recent evidence from a pretest, post-test contact intervention, and from a 3-month longitudinal correlational study, demonstrated that contact effectively lowers levels of SDO (Dhont, Van Hiel, & Hewstone, 2014). Nonetheless, examining these processes over longer time intervals, and exploring mediation mechanisms (e.g. T1 contact → T2 mediators [e.g. anxiety] → T3 ideology [e.g. SDO/RWA]), would be valuable for the field. (For related contact analyzes without ideology, see Swart, Hewstone, Christ, & Voci, 2011).

Non-attitude outcomes

Another avenue for expansion is to move beyond an emphasis on attitudes as criteria. Some have rightfully criticized the field for an overly strong emphasis on out-group evaluations that may overlook other important outcomes, such as policy support (e.g. Dixon et al., 2005). There are reasons to anticipate that heeding such advice might pay dividends. Consider that HPs often show stronger benefits of contact than LPs in terms of anti-gay *attitudes* (Cunningham & Melton, 2013; Hodson, Harry, et al., 2009), but LPs often show stronger effects than HPs when gay *rights* are considered (Lewis, 2011; Skipworth, Garner, & Dettrey, 2010). In addition, physiological measures, particularly as mediators, can shed more light on how contact unfolds in real time (e.g. West, Turner, & Levita, 2015). This would help reconcile the intergroup interaction literature, highlighting negative stresses of contact in the immediate term, with the intergroup contact literature, highlighting the positive effects of contact over time, including the reduction of intergroup anxiety (MacInnis & Page-Gould, 2015). Another strong candidate for consideration is out-group (de)humanization following contact (e.g. Vezzali, Capozza, Stathi, & Giovannini, 2012), particularly as a function of individual differences.

Additional (and unique) individual differences

Addressing which individual differences are most (and least) receptive to positive contact effects is also an important direction for future research. Such information can inform about the nature of these individual difference constructs, and better inform contact interventions by isolating mediators to target. We encourage researchers to follow the lead of Asbrock and colleagues (2012, 2013) in statistically isolating the unique effects of individual differences against each other. Moreover, additional individual differences relevant to contact can be further considered. As an example, Hodson and colleagues (2015) sought to better understand individual differences in intergroup disgust sensitivity, whereby those scoring higher (vs. lower) are more repulsed by contact with out-groups. This variable, being rooted in disgust but with a distinctly intergroup element, is ultimately concerned with *contact*. In contrast to past interventions that failed to weaken or sever the link between intergroup disgust sensitivity and prejudice (Choma et al., 2012), in this investigation imagined contact interventions facilitated this function. In particular, elaborated imagined contact that involved deep breathing, relaxation and guided imagery, significantly weakened the prediction of anti-homeless attitudes through increasing out-group trust with the homeless. Through such exercises, the field learns more about both the individual difference construct contributing to prejudice, and the features of contact settings that best alleviate tension, conflict and bias.

Structural features of the contact setting

Other aspects of the contact setting itself warrant further exploration. Recent research reveals that, across nations, positive contact is more common but less impactful than negative contact (Graf, Paolini, & Rubin, 2014). Although Dhont and Van Hiel (2009) considered positive and negative contact separately, future research would benefit from better understanding how contact valence matters as a function of various individual differences. It is possible (if not probable) that HPs might benefit from more frequent and more positive contact (as our review reflects), but be particularly susceptible to the negative impact of negative or inflamed contact. Although contact is associated with lower prejudice in prison (Hodson, 2008) and Middle-East conflict (Maoz, 2003) settings, even among HPs, it is not clear the extent to which this finding generalizes. For instance, in both the Hodson and Maoz studies participants were in the *majority* or dominant group, either White inmates or Israelis. Collapsing across individual differences, meta-analytic research demonstrates that contact works best among the majority group (Tropp & Pettigrew, 2005). It is unclear, therefore, whether HPs who are members of minority or disadvantaged groups would benefit from contact, particularly if they are being mistreated or dominated (or whether society would actually benefit from them developing positive attitudes towards the dominant group at the cost of instigating social change; see Dixon, Tropp, Durrheim, & Tredoux, 2010). Thus, a more fine-grained analysis of contact features, such as group status and negativity of contact, will shed more light on the person-based contact question. In addressing such questions, researchers are encouraged to take advantage of the slate of sophisticated statistical procedures currently available that can, for instance, parse variance from individuals and contexts (e.g. multilevel modelling; see Christ & Wagner, 2013).

Researchers can also take advantage of modern technology to examine contact through virtual means. For example, researchers can engage participants in realistic intergroup contact through videogames that simulate actual life experiences (see Adachi, Hodson, & Hoffarth, 2015; Adachi, Hodson, Willoughby, Blank, & Ha, 2016; Adachi, Hodson, Willoughby, & Zanette, 2015). Not only can researchers systematically modify aspects of the situation (e.g. status) but also outcomes (e.g. winning vs. losing), duration of contact, positivity–negativity, etc. Moreover, participants can also gain experience through out-group avatars, that is, "contact" with an out-group by experiencing life *as* an out-group member. Role-playing as the out-group in the non-virtual environments has already proven effective at reducing prejudice, even among HPs (e.g. Hodson, Choma, & Costello, 2009). Such methods can also offer help with the ultimate challenge that contact researchers face in the future—given that contact reduces prejudice among HPs but they naturally avoid contact, how do we encourage such persons to engage in contact? Precursors to actual contact, such as imagined contact (Crisp & Turner, 2009), online intergroup friendship formation (e.g. MacInnis & Hodson, 2015), or video gaming (Adachi et al., 2016; Adachi, Hodson, Willoughby, et al., 2015) offer promise as tools to bring the proverbial horse to the water, even if the horse does not want to drink.

Closing remarks

Through this review, we have shown that individual differences matter in predicting who will approach or avoid intergroup contact. We have also demonstrated that contact, when experienced, improves intergroup attitudes among those most in need of intervention (HPs), through many of the mechanisms generally known to operate in contact settings (e.g. reduced anxiety and threat, increased trust). At this juncture, it comes as little surprise that individual differences matter to intergroup contact given that they matter to prejudice (Hodson & Dhont, 2015). It might be naïve to propose, as did Lincoln, that disliking others instigates a motive to seek out the other and learn more about the person and their group. Yet the evidence to date suggests that engaging in contact with out-groups is a worthwhile pursuit; those predisposed towards bias have the most to gain and are clearly susceptible to the power of contact.

Notes

1 By most accounts, Lincoln was considered a bright and perceptive man. His statement was most likely part tongue-in-cheek, part optimism, and part prescriptive.
2 In these studies reviewed, Agreeableness was operationalized and measured in keeping with the Big Five framework. Studies employing the HEXACO 6-factor framework and measure observe less role of Agreeableness and more influence by Honesty-Humility predicting lower prejudice (Hodson & Dhont, 2015).
3 Nonetheless, the other focus is equally valid (and primarily of interest to individual difference researchers).
4 As an illustration of the point we raise in Figure 1.2, these authors plotted religious fundamentalism on the x-axis and considered contact as the moderator (instead of the converse). Regardless, contact among HPs was associated with less prejudice.
5 The first author (GH) first realized the challenges of working in this field when reviewers of Hodson (2008) were visibly split over whether contact can work well among HPs—some insisted that *this cannot be the case*, whereas others asserted that *this is so obviously the case that this research question tells us nothing new.*
6 Other large-sample studies have provided mixed support contact benefits among SDOs. Schmid, Hewstone, Kupper, Zick and Wagner (2012) examined whether contact-based attitudes towards the contact group generalize to other groups, employing two-item SDO (and contact) scales out of necessity for the sample size and methodology. Such studies are extremely valuable to the field but inherently trade off construct measurement for large *n*s and nationally representative participants. Conclusions about the constructs should be interpreted with this in mind.

References

Adachi, P.J.C., Hodson, G., & Hoffarth, M.R. (2015). Video game play and intergroup relations: Real world implications for prejudice and discrimination. *Aggression and Violent Behavior.* doi: 10.1016/j.avb.2015.09.008

Adachi, P.J.C., Hodson, G., Willoughby, T., Blank, C., & Ha, A. (2016). From outgroups to allied forces: The effect of intergroup cooperation in violent and non-violent video games on boosting favorable outgroup attitudes. *Journal of Experimental Psychology: General, 145,* 259–65. doi: 10.1037/xge0000145

Adachi, P.J.C., Hodson, G., Willoughby, T., & Zanette, S. (2015). Brothers or sisters in arms: Intergroup cooperation in a violent shooter game can reduce intergroup prejudice. *Psychology of Violence, 5,* 455–62. doi: 10.1037/a0037407

Al Ramiah, A., & Hewstone, M. (2013). Intergroup contact as a tool for reducing, resolving, and preventing intergroup conflict: Evidence, limitations, and potential. *American Psychologist, 68,* 527–42. doi: 10.1037/a0032603

Allport, G.W. (1954). *The nature of prejudice*. Cambridge, MA: Addison-Wesley.

Altemeyer, B. (1996). *The authoritarian specter*. Cambridge, MA: Harvard University Press.

Asbrock, F., Christ, O., Duckitt, J., & Sibley, C.G. (2012). Differential effects of intergroup contact for authoritarians and social dominators: A Dual Process Model perspective. *Personality and Social Psychology Bulletin, 38*, 477–90. doi: 10.1177/0146167211429747

Asbrock, F., Gutenbrunner, L., & Wagner, U. (2013). Unwilling, but not unaffected – Imagined contact effects for authoritarians and social dominators. *European Journal of Social Psychology, 43*, 404–12. doi: 10.1002/ejsp.1956

Beelmann, A., & Heinemann, K.S. (2014). Preventing prejudice and improving intergroup attitudes: A meta-analysis of child and adolescent training programs. *Journal of Applied Developmental Psychology, 35*, 10–24. doi: 10.1016/j.appdev.2013.11.002

Brown, R., & Hewstone, M. (2005). An integrative theory of intergroup contact. In M. Zanna (Ed.), *Advances in experimental social psychology* (Vol. 37, pp. 255–343). San Diego, CA: Academic Press.

Choma, B.L., Hodson, G., & Costello, K. (2012). Intergroup disgust sensitivity as a predictor of Islamophobia: The modulating effect of fear. *Journal of Experimental Social Psychology, 48*, 499–506. doi: 10.1016/j.jesp.2011.10.014

Christ, O. & Wagner, U. (2013). Methodological issues in the study of intergroup contact: Towards a new wave of research. In G. Hodson & M. Hewstone (Eds.), *Advances in Intergroup Contact* (pp. 233–61). London, UK: Psychology Press.

Crisp, R.J., & Turner, R.N. (2009). Can imagined interactions produce positive perceptions? Reducing prejudice through simulated social contact. *American Psychologist, 64*, 231–40. doi: 10.1037/a0014718

Cunningham, G.B., & Melton, E.N. (2013). The moderating effects of contact with lesbians and gay friends on the relationships among religious fundamentalism, sexism, and sexual prejudice. *Journal of Sex Research, 50*, 401–08. doi: 10.1080/00224499.2011.648029

Dhont, K., Roets, A., & Van Hiel, A. (2011). Opening closed minds: The combined effects of intergroup contact and Need for Closure on prejudice. *Personality and Social Psychology Bulletin, 37*, 514–28. doi: 10.1177/0146167211399101

Dhont, K., & Van Hiel, A. (2009). We must not be enemies: Interracial contact and the reduction of prejudice among authoritarians. *Personality and Individual Differences, 46*, 172–7. doi: 10.1016/j.paid.2008.09.022

Dhont, K., & Van Hiel, A. (2011). Direct contact and authoritarianism as moderators between extended contact and reduced prejudice: Lower threat and greater trust as mediators. *Group Processes & Intergroup Relations, 14*, 223–7. doi: 10.1177/1368430210391121

Dhont, K., Van Hiel, A., & Hewstone, M. (2014). Changing the ideological roots of prejudice: Longitudinal effects of ethnic intergroup contact on social dominance orientation. *Group Processes and Intergroup Relations, 17*, 27–44. doi: 10.1177/1368430213497064

Dixon, J., Durrheim, K., & Tredoux, C. (2005). Beyond the optimal contact strategy: A reality check for the contact hypothesis. *American Psychologist, 60*, 697–711. doi: 10.1037/0003-066X.60.7.697

Dixon, J., Tropp, L.R., Durrheim, K., & Tredoux, C. (2010). "Let them eat harmony": Prejudice-reduction strategies and attitudes of historically disadvantaged groups. *Current Directions in Psychological Science, 19*, 76–80. doi: 10.1177/0963721410363366

Graf, S., Paolini, S., & Rubin, M. (2014). Negative intergroup contact is more influential, but positive contact is more common: Assessing contact prominence and contact prevalence in five Central European countries. *European Journal of Social Psychology, 44*, 536–47. doi: 10.1002/ejsp.2052

Graham, H.E., Frame, M.C., & Kenworthy, J.B. (2014). The moderating effect of prior attitudes on intergroup face-to-face contact. *Journal of Applied Social Psychology, 44*, 547–56. doi: 10.1111/jasp.12246

Hayes, A.F. (2009). Beyond Baron and Kenny: Statistical mediation analysis in the new millennium. *Communication Monographs, 76,* 408–20. doi: 10.1080/03637750903310360

Hodson, G. (2008). Interracial prison contact: The pros for (socially dominant) cons. *British Journal of Social Psychology, 47,* 325–51. doi: 10.1348/014466607X231109

Hodson, G. (2011). Do ideologically intolerant people benefit from intergroup contact? *Current Directions in Psychological Science, 20,* 154–9. doi: 10.1177/0963721411409025

Hodson, G. (in press). Authoritarian contact: From "tight circles" to cross-group friendships. In F. Funke, T. Petzel, J.C. Cohrs, & J. Duckitt (Eds.), *Perspectives on authoritarianism.* Wiesbaden, Germany: VS-Verlag.

Hodson, G., & Busseri, M.A. (2012). Bright minds and dark attitudes: Lower cognitive ability predicts greater prejudice through right-wing ideology and low intergroup contact. *Psychological Science, 23,* 187–95. doi: 10.1177/0956797611421206

Hodson, G., Choma, B.L., Boisvert, J., Hafer, C., MacInnis, C.C., & Costello, K. (2013). The role of intergroup disgust in predicting negative outgroup evaluations. *Journal of Experimental Social Psychology, 49,* 195–205. doi: 10.1016/j.jesp.2012.11.002

Hodson, G., Choma, B.L., & Costello, K. (2009). Experiencing Alien-Nation: Effects of a simulation intervention on attitudes toward homosexuals. *Journal of Experimental Social Psychology, 45,* 974–8. doi: 10.1016/j.jesp.2009.02.010

Hodson, G., Costello, K., & MacInnis, C.C. (2013). Is intergroup contact beneficial among intolerant people? Exploring individual differences in the benefits of contact on attitudes. In G. Hodson & M. Hewstone (Eds.), *Advances in intergroup contact* (pp. 49–80). London, UK: Psychology Press.

Hodson, G., & Dhont, K. (2015). The person-based nature of prejudice: Individual difference predictors of intergroup negativity. *European Review of Social Psychology, 26,* 1–42. doi: 10.1080/10463283.2015.1070018

Hodson, G., Dube, B., & Choma, B.L. (2015). Can (elaborated) imagined contact interventions reduce prejudice among those higher in intergroup disgust sensitivity (ITG-DS)? *Journal of Applied Social Psychology, 45,* 123–31. doi: 10.1111/jasp.12281.

Hodson, G., Harry, H., & Mitchell, A. (2009). Independent benefits of contact and friendship on attitudes toward homosexuals among authoritarians and highly identified heterosexuals. *European Journal of Social Psychology, 39,* 509–25. doi: 10.1002/ejsp.558

Hodson, G., & Hewstone, M. (Eds.) (2013a). *Advances in intergroup contact.* London, UK: Psychology Press.

Hodson, G., & Hewstone, M. (2013b). Introduction: Advances in intergroup contact. In G. Hodson & M. Hewstone (Eds.), *Advances in intergroup contact* (pp. 3–20). London, UK: Psychology Press.

Hodson, G., Hewstone, M., & Swart, H. (2013). Advances in intergroup contact: Epilogue and future directions. In G. Hodson & M. Hewstone (Eds.), *Advances in intergroup contact* (pp. 262–305). London, UK: Psychology Press.

Hodson, G., & Skorska, M.N. (2015). Tapping generalized essentialism to predict outgroup prejudices. *British Journal of Social Psychology, 54,* 371–82. doi: 10.1111/bjso.12083

Hoffarth, M.R., & Hodson, G. (2016). Who needs imagined contact? Replication attempts examining previous contact as a potential moderator. *Social Psychology, 47,* 118–24. doi: 10.1027/1864-9335/a000258

Islam, M.R., & Hewstone, M. (1993). Dimensions of contact as predictors of intergroup anxiety, perceived outgroup variability, and out-group attitude: An integrative model. *Personality and Social Psychology Bulletin, 19,* 700–10. doi: 10.1177/0146167293196005

Jackson, J.W., & Poulsen, J.R. (2005). Contact experiences mediate the relationship between Five-Factor Model of personality traits and ethnic prejudice. *Journal of Applied Social Psychology, 35,* 667–85. doi: 10.1111/j.1559–1816.2005.tb02140.x

John, O.P., Donahue, E.M., & Kentle, R.L. (1991). The "Big Five" inventory – Versions 4a and 54 (Tech. Rep.). Berkeley: Institute of Personality and Social Research, University of California, Berkeley.

Kline, R.B. (2011). *Principles and practice of structural equation modeling* (3rd ed). New York, NY: Guilford Press.

Kruglanski, A.W. (1990). Motivations for judging and knowing: Implications for causal attribution. In E.T. Higgins & R.M. Sorrentino (Eds.), *The handbook of motivation and cognition: Foundation of social behavior* (Vol. 2, pp. 333–68). New York, NY: Guilford Press.

Lemmer, G., & Wagner, U. (2015). Can we really reduce ethnic prejudice outside the lab? A meta-analysis of direct and indirect contact interventions. *European Journal of Social Psychology, 45*, 152–68. doi: 10.1002/ejsp.2079

Lewis, G.B. (2011). The friends and family plan: Contact with gays and support for gay rights. *The Policy Studies Journal, 39*, 217–38.

Liebkind, K., Haaramo, J., & Jasinskaja-Lahti, I. (2000). Effects of contact and personality on intergroup attitudes of different professionals. *Journal of Community and Applied Social Psychology, 10*, 171–81.

MacInnis, C.C., & Hodson, G. (2015). The development of online cross-group relationships among university students: Benefits of earlier (*vs.* later) disclosure of stigmatized group membership. *Journal of Social and Personal Relationships, 32*, 788–809. doi: 10.1177/0265407514548394

MacInnis, C.C., & Page-Gould, E. (2015). How can intergroup interaction be bad if intergroup contact is good? Exploring and reconciling an apparent paradox in the science of inter-group relations. *Perspectives on Psychological Science, 10*, 307–27. doi: 10.1177/1745691614568482

Maoz, I. (2003). Peace-building with the hawks: Attitude change of Jewish-Israeli hawks and doves following dialogue encounters with Palestinians. *International Journal of Intercultural Relations, 27*, 701–14. doi: 10.1016/j.ijintrel.2003.08.004

McCrae, R.R., & Costa, P.T.C., Jr. (1987). Validation of the five-factor model of personality across instruments and observers. *Journal of Personality and Social Psychology, 52*, 81–90. http://dx.doi.org.proxy.library.brocku.ca/10.1037/0022–3514.52.1.81

Miller, D.A., Smith, E.R., & Mackie, D.M. (2004). Effects of intergroup contact and political predispositions on prejudice: Role of intergroup emotions. *Group Processes and Intergroup Relations, 7*, 221–37. doi: 10.1177/1368430204046109

Munniksma, A., Stark, T.H., Verkuyten, M., Flache, A., & Veenstra, R. (2013). Extended intergroup friendships within social settings: The moderating role of initial outgroup attitudes. *Group Processes and Intergroup Relations, 16*, 752–70. doi: 10.1177/1368430213486207

Pettigrew, T.F., & Tropp, L.R. (2006). A meta-analytic test of intergroup contact theory. *Journal of Personality and Social Psychology, 90*, 751–83. doi: 10.1037/0022–3514.90.5.751

Pettigrew, T.F., & Tropp, L.R. (2008). How does intergroup contact reduce prejudice? Meta-analytic tests of three mediators. *European Journal of Social Psychology, 38*, 922–34. doi: 10.1002/ejsp.504

Pettigrew, T.F., & Tropp, L.R. (2011). *When groups meet: The dynamics of intergroup contact.* New York, NY: Psychology Press.

Reynolds, K.J., Turner, J.C., Haslam, A., & Ryan, M.K. (2001). The role of personality and group factors in explaining prejudice. *Journal of Experimental Social Psychology, 37*, 427–34. doi: 10.1006/jesp.2000.1473

Roets, A., & Van Hiel, A. (2011). Allport's prejudiced personality today: Need for closure as the motivated cognitive basis of prejudice. *Current Directions in Psychological Science, 20*, 349–54. doi: 10.1177/0963721411424894

Schmid, K., Hewstone, M., Küpper, B., Zick, A., & Wagner, U. (2012). Secondary transfer effects of intergroup contact: A crossnational comparison in Europe. *Social Psychology Quarterly, 75,* 28–51. doi: 10.1177/0190272511430235

Sidanius, J., & Pratto, F. (1999). *Social dominance: An intergroup theory of social hierarchy and oppression.* Cambridge, UK: Cambridge University Press.

Skipworth, S.A., Garner, A., & Dettrey, B.J. (2010). Limitations of the contact hypothesis: Heterogeneity in the contact effect on attitudes toward gay rights. *Politics and Policy, 38,* 887–906. doi: 10.1111/j.1747-1346.2010.00262.x/enhanced/exportCitation/doi/10.1111/j.1747-1346.2010.00262.x

Swart, H., Hewstone, M., Christ, O., & Voci, A. (2011). Affective mediators of intergroup contact: A longitudinal analysis in South Africa. *Journal of Personality and Social Psychology, 101,* 1221–38. doi: 10.1037/a0024450

Tajfel, H., & Turner, J.C. (1979). An integrative theory of intergroup conflict. In W.G. Austin & S. Worchel (Eds.), *The social psychology of intergroup relations* (pp. 33–47). Monterey, CA: Brooks/Cole Publishing Company.

Tropp, L.R., & Pettigrew, T.F. (2005). Relationships between intergroup contact and prejudice among minority and majority status groups. *Psychological Science, 16,* 951–7. doi: 10.1111/j.1467–9280.2005.01643.x

Turner, R.N., Dhont, K., Hewstone, M., Prestwich, A., & Vonofakou, C. (2014). The role of personality factors in the reduction of intergroup anxiety and amelioration of outgroup attitudes via intergroup contact. *European Journal of Personality, 28,* 180–92. doi: 10.1002/per.1927

Turner, R.N., Hewstone, M., & Voci, A. (2007). Reducing explicit and implicit outgroup prejudice via direct and extended contact: The mediating role of self-disclosure and intergroup anxiety. *Journal of Personality and Social Psychology, 93,* 369–88. doi: 10.1037/0022–3514.93.3.369

Vezzali, L., Capozza, D., Stathi, S., & Giovannini, D. (2012). Increasing outgroup trust, reducing infrahumanization, and enhancing future contact intentions via imagined intergroup contact. *Journal of Experimental Social Psychology, 48,* 437–40. doi: 10.1016/j.jesp.2011.09.008

Voci, A., & Hewstone, M. (2003). Intergroup contact and prejudice toward immigrants in Italy: The mediational role of anxiety and the moderational role of group salience. *Group Processes and Intergroup Relations, 6,* 37–54. doi: 10.1177/1368430203006001011

Voci, A., Hewstone, M., Swart, H., & Veneziani, C.A. (2015). Refining the association between intergroup contact and intergroup forgiveness in Northern Ireland: Type of contact, prior conflict experience, and group identification. *Group Processes and Intergroup Relations. 18,* 589–608. doi: 10.1177/1368430215577001

West, K., Turner, R.N., & Levita, L. (2015). Applying imagined contact to improve physiological responses in anticipation of intergroup interactions and the perceived quality of these interactions. *Journal of Applied Social Psychology, 45,* 425–36. doi: 10.1111/jasp.12309

3

THE INFLUENCE OF DIRECT AND EXTENDED CONTACT ON THE DEVELOPMENT OF ACCULTURATION PREFERENCES AMONG MAJORITY MEMBERS

Roberto González and Rupert Brown

Key words: cross-group friendship, extended contact, ingroup norms, trust, intergroup similarities and acculturation preferences

There is no doubt that human migration has become one of the most visible and relevant social issues in recent decades. According to recent international statistics, approximately 3.2% of the world's population, over 232 million people, are defined as immigrants, that is, living in a country other than where they were born (United Nations, Department of Economic and Social Affairs, 2013). Such massive migration flows inevitably bring members of different groups into contact with one another, and such encounters will often require groups—both the migrant groups and those in the receiving society—to overcome several challenges. Immigrants will often need to learn about a new culture, probably develop a new social identity and, in some cases, face discrimination in social environments that are not always welcoming. Majority members are often confronted by groups with different cultural backgrounds and practices, which they may perceive as threatening to their social identities. Within social psychology, this process is called acculturation, the manifold ways in which members of different cultures mutually influence and accommodate to each other (Brown & Zagefka, 2011; Redfield, Linton, & Herskovits, 1936).

Though there has been a growth of acculturation research in different cultural contexts (Brown & Zagefka, 2011), there are still some important research gaps. First, the vast majority of acculturation studies have been concerned with *consequences* of acculturation preferences, rather than their *antecedents* (Sam & Berry, 2010). Thus, the trend has been to conceptualize acculturation preferences as an independent, rather than a dependent variable. As a whole, the evidence suggests that holding an acculturation orientation of "integration" usually is associated with positive health outcomes in minorities (e.g. Berry, 1997) and more favorable intergroup relationships (e.g. González, Sirlopú, & Kessler, 2010; Pfafferott & Brown, 2006; Verkuyten, 2005; Zagefka, Brown, & González, 2009). Yet, we know little less about how to foster the acculturation preferences that bring about these positive outcomes.

Second, most research has focused attention on the immigrants' acculturation preferences; however, it seems obvious that majority members might also have expectations about how immigrants should live in the country (Berry, 1997; González et al. , 2010; Piontkowski, Florack, Hoelker, & Obdrzálek, 2000; Zagefka et al., 2009). Even though this issue has been highlighted as theoretically important, there is still more research on immigrants' acculturation preferences than of majority members, even though the latter are able to exert a decisive influence over the nature of intergroup relations in a society due to their greater numerical size and political power. Therefore, it is critical to understand the majority's point of view as the preferences of its members make an important contribution to the promotion of multiculturalism.

Third, despite the close conceptual relationships that exist between Acculturation Theory (e.g. Berry, 1997) and Intergroup Contact Theory (Allport, 1954; Brown & Hewstone, 2005; Gaertner, Dovidio, Anastasio, Bachman, & Rust, 1993), the integration between these two lines of work has only recently received attention (e.g. Brown & Zagefka, 2011; Van Acker & Vanbeselaere, 2011). In this chapter, therefore, we will explore how majority members' acculturation preferences can be predicted from both direct and indirect experiences of intergroup contact.

Fourth, the vast majority of acculturation research has focused, not surprisingly, on immigration contexts in North America and Europe. However, as Henrich, Heine and Norenzayan (2010) have persuasively argued, not everyone is so *WEIRD* (Western, Educated, Industrialized, Rich and Democratic). Accordingly, here we will review some of our work in Chile, looking particularly at the Chilean–Peruvian intergroup relationship.

In the next sections, we review our research program (three studies) that has tested the impact of direct and indirect contact experiences of majority members on the development of their acculturation preferences. We believe that our research program has contributed to the development of the contact–acculturation research agenda by conducting innovative *longitudinal* research in the Chilean-Peruvian immigrant context. These longitudinal designs permitted us to learn about the dynamic and cumulative process underlying changes in acculturation preferences from the majority group's perspective, with a particular focus on future research challenges and policy implications. As we hope will become apparent, this integration of the contact and acculturation traditions is both timely and important, which opens up many new research avenues.

Research context

After democracy was regained in Chile in 1989, migration to Chile underwent important transformations (Stefoni, 2011). Chile became an attractive place for Latin

American migrants due to its comparatively high quality of life and work opportunities (Mora, 2008). Since then, immigration has increased 200% and is expected to continue increasing. According to estimates of the Ministerio del Interior, Chile (2009), by 2009, 352,344 migrants lived in Chile (2.08% of the total population). Among these, the largest immigrant groups come from Peru (37.1%), Argentina (17.2%) and Bolivia (6.8%). The majority of Peruvian immigrants has indigenous origins and belongs to low socioeconomic groups, with a disproportionally high proportion of women between 15 and 44 years of age. The migration process has accentuated differences between nationals and immigrants bringing about both negative and positive outcomes (González et al., 2010). Thus, this context offers an opportunity to analyze several social-psychological factors that explain attitudes and behavior towards immigrants in general, and Peruvian immigrants in particular.

Intergroup attitudes between Peruvian immigrants and Chileans may be affected by both realistic and symbolic threats (Stephan & Stephan, 2000). Realistic threat derives from perceptions that the in-group's material well-being, as well as its economic and political power, may deteriorate because of the presence of immigrant groups (e.g. competition between Peruvian immigrants and lower-class Chileans for low-skilled jobs; González et al., 2010). On the other hand, at the symbolic level, while Peruvians and Chileans share many cultural characteristics (such as language and religion), there are noticeable differences when it comes to ethnic origins: while Chileans have a stronger White-European descent, Peruvian immigrants have a stronger Andean indigenous origin (González et al., 2010).

Direct cross-group friendship and the development of acculturation preferences

Study 1

Our first longitudinal study examines the relationship between contact and acculturation preferences among majority members in the context of the Peruvian immigration to Chile (Hässler et al., 2015). Here, we analyze the dynamic process that occurs when actual friendship between Peruvian immigrants and Chileans (majority) takes place within school contexts. We explore how quality and quantity of cross-group friendship can be conceived as causal factors, facilitating Chileans' desire for Peruvians' culture maintenance and culture adoption over time. We also seek to explain *why* acculturation preferences might be influenced by experiences of intergroup contact by exploring the mediational role that intergroup trust (Tam, Hewstone, Kenworthy, & Cairns, 2009) and perceived group similarities (Gaertner et al., 1993) play in influencing acculturation preferences of Chilean majority members. Thus, we focused on both the antecedents (quantity and quality of contact) and mechanisms (intergroup trust and perceived intergroup similarity) that might explain the development of desired acculturation preferences (cultural maintenance and cultural adoption) of the Chilean majority.

Following Berry's acculturation model (Berry, 1997) and its subsequent developments (Bourhis, Moïse, Perrault & Senécal, 1997; Brown & Zagefka, 2011), we first assume that majority members have their own preferences for immigrants to either be "integrated", "assimilated", "segregated" or "marginalized" from the society (Piontkowski et al., 2000). These acculturation orientations stem from their attitudes towards or desire that immigrants should be able to maintain their culture of origin and the extent to which they want immigrants to adopt their mainstream culture (Bourhis et al., 1997).

Now, we know that majority members sometimes disapprove of immigrants' cultural maintenance (Van Acker & Vanbeselaere, 2011; Zagefka et al., 2009). So, the question is: what factors might stimulate members of the majority to support immigrants' cultural maintenance? Positive forms of contact experiences, we suggest, are an important factor when predicting support for cultural maintenance. There is evidence that Chilean adult majority members that support integration of Peruvian immigrants report having more Peruvian immigrant friends than those preferring separation (González et al., 2010). Additionally, cross-group friendship has been identified as a key element for improving intergroup attitudes towards immigrants (Binder et al., 2009; Paolini, Hewstone, Cairns, & Voci, 2004), as well as towards majority members from the perspective of minority groups (González et al., 2010).

There is also evidence suggesting that the mere perception that immigrants are striving for contact and are making an effort to adopt the mainstream culture leads to positive attitudes among majority members (Van Acker & Vanbeselaere, 2011; Zagefka, Brown, Broquard, & Martin, 2007) which, in turn, increase their support for cultural maintenance, suggesting a virtuous circle. Yet, in order for positive attitudes to develop, the majority's preference for culture maintenance also needs to be coupled with a desire for intergroup contact or cultural adoption ("integration"). Thus, contact could be conceived as a factor that might increase support for immigrants' cultural maintenance as well as cultural adoption.

Contact has been said to reduce prejudice because it *reduces* feelings of intergroup anxiety and realistic threat (Binder et al., 2009; González et al., 2010; Paolini et al., 2004; Turner, Hewstone, Voci, Paolini, & Christ, 2007) and *increases* knowledge and empathy towards out-group members (Pettigrew & Tropp, 2008). Frequent and in-depth contact with out-group members provides the potential to learn about the other's background, history, values, customs and traditions. Thus, increasing knowledge about the out-group may help to decrease intergroup anxiety, increase intergroup trust through the experience of positive contact (Tam et al., 2009; Turner, Hewstone, & Voci, 2007) and foster perceived group similarities (Gaertner et al., 1993).

Research on interpersonal similarity has shown that similarity may lead to greater attraction as well as to greater willingness to associate with others (Byrne, 1971). Further, evidence suggests that perceived similarity also leads to greater willingness to associate with other ethnic groups (Osbeck, Moghaddam, & Perreault, 1997). People who prefer integration strategies perceive immigrants to be more similar to their own group, feel enriched by the influence of the minorities group's culture and show reduced in-group bias, in contrast to people preferring other acculturation strategies (Piontkowski et al., 2000). These results are in line with the role that perceived similarity with out-group members plays in the contact–attitude link (Stathi, Cameron, Hartley, & Bradford, 2014; Wolsko, Park, Judd, & Bachelor, 2003). Based on this evidence, we argued that the development of intergroup friendship may lead to an increase in perceived similarity, which may subsequently positively predict both acculturation preferences, cultural maintenance and cultural adoption.

Trusting the out-group may be a second mediator for the contact–acculturation link. Out-group trust can be defined as a positive expectation about the intentions and behaviors of a specific out-group towards the in-group (Lewicki, McAllister, & Bies, 1998). Cross-group friendship has been shown to impact intergroup attitudes positively through increased trust in the out-group (Tam et al., 2009; Turner, Hewstone, & Voci, 2007). Given this role of trust in influencing general attitudes towards the out-group, it may also be an important precursor of the majority's support for the minority group engaging in culture maintenance and cultural adoption. First, because the majority feels confident that the minority will not exploit the situation and, second, because trust should increase the willingness to cooperate, which may lead to preferences to have an out-group friend. Thus, having trustworthy immigrant friends might allow Chileans to feel more secure and ready to support cultural maintenance and cultural adoption to the extent they do not see immigrants as threatening the existence of their mainstream culture (Van Acker & Vanbeselaere, 2011).

Study 1 was conducted in secondary schools in Chile, an environment in which young Chilean and Peruvian immigrants have many opportunities for contact. Participants were recruited from ten schools in immigrant-dense neighbourhoods in Santiago. The schools were either public municipal or subsidized schools, which are attended mainly by students of socio-economically disadvantaged or middle-income families. All the students in classes with at least three Peruvian students were invited to participate, after obtaining informed consent from their parents and/or guardians. In total, 467 Chilean high school students (roughly equal numbers of boys and girls) filled out the questionnaires at three different time points during the academic year (with a lag of two months between time points).

Using structural equation modelling (SEM), we explored the longitudinal effects of the independent variables, number and quality of cross-group friendships, the two mediators, intergroup similarity and out-group trust, and the dependent variables concerning acculturation preferences, culture maintenance and culture adoption, across the three waves (Muthén & Muthén, 2012). Statistically, we tested our hypotheses running multivariate longitudinal cross-lagged analyzes starting with the most basic longitudinal model. This basic model was then compared step-by-step with more restrictive models (Hässler et al., 2015).

The study revealed several interesting findings. First, the Chilean students reported that they had had positive experiences of contact (>= 5 on a 7-point scale at all three time points) and also high levels of trust in their Peruvians friends (> 4), though they did also report a slight reduction in the number of Peruvian friends within the school over time. They also perceived only a moderate level of intergroup similarities between Peruvian and Chilean students (between 3 and 4). With regard to the acculturation preferences, Chilean students were moderately in favor of Peruvian immigrants maintaining their culture (> 4) and adopting the Chilean culture (~4).

Second, as can be seen from Figure 3.1, quality of cross-group friendship on its own influenced acculturation preferences of the students: the better the quality of the friendship that Chilean students established with Peruvian immigrants at school, the more they wanted them to maintain their original culture. This effect, as we predicted, was partially mediated by changes in the level of intergroup trust over time. Thus, the better the quality of their friendship, the more they trusted Peruvians as a whole and, subsequently, the more they wanted them to maintain their culture. However, contrary to our expectations, intergroup similarity did not mediate the relationship between quality of contact and cultural maintenance, but it did play a role when predicting cultural adoption. Thus, quality of intergroup friendship significantly increased the level of perceived intergroup similarities, which in turn significantly increased their preferences of culture adoption.

Third, quantity of out-group friends had no direct effect on either culture maintenance or cultural adoption. Instead, its effects on culture maintenance and culture adoption were marginally mediated by out-group trust and perceived intergroup similarity, respectively. Though marginal, the effect of these mediators mirrored those observed for quality of contact on both acculturation preferences.

Finally, we ran a bidirectional model (in which we combined the unidirectional forward and reverse effects of the variables in the model) and compared its pattern of results with the one obtained in the unidirectional model (the bidirectional model is not depicted in the Figure). A strength of the bidirectional model was that it allowed us to better understand the dynamic of changes over time. Interestingly, the pattern for the mediation effects holds even though the longitudinal indirect effect from quality of cross-group friendship to culture adoption via intergroup similarity was now only marginally significant. Furthermore, the total longitudinal indirect effect from number of intergroup friends to culture maintenance became significant in the bidirectional model, when it was only marginally significant in the unidirectional one. Out-group trust seemed to play a role in this process, since it was predicted by cross-group friendship and preferences for culture maintenance. Further, there appears to be a bidirectional cross-lagged relationship between perceived intergroup similarity and culture adoption; that is, culture adoption predicted greater perception of intergroup similarity, which in turn predicted a stronger preference for culture adoption and vice versa.

These results are especially important, because they contradict other findings that the majority does not support culture maintenance (Tip et al., 2012; Van Acker & Vanbeselaere, 2011), and highlight the role of trust as an essential part in explaining

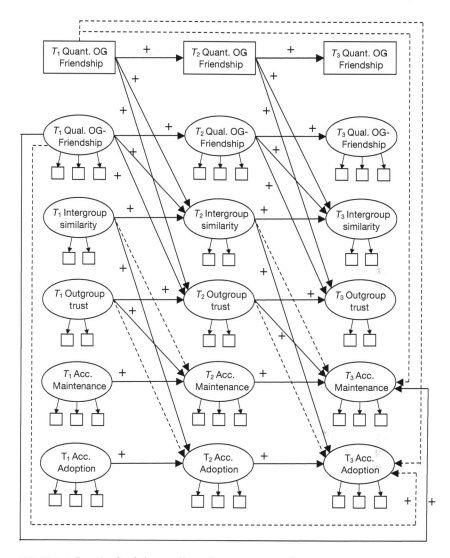

FIGURE 3.1 Longitudinal direct effect of contact on acculturation preferences
(Study 1). Dotted paths indicate non-significant relationships.

this contrasting pattern. In the immigrant context, majority members commonly experience anxiety and threat (Stephan & Stephan, 2000), a pattern that was also found in the Chilean context (González et al., 2010; Sirlopú & Van Oudenhoven, 2013). What the current results reveal is that, even though majority members might experience these negative emotions, cross-group friendship could exert a significant change: becoming friends with Peruvian immigrants allowed majority Chilean students to develop trust for them, which, in turn, significantly predicted an increase in their desire for Peruvian immigrants to maintain their culture.

The mediating role of intergroup similarity, on the other hand, differed from that of trust. This time, quality of cross-group friendship (and marginally quantity of contact) increased perceived intergroup similarity over time and, through this mechanism, it increased culture adoption. No significant effects were found for perceived similarity when predicting cultural maintenance. One reason for this asymmetrical pattern of the mediator variables may be that the maintenance of the heritage culture by the minority might emphasize differences between the two groups. Therefore, it seems reasonable to assume that perceived similarity would likely predict culture adoption but not culture maintenance. In addition, this asymmetrical role of the mediators underlines the importance of taking into account the distinct effects on both acculturation preference dimensions, although quality of cross-group friendship was associated with both of them.

In conclusion, Study 1 not only provided substantial longitudinal evidence about the central role that contact with immigrants plays in promoting the development of acculturation preferences of cultural maintenance and cultural adoption among majority members, but also it shed light on reasons why it does so. Contact affected acculturation preferences of majority members by increasing the psychological feeling of intergroup trust and perceived intergroup similarities with immigrants groups.

Direct and extended contact and the development of acculturation preferences

In this section, we present two other longitudinal studies from our research program. This time, our focus was on understanding the role that both direct and extended contact experiences may have in promoting changes on acculturation preferences among Chilean majority members (González et al., 2015). There has been some recent interest in exploring the relationship between direct and extended contact (e.g. Christ et al., 2010), and we wished to extend those research developments to examine the independent and joint effects of both kinds of contact on the development of majority acculturation preferences.

Study 2

One of the most fruitful extensions of the contact hypothesis has been that observing cross-group friendship (extended contact) also improves intergroup attitudes (Wright, Aron, McLaughlin-Volpe, & Ropp, 1997). Thus, the mere knowledge that an in-group member has close contact with an out-group member positively affects how in-group members feel about, think about and behave towards the respective out-group (Turner, Hewstone, Voci, et al., 2007).

The positive effect of extended contact has been demonstrated among adults (e.g. Wright et al., 1997) and adolescents (e.g. De Tezanos-Pinto, Bratt, & Brown,

2010). Extended contact has been said to prepare people for future direct contact and may actually promote intergroup friendship (Gómez, Tropp, & Fernandez, 2011; Mazziota, Rohmann, Wright, De Tezanos-Pinto, & Lutterbach, 2015; Turner, Hewstone, & Voci, 2007). In addition, extended contact effects can sometimes be observed over and above direct contact (e.g. Pettigrew, Christ, Wagner, & Stellmacher, 2007).

Now, assuming that the acculturation preferences can be considered as attitudinal constructs, and that actual contact and the contact acculturation preferences are conceptually related, we then expected direct contact to be particularly relevant to explain the acculturation–contact link in Study 2. We reasoned that the more Chilean majority members have Peruvian immigrant friends, the more they would desire them to have contact with them. Cross-group friendship was then expected to motivate members of the majority to continue their relationships and foster positive expectations for future contact (Binder et al., 2009; Pettigrew & Tropp, 2006).

However, direct and extended contact may affect intergroup relations through different pathways. Affective processes may mediate both direct and extended contact effects (Pettigrew & Tropp, 2008), yet extended contact may be particularly associated with changes in perceived norms (De Tezanos-Pinto et al., 2010; Turner, Hewstone, Voci, & Vonofakou, 2008; Vezzali, Hewstone, Capozza, Giovanini, & Wölfer, 2014). In extended friendship, group membership might be expected to be salient to the observer, whereas observing a cross-group interaction should not evoke anxiety or other negative affective reactions.

Within the contact literature, there has been a growing realization of the important role that in-group norms can play as a mediator of extended contact effects. Inspired by Allport (1954), several studies have shown that extended contact plays a significant role in the generation of new social norms in favor of intergroup tolerance (De Tezanos Pinto et al., 2010; Turner et al., 2008; Vezzali et al., 2014). Studies of multiculturalism have also revealed that in-group norms about what are appropriate acculturation behaviors are correlated with support for multiculturalism (Tip et al., 2015).

Thus, in Study 2 we hypothesized that extended experiences of contact would promote changes in the majority's acculturation preferences because they change in-group norms regarding contact experiences with out-group members. Cross-group friendship, on the other hand, was expected to directly influence acculturation preference for cultural maintenance and contact (Berry, 1997). A person's direct experience with an out-group member might well be expected to influence his/her own feelings and attitudes, but would not necessarily convey much information about what others in the in-group do or think about such cross-group friendships. The *indirect* experience of extended contact, on the other hand, does say something about what the other(s) in the in-group thinks about such relationships.

Study 2 used data from a different longitudinal survey with two time points (with a lag of 6 months). The data was collected among low-income urban high school students in several downtown neighbourhoods of Santiago, Chile (as in Study 1). Participants in this study included 654 Chilean school students (again with an approximately equal number of boys and girls). Using a 0 (*none*) to 6 (*6 or more*) scale, students reported direct contact (number of Peruvian friends) and extended contact (the extent to which their fellow Chilean friends have Peruvian friends). In-group norms supporting cross-group friendship, on the other hand, were assessed by asking Chilean students on a 5-point scale to report the extent to which their fellow in-group members would be happy if they have Peruvian friends.

We now present the main results. First, Chilean students reported having rather few Peruvian friends (only one on average) and slightly more extended contact experiences (between one and two). They also reported a moderate level of perceived in-group norms favoring contact with Peruvian immigrants (~ 2.5). As in Study 1, these Chilean students were moderately in favor of Peruvian immigrants maintaining their culture (~ 3) and having contact with majority members (> 3). These data indicate an orientation towards "integration".

Second, as predicted, extended contact positively influenced perceived in-group norms in favor of intergroup contact. Thus, the more Chilean students reported having in-group friends who have Peruvian friends, the more they

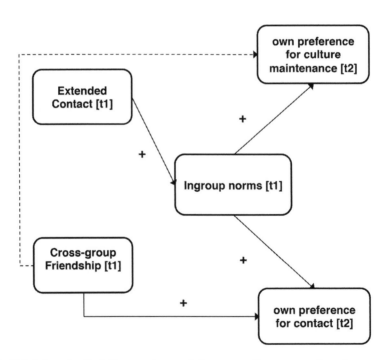

FIGURE 3.2 Longitudinal direct and extended contact effects on acculturation preferences (Study 2). Dotted paths indicate non-significant relationships.

thought their friends valued and liked them to have Peruvian friends. In turn, those in-group norms longitudinally fostered the development of acculturation preferences of contact and culture maintenance (Figure 3.2). Thus, as expected, in-group norms longitudinally mediated the extended contact–acculturation preferences association. This new longitudinal evidence complements the cross-sectional results obtained in previous studies (De Tezanos-Pinto et al., 2010; Turner et al., 2008; Wright et al., 1997). Direct cross-group friendship, on the other hand, predicted changes in the acculturation preferences but only regarding the desire for contact dimension (mirroring the effects observed in Binder et al., 2009).

Thus, in conclusion, Study 2 provided longitudinal evidence about the roles that direct and extended contact with immigrants play in promoting the development of acculturation preferences of cultural maintenance and contact among majority members. Extended contact influenced both acculturation preferences by increasing the perception that in-group members value majority members to have contact with immigrants groups (perceived in-group norms supporting cross-group friendship).

Study 3

Study 3 was an extension of Study 2, but differed from it in several respects. First, cross-group friendship and extended contact were measured with the same items used in Study 2 but with a different scale (from 0 "*none*" to 10 "*10 or more*"). Second, rather than analyzing the acculturation measure of cultural adoption, we chose desire for contact (the original dimension proposed by Berry, 1997, measured on a 5-point scale). Finally, we expanded the time lag between data points. Data collection took place over a 6-month period. Each of the three time points was assessed with a lag of 3 months. Here we were interested in testing a slightly different model: the direct and extended contact effects on acculturation preferences of cultural maintenance and desire for contact (and not cultural adoption) using a three-wave longitudinal design. As in Study 2, we also tested the longitudinal mediational role of in-group norms.

Study 3 was conducted in the same school as Study 1 (same sample but different variables and new time lag), in which young Chileans and Peruvian immigrants had many opportunities for contact. There were 475 Chilean high school students (roughly equal numbers of boys and girls) who participated in the study and filled out the questionnaires in Spanish in three different time points during the academic year.

The main results were as follows. First, Chilean students reported a reduction in the numbers of Peruvian friends over time (from > 3.5 at T1 to < 2.7 at T3) and extended contact experiences (> 3 at T1 to < 2.5 at T3). They also reported moderate and stable level of perceived in-group norms favoring contact with Peruvian immigrants (between 3.5 and 4 on a 7-point scale). They were also fairly positive in favor of Peruvian immigrants maintaining their culture (3–4.7 on a

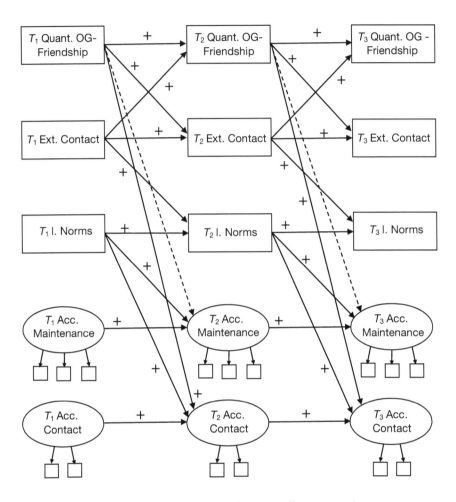

FIGURE 3.3 Longitudinal direct and extended contact effects on acculturation preferences (Study 3). Dotted paths indicate non-significant relationships.

7-point scale) and experiencing contact with majority members of the Chilean society (4–4.7 on a 7-point scale).

As predicted, and confirming the results of Study 2, extended contact longitudinally predicted changes in acculturation preferences of majority members (cultural maintenance and desire for contact) by changing perceived in-group norms supporting cross-group friendship (Figure 3.3). Similar to Study 1, direct cross-group friendship predicted changes in acculturation attitudes over time but it only affected the contact dimension. Finally, as expected, extended contact was a significant precursor of cross-group friendship development (Gómez et al., 2011; Mazziotta et al., 2015; Turner, Hewstone, Voci, et al., 2007).

Because these were longitudinal effects, they are suggestive of causal effects, that is, *from* extended contact *to* acculturation attitudes. As a whole, the results of all three studies confirmed the dynamic relationships that typify links between direct and extended contact when predicting acculturation attitudes.

Future research: challenges for the contact–acculturation research agenda

Our research has produced substantial evidence confirming the central role that direct and extended forms of intergroup contact play in facilitating the development of acculturation preferences. Yet, there are still several challenges we need to face in the next step of development of this research agenda.

First, there has been a debate in the contact literature about whether contact works in the same way for majority and minority groups. Indeed, evidence has generally shown an asymmetrical pattern for the effects of contact (Binder et al., 2009; Tropp & Pettigrew, 2005). Therefore, understanding the minority perspective seems to be a critical aspect to tackle in future research linking contact and acculturation theorizing (Zagefka, González, & Brown, 2011). Indeed, our research program (Studies 1 and 3) included equivalent measures for Peruvian immigrants but the number of participants was not high enough to allow the use of more sophisticated techniques such as longitudinal cross-lagged analyzes. We hope to shed light on this issue when completing a bigger longitudinal study, this time involving indigenous and non-indigenous Chilean participants in school contexts.

We know now that intergroup friendship brings about positive intergroup attitude change, partly because it reduces intergroup anxiety and feelings of symbolic and realistic threat, and increases empathy and knowledge about the outgroup (Binder et al., 2009; González et al., 2010; Pettigrew & Tropp, 2008; Tropp & Pettigrew, 2005). The question now is how people who belong to different groups—be they religious, political, ethnic, racial—ever become friends?! What drives their intentions and behaviors to cross over their group boundaries and establish relationships with out-group members? What are the central mechanisms that explain the development or breakdown of intergroup friendship? For instance, feelings of intergroup anxiety (Stephan & Stephan, 2000) are expected to influence the way people navigate in intergroup relations, so they might prevent people to carry on seeing each other if they arise significantly during contact. The extent to which the contact situation allows the development of self-disclosure (Turner, Hewstone, & Voci, 2007) and favors pro-contact in-group norms (Christ et al., 2014; De Tezanos-Pinto et al., 2010; Turner et al., 2008) is also important, since these two variables seem to be relevant mechanisms that might foster the development of friendship and trust. These questions should also guide the research agenda of the contact–acculturation area (Tropp et al., 2016).

In addition, understanding the conditions that might influence the way contact can affect the development of acculturation preferences is also relevant to consider. Here, we are interested in answering the question of what factors may increase or decrease the effect of intergroup contact on acculturation attitudes. There are at least three major potential factors (moderators) of this relationship: perceived social climate, negative experiences of contact and the status of the immigrant groups.

Social climate has been considered a critical aspect when understanding the development of acculturation preferences (Brown & Zagefka, 2011). By "social climate" here we mean both the wider societal climate (e.g. for or against multi-culturalism) and the more "micro" contexts of the school classroom or playground (which may be characterized by discrimination or tolerance). As we have already noted, majority members often demand that minority members adopt the mainstream culture, while not supporting their cultural maintenance. This seems to be particularly true when negative attitudes towards immigrants are widespread (Van Acker & Vanbeselaere, 2011; Zagefka et al., 2009). Further, the perception that immigrants prefer culture maintenance may negatively influence majorities' own acculturation preferences for integration if negative climate predominates (Zagefka et al., 2007). On the other hand, from the minority's perspective, in a climate where its members feel permitted to maintain an important aspect of their identity, they are less likely to feel threatened and more likely to feel accepted by majority members. This should lead to lessened intergroup anxiety (Stephan & Stephan, 2000) and hence to enhanced attitudes towards majority members (Brown & Hewstone, 2005). Therefore, including the nature of social climate into the model seems necessary to better understand the process by which acculturation preferences develop.

Negative forms of intergroup contact, on the other hand, could significantly increase tension and conflict between groups, rendering social cohesion a major challenge for policy makers in social environments that are characterized by such encounters. Thus, it is relevant to study conditions associated with the arrival of newcomers that might bring about negative experiences of contact. Focusing on their antecedents as well as consequences would be very relevant. As we have argued, a huge body of research has shown that contact can reduce prejudice (Pettigrew & Tropp, 2006). However, these effects are mostly driven by positive forms of contact that meet Allport's (1954) optimal conditions. As Pettigrew and Tropp (2006) pointed out, research on negative intergroup contact has been rather neglected, rendering it an important topic to address, particularly in social contexts that involve an encounter between members of advantaged majority and devalued minority groups (Paolini, Harwood, & Rubin, 2010). Indeed, recent research shows that negative contact could be more influential in shaping out-group attitudes than positive contact (Barlow et al., 2012).

It could also be very valuable to explore longitudinal contact–acculturation models involving contact between the majority host members and immigrant groups with different status. As is well documented, the status of the group could potentially have a significant impact on intergroup attitudes (Ellemers, 1993). Those immigrant group members that belong to high status groups might trigger different attitudes in the receiving population than the ones coming from devalued low status groups (low socioeconomic status, with low qualifications), as the stereotype content model suggests (Fiske, Cuddy, Glick, & Xu, 2002). On the other hand, there is also research showing the importance of studying contact between minority groups (Jasinskaja-Lahti, Liebkind, Horenczyk, & Schmitz, 2003). This could be the context where we study, for instance, contact and acculturation orientations involving low social class groups such as immigrants and local groups living in deprived neighbourhoods.

Research challenges should also concern other potential mediators of the contact–acculturation link. One potential mediator seems to be perceived discrimination from the minority perspective. Indeed, there is an emerging body of research emphasizing important ways in which ethnic minorities' contact experiences with majority members can diminish minority perceptions of discrimination and support for social change (Dixon, Tropp, Durrheim, & Tredoux, 2010; Saguy, Shchori-Eyal, Hasan-Aslih, Sobol, & Dovidio, this volume). However, this effect has been shown to be moderated by the status among members of different ethnic minority groups (e.g. African, Latino and Asian-American participants exhibited changes in support for ethnic activism as a function of cross-group friendship with White Americans and perceived discrimination; Tropp, Hawi, Van Laar, & Levin, 2011). It is precisely this positive effect of contact on the reduction of perceived discrimination that opens the door for new theorizing involving acculturation preferences in minority immigrant groups. Immigrants in many societies are often under pressure to assimilate into the main society and to relinquish their identity. Depending on the climate, if they feel threatened by the situation, they might be willing to abandon their identity because of the persistent feelings of being discriminated against due to their ethnicity, cultural values or way of life. Thus, if positive contact with members of the majority has been shown to reduce the feeling of perceived discrimination, then that could be the route to foster immigrants' "desire to maintain" rather than abandon their identity. So contact could be a facilitator of cultural maintenance via reducing perceived discrimination among immigrant minorities. But, on the other hand, according to Saguy et al. (this volume) and others (Dixon et al., 2010), reducing perceived discrimination in the minority may ironically result in a lower desire of minority members to engage in collective action in order to improve their position. This is certainly a matter we need to study in the future.

Looking for other potential mediators of the extended contact–acculturation link is also an interesting challenge for this research area. The intergroup contact literature has shown the importance of considering the mediators when trying to understand why contact does indeed affect intergroup attitudes. In the same vein, it would be informative to explore other mediators in addition to intergroup trust (Hässler et al., 2015; Tam et al., 2009), perceived similarity (Brown & Hewstone, 2005; Gaertner et al., 1993) and in-group norms, already studied in our research program, such as inclusion of the other in the self, intergroup anxiety and self-disclosure (Christ et al., 2014; González et al., 2010; Turner, Hewstone, & Voci, 2007; Turner et al., 2008). By focusing on a cognitive mechanism like inclusion of the other in the self, we will complement the role that intergroup anxiety and self-disclosure play in mediating the direct and extended contact–acculturation association (Wright et al., 1997).

Another challenge in this research area is the need to implement more and extensive longitudinal contact–acculturation studies and particularly involving the rather neglected real intergroup contexts such as indigenous and non-indigenous or immigrant groups in countries other than the United States or European countries. Indeed many Latin American and Caribbean countries (e.g. Peru, Bolivia and Ecuador) are now facing similar social challenges as the ones described in this chapter when integrating newcomers or dealing with integration of indigenous communities. This issue is also relevant in developed countries such as Canada, New Zealand and Australia where indigenous populations seek a social system that recognizes and values their group and cultural distinctiveness. Researching in this area is conceptually valuable and particularly because of its policy implications.

Policy implications

Let us now discuss some policy implications that can be drawn from our research program and, of course, from the literature involving contact and acculturation preferences already discussed.

First, one of the take home messages from the great meta-analysis conducted by Lemmer and Wagner (2015) is that contact researchers should work more closely with policy makers. Almost all the effective interventions reported in this meta-analysis were aimed at improving intergroup relations in real intergroup contexts (outside the labs) involving direct (contact meetings and cooperative group learning) and indirect contact (extended and virtual) among in-group and out-group members (minority, majority or both) in school and college contexts (see also Brown & Hewstone, 2005). Indeed, educational contexts provide great opportunities to foster collaboration between contact researchers and teachers and school/college authorities and leaders that can inform each other about the need and usefulness of contact interventions.

Second, interventions aimed at improving intergroup relations and fostering positive acculturation preferences (e.g. integration), particularly in the majority, should focus their attention on stimulating both high quality and frequent experiences of contact with out-group members. As we have reviewed in this chapter, there is substantial evidence confirming the importance of developing cross-group friendships involving members of the majority and immigrants as a way of creating the psychological foundation for intergroup trust, perceived similarity, value of diversity and commitment with out-group members (Binder et al., 2009; Paolini et al., 2004). Focusing the attention on these mechanisms related to changes in acculturation preferences would allow group members to value diversity and recognize the importance of keeping group distinctiveness as a fundamental aspect of group well-being and positive intergroup attitudes (Brown & Hewstone, 2005). Recognizing and valuing immigrants to keep their culture and traditions will allow members of the minority to feel less threatened and will prepare them to integrate into the mainstream society. For majority members, instead, it would allow them to feel more comfortable and less anxious and threatened by the arrival of immigrants to the extent that they add value to the mainstream society (multiculturalism). Thus, creating opportunities for contact to develop should be a priority starting point. Contact, however, should meet Allport's (1954) optimal conditions if it is expected to foster positive intergroup attitudes and acculturation preferences such as integration.

Fostering positive experiences of contact, as shown in our research program, was also a significant predictor of extended contact (Gómez et al., 2011) and vice versa (see Study 3; González et al., 2015). This finding is highly relevant for its policy implications: extended contact can be conceived as a source of acculturation preference change via changing perceived injunctive in-group norms (what other in-group members approve of) supporting the development of friendship. Thus, it is important to highlight the fact that, if we do not start by creating opportunity for contact to emerge in the first place, there is less chance for extended contact to operate in the expected positive direction.

Interventions could also benefit significantly by looking at several vicarious forms of intergroup contact. By inspecting the impressive meta-analyzes by Lemmer and Wagner (2015), we can see that many interventions reviewed by them indeed involve vicarious forms of contact (Vezzali et al., 2014, see also Vezzali & Stathi, this volume). Therefore, interventions aimed at improving intergroup relations and fostering positive acculturation preferences, especially in social environments with either fewer opportunities for contact or more problematic relationships between members of the receiving society and immigrants, could capitalize a lot from vicarious forms of contact. Critically, such vicarious interventions should be concerned with selecting very distinctive and recognized in-group characters to play the role models in storytelling, radio programs or films, etc. (e.g. Paluck, 2009). These initiatives could be significant ways of portraying contact situations. Vicarious in-group role models are not "actual friends" but throughout the story, film or radio program, they should be perceived as fellow in-group members, experiencing positive contact with out-group members. The main assumption is that this vicarious form of contact would promote more positive intergroup attitudes—not as a consequence of having direct experiences of contact with out-group (immigrant) members but rather through sympathizing and identifying with the role model. By this identification process, members of the majority will take the perspective of the role model protagonist when facing contact experiences with immigrants. One potential limitation of vicarious interventions is that they may be more effective with young children rather than adolescents. It seems easier for young children to believe in the role model than it is for older children (Aronson et al., 2016; Cameron, Rutland, Hossain, & Petley, 2011). Finding ways of increasing perceived similarity with the role model seems to be a critical aspect that might increase identification with the protagonist. Research on applying interventions should help to identify the optimal conditions that facilitate the process for vicarious interventions to be effective.

Finally, assuming that many of the vicarious forms of contact interventions could be relevant in school contexts, considering the teacher's perspective is very relevant. The challenge and temptation of color-blind versus multiculturalism approaches is an issue in educational contexts, where in order to avoid the potential "problems" that might emerge as a function of making different groups salient within classrooms, teachers may not talk about or address group diversity issues (fostering the use of color-blind methods). Interventions should facilitate and provide pedagogic materials to enable teachers to address the issue of diversity within classrooms using social psychological tools. Vicarious forms of contact interventions could be an easy way to do it.

Closing remarks

There is no doubt that in order to increase our understanding of the nature of the intergroup relations involving majority and minority members in the context of the immigration process across the globe, intergroup contact and acculturation theories need to be integrated. Based on the evidence we have produced in our research program and the many other contributions addressed in this chapter, we advanced some conceptual relations and policy implications that we hope will illuminate the future research challenges in the contact–acculturation domain.

Notes

This research was supported by grants from the Chilean National Foundation for Scientific and Technological Development (FONDECYT #11210009), the Center for Social Conflict and Cohesion Studies (FONDAP #15130009), the Interdisciplinary Center for Intercultural and Indigenous Studies (FONDAP #15110006) and Anillos (CONICYT #SOC1103) awarded to Roberto González.

References

Allport, G.W. (1954). *The nature of prejudice*. Reading, MA: Addison-Wesley.

Aronson, K.M., Stefanile, C., Matera, C., Nerini, A., Grisolaghi, J., Romani, G., . . . & Brown, R. (2016). Telling tales in school: Extended contact interventions in the classroom. *Journal of Applied Social Psychology, 46*, 229–41. doi: 10.1111/jasp.12358

Barlow, F.K., Paolini, S., Pedersen, A., Hornsey, M.J., Radke, H.R.M., Harwood, J. & Sibley, C.G. (2012). The contact caveat: Negative contact predicts increased prejudice more than positive contact predicts reduced prejudice. *Personality and Social Psychology Bulletin, 38*, 1629–43. doi: 10.1177/0146167212457953

Berry, J.W. (1997). Immigration, acculturation, and adaptation. *Applied Psychology: An International Review, 46*, 5–34. doi: 10.1111/j.1464-0597.1997.tb01087.x

Binder, J., Zagefka, H., Brown, R., Funke, F., Kessler, T., & Mummendey, A. (2009). Does contact reduce prejudice or does prejudice reduce contact? A longitudinal test of the contact hypothesis among majority and minority groups in three European countries. *Journal of Personality and Social Psychology, 96*, 843–56. doi: 10.1037/a0013470

Bourhis, R.Y., Moïse, L.C., Perreault, S., & Senécal, S. (1997). Towards an interactive acculturation model: A social psychological approach. *International Journal of Psychology*, *32*, 369–86. doi: 10.1080/002075997400629

Brown, R., & Hewstone, M. (2005). An integrative theory of intergroup contact. *Advances in Experimental Social Psychology*, *37*, 255–343. doi: 10.1016/S0065-2601(05)37005-5

Brown, R., & Zagefka, H. (2011). The dynamics of acculturation: An intergroup perspective. *Advances in experimental social psychology*, *44*, 129–84. doi: 10.1016/B978-0-12-385522-0.00003-2

Byrne, D. (1971). *The attraction paradigm.* New York, NY: Academic Press.

Cameron, L., Rutland, A., Hossain, R., & Petley, R. (2011). When and why does extended contact work? The role of high quality direct contact and group norms in the development of positive ethnic intergroup attitudes amongst children. *Group Processes and Intergroup Relations*, *14*, 193–206. doi: 10.1016/j.sbspro.2013.12.698

Christ, O., Hewstone, M., Tausch, N., Wagner, U., Voci, A., Hughes, J., & Cairns, E. (2010). Direct contact as a moderator of extended contact effects: Cross-sectional and longitudinal impact on outgroup attitudes, behavioral intentions, and attitude certainty. *Personality and Social Psychology Bulletin*, *36*, 1662–74. doi: 10.1177/0146167210386969

Christ, O., Schmid, K., Lolliot, S., Swart, H., Stolle, D., Tausch, N., & Hewstone, M. (2014). Contextual effect of positive intergroup contact on outgroup prejudice. *Proceedings of The National Academy of Sciences of The United States of America*, *111*, 3996–4000. doi: 10.1073/pnas.1320901111

De Tezanos-Pinto, P., Bratt, C., & Brown, R. (2010). What will the others think? In-group norms as a mediator of the effects of intergroup contact. *British Journal of Social Psychology*, *49*, 507–23. doi: 10.1348/014466609X471020

Dixon, J., Tropp, L.R., Durrheim, K., & Tredoux, C. (2010). "Let them eat harmony": Prejudice reduction strategies and attitudes of historically disadvantaged groups. *Current Directions in Psychological Science*, *19*, 76–80. doi: 10.1177/0963721410363366

Ellemers, N. (1993). The influence of socio-structural variables on identity enhancement strategies. *European Review of Social Psychology*, *4*, 27–57. doi: 10.1080/14792779343000013

Fiske, S., Cuddy, A.J., Glick, P., & Xu, J. (2002). A model of (often mixed) stereotype content: Competence and warmth respectively follow from perceived status and competition. *Journal of Personality and Social Psychology*, *82*(6), 878–902. doi: 10.1037//0022-3514.82.6.878

Gaertner, S.L., Dovidio, J., Anastasio, P.A., Bachman, B.A., & Rust, M.C. (1993). The common ingroup identity model: Recategorization and the reduction of intergroup bias. *European Review of Social Psychology*, *4*, 1–26. doi: 10.1080/14792779343000004

Gómez, A., Tropp, L.R., & Fernandez, S. (2011). When extended contact opens the door to future contact: Testing the effects of extended contact on intergroup attitudes and expectancies among minority and majority groups. *Group Processes and Intergroup Relations*, *14*, 161–73. doi: 10.1177/1368430210391119

González, R., Brown, R., Manzi, J., Lay, S., Hässler, Miranda, D., & Tropp, L.R. (2015). *Longitudinal consequences of direct and extended contact: The role of perceived in-group norms in developing acculturation preferences among majority members.* Manuscript in preparation.

González, R., Sirlopú, D., & Kessler, T. (2010). Prejudice among Peruvians and Chileans as a function of identity, intergroup contact, acculturation preferences, and intergroup emotions. *Journal of Social Issues*, *66*, 803–24. doi: 10.1111/j.1540-4560.2010.01676.x

Hässler, T., González, R., Lay, S., Lickel, B., Zagefka, H., Brown, R., & Bernardino, M. (2015). *With a little help from our friends: The impact of cross-group friendship on acculturation preferences.* Manuscript submitted for publication.

Henrich, J., Heine, S.J., & Norenzayan, A. (2010). Most people are not WEIRD. *Nature*, *466*(7302), 29–9. doi: 10.1038/466029a

Jasinskaja-Lahti, I., Liebkind, K., Horenczyk, G., & Schmitz, P. (2003). The interactive nature of acculturation: Perceived discrimination, acculturation attitudes and stress among young ethnic repatriates in Finland, Israel and Germany. *International Journal of Intercultural Relations*, *27*, 79–97. doi: 10.1016/S0147-1767(02)00061-5

Lemmer, G., & Wagner, U. (2015). Can we really reduce ethnic prejudice outside the lab? A meta-analysis of direct and indirect contact interventions. *European Journal of Social Psychology*, *45*, 152–68. doi: 10.1002/ejsp.2079

Lewicki, R.J., McAllister, D.J., & Bies, R.J. (1998). Trust and distrust: New relationships and realities. *Academy of Management Review*, *23*, 438–58. doi: 10.5465/AMR.1998. 926620

Mazziotta, A., Rohmann, A., Wright, S.C., De Tezanos-Pinto, P., & Lutterbach, S. (2015). (How) does positive and negative extended cross-group contact predict direct cross-group contact and intergroup attitudes? *European Journal of Social Psychology*, *45*, 653–67. doi: 10.1002/ejsp.2110

Ministerio del Interior, C. (2009). *Informe Estadístico: Estimación de Población de Extranjeros en Chile a Diciembre de 2008*. Santiago, Chile. Retrieved on July 20, 2015, from www.extranjeria.gob.cl/filesapp/Informe%20Estimacion%20Poblacion%20Extranjeros%2 02008.pdf

Mora, C. (2008). The Peruvian community in Chile. *Peace Review: A Journal of Social Justice*, *20*, 339–47.

Muthen, L.K., & Muthen, B.O. (2012). *Mplus User's Guide* (7th ed). Los Angeles, CA: Muthen & Muthen.

Osbeck, L.M., Moghaddam, F.M., & Perreault, S. (1997). Similarity and attraction among majority and minority groups in a multicultural context. *International Journal of Intercultural Relations*, *21*, 113–23. doi: 10.1016/S0147-1767(96)00016-8.

Paluck, E.L. (2009). Reducing intergroup prejudice and conflict using the media: A field experiment in Rwanda. *Journal of personality and social psychology*, *96*, 574–87. doi: 10. 1037/a0011989

Paolini, S., Harwood, J., & Rubin, M. (2010). Negative intergroup contact makes group memberships salient: Explaining why intergroup conflict endures. *Personality and Social Psychology Bulletin*, *36*, 1723–38. doi: 10.1177/0146167210388667

Paolini, S., Hewstone, M., Cairns, E., & Voci, A. (2004). Effects of direct and indirect cross-group friendships on judgments of Catholics and Protestants in Northern Ireland: The mediating role of an anxiety-reduction mechanism. *Personality and Social Psychology Bulletin*, *30*, 770–86. doi: 10.1177/0146167203262848

Pettigrew, T.F., Christ, O., Wagner, U., & Stellmacher, J. (2007). Direct and indirect intergroup contact effects on prejudice: A normative interpretation. *International Journal of Intercultural Relations*, *31*, 411–25. doi: 10.1016/j.ijintrel.2006.11.003

Pettigrew, T.F., & Tropp, L.R. (2006). A meta-analytic test of intergroup contact theory. *Journal of Personality and Social Psychology*, *90*, 751–83. doi: 10.1037/0022–3514.90.5.751

Pettigrew, T.F., & Tropp, L.R. (2008). How does intergroup contact reduce prejudice? Meta-analytic tests of three mediators. *European Journal of Social Psychology*, *38*, 922–34. doi: 10.1002/ejsp.504

Pfafferott, I., & Brown, R. (2006). Acculturation preferences of majority and minority adolescents in Germany in the context of society and family. *International Journal of Intercultural Relations*, *30*, 703–17. doi: 10.1016/j.ijintrel.2006.03.005

Piontkowski, U., Florack, A., Hoelker, P., & Obdrzálek, P. (2000). Predicting acculturation attitudes of dominant and non-dominant groups. *International Journal of Intercultural Relations*, *24*, 1–26. doi: 10.1016/S0147–1767(99)00020-6

Redfield, R., Linton, R., & Herskovits, M.J. (1936). Memorandum for the study of acculturation. *American anthropologist, 38*, 149–52. doi: 10.1525/aa.1936.38.1.02a.00330

Sam, D.L., & Berry, J.W. (2010). Acculturation: When individuals and groups of different cultural backgrounds meet. *Perspectives on Psychological Science, 5*, 472–81. doi: 10.1177/1745691610373075

Sirlopú, D., & Van Oudenhoven, J.P. (2013). Is multiculturalism a viable path in Chile? Intergroup and acculturative perspectives on Chilean society and Peruvian immigrants. *International Journal of Intercultural Relations, 37*, 739–49. doi: 10.1016/j.ijintrel.2013.09.011

Stathi, S., Cameron, L., Hartley, B., & Bradford, S. (2014). Imagined contact as a prejudice-reduction intervention in schools: The underlying role of similarity and attitudes. *Journal of Applied Social Psychology, 44*, 536–46. doi: 10.1111/jasp.12245

Stefoni, C. (2011). Ley y política migratoria en Chile. La ambivalencia en la comprensión del migrante. In B. Feldman-Bianco, B.L. Rivera Sánchez, C. Stefoni, & M. Villa Martínez (Eds.), *La construcción social del sujeto migrante en América Latina. Prácticas, representaciones y categorías* (pp. 79–110). Quito, FLACSO, Sede Ecuador: Consejo Latinoamericano de Ciencias Sociales, CLACSO: Universidad Alberto Hurtado.

Stephan, W.G., & Stephan, C.W. (2000). An integrated threat theory of prejudice. In S. Oskamp (Ed.), *Reducing prejudice and discrimination* (pp. 23–45). Mahwah, NJ: Erlbaum.

Tam, T., Hewstone, M., Kenworthy, J., & Cairns, E. (2009). Intergroup trust in Northern Ireland. *Personality and Social Psychology Bulletin, 35*, 45–59. doi: 10.1177/014616 7208325004

Tip, L.K., González, R., Brown, R., De Tezanos-Pinto, P., Saavedra, P., Sagredo, V., . . . & Celeste, L. (2015). Effects of ingroup norms on domain-specific acculturation preferences: Experimental evidence from two cultural contexts. *International Journal of Intercultural Relations, 47*, 113–30. doi: 10.1016/j.ijintrel.2015.03.027

Tip, L.K., Zagefka, H., González, R., Brown, R., Cinnirella, M., & Na, X. (2012). Is support for multiculturalism threatened by . . . threat itself? *International Journal of Intercultural Relations, 36*, 22–30. doi: 10.1016/j.ijintrel.2010.09.011

Tropp, L.R., Hawi, D.R., Van Laar, C., & Levin, S. (2011). Cross-ethnic friendships, perceived discrimination, and their effects on ethnic activism over time: A longitudinal investigation of three ethnic minority groups. *British Journal of Social Psychology, 51*, 257–72. doi: 10.1111/j.2044-8309.2011.02050.x

Tropp, L.R., O'Brien, T., González, R., Valdenegro, D., Migacheva , K., De Tezanos Pinto, P., & Cayul, O. (2016). How school norms, peer norms and discrimination predict interethnic experiences among ethnic minority and majority youth. *Child Development, 87*, 1436–51. doi: 10.1111/cdev.12608

Tropp, L.R., & Pettigrew, T.F. (2005). Relationships between intergroup contact and prejudice among minority and majority status groups. *Psychological Science, 16*, 951–7. doi: 10.1111/j.1467-9280.2005.01643.x

Turner, R.N., Hewstone, M., & Voci, A. (2007). Reducing explicit and implicit outgroup prejudice via direct and extended contact: The mediating role of self-disclosure and inter-group anxiety. *Journal of Personality and Social Psychology, 93*, 369–88. doi: 10.1037/0022-3514.93.3.369

Turner, R.N., Hewstone, M., Voci, A., Paolini, S., & Christ, O. (2007). Reducing prejudice via direct and extended cross-group friendship. *European Review of Social Psychology, 18*, 212–55. doi: 10.1080/10463280701680297

Turner, R.N., Hewstone, M., Voci, A., & Vonofakou, C. (2008). A test of the extended intergroup contact hypothesis: The mediating role of intergroup anxiety, perceived ingroup and outgroup norms, and inclusion of the outgroup in the self. *Journal of Personality and Social Psychology, 95*, 843–60. doi: 10.1037/a0011434

United Nations, Department of Economic and Social Affairs. (2013). *Trends in international migrant stock: The 2013 Revision.* Retrieved June 2014 from: http://esa.un.org/unmigration/TIMSA2013/migrantstocks2013.htm?mtotals

Van Acker, K., & Vanbeselaere, N. (2011). Bringing together acculturation theory and inter-group contact theory: Predictors of Flemings' expectations of Turks' acculturation behavior. *International Journal of Intercultural Relations, 35,* 334–45. doi: 10.1016/j.ijintrel. 2010.06.004

Verkuyten, M. (2005). Ethnic group identification and group evaluation among minority and majority groups: Testing the multiculturalism hypothesis. *Journal of Personality and Social Psychology, 88,* 121–38. doi: 10.1037/0022-3514.88.1.121

Vezzali, L., Hewstone, M., Capozza, D., Giovannini, D., & Wölfer, R. (2014). Improving intergroup relations with extended and vicarious forms of indirect contact. *European Review of Social Psychology, 24,* 314–89. doi: 10.1080/10463283.2014.982948

Wolsko, C., Park, B., Judd, C., & Bachelor, J. (2003). Intergroup contact: Effects on group evaluations and perceived variability. *Group Processes and Intergroup Relations, 6,* 93–110. doi: 10.1177/1368430203006001014

Wright, S.C., Aron, A., McLaughlin-Volpe, T., & Ropp, S.A. (1997). The extended contact effect: Knowledge of cross-group friendships and prejudice. *Journal of Personality and Social Psychology, 73,* 73–90. doi: 10.1037/0022–3514.73.1.73

Zagefka, H., Brown, R., Broquard, M., & Martin, S.L. (2007). Predictors and consequences of negative attitudes toward immigrants in Belgium and Turkey: The role of acculturation preferences and economic competition. *British Journal of Social Psychology, 46,* 153–69. doi: 10.1348/014466606X111185

Zagefka, H., Brown, R., & González, R. (2009). Antecedents and consequences of acculturation preferences of non-indigenous Chileans in relation to an indigenous minority: Longitudinal survey evidence. *European Journal of Social Psychology, 39,* 558–75. doi: 10.1002/ejsp.550

Zagefka, H., González, R., & Brown, R. (2011). How minority members' perceptions of majority members' acculturation preferences shape minority members' own acculturation preferences: Evidence from Chile. *British Journal of Social Psychology, 50,* 216–33. doi: 10.1348/014466610X512211

4

THE IRONY OF HARMONY

Past and new developments

*Tamar Saguy, Noa Shchori-Eyal, Siwar Hasan-Aslih,
Danit Sobol and John F. Dovidio*

Key words: prejudice, intergroup relations, social change, collective action, intergroup contact

One of the most critical aims of social psychological science is to inform practical solutions to pressing social problems, many of which are associated with tensions between groups in society (Demoulin, Leyens, & Dovidio, 2009). Among the most studied interventions for ameliorating tension between groups is intergroup contact (Allport, 1954; Dovidio, Gaertner, & Kawakami, 2003; Paluck & Green, 2009; Pettigrew, 1998). The central notion in contact theory is that intergroup bias can be substantially reduced via positive encounters between members of different groups. Decades of research within the framework of intergroup contact have focused on the processes that are responsible for the effects of contact on attitudes, and on the underlying principles of what constitutes a "positive", or optimal, encounter (Pettigrew & Tropp, 2006). A central element that emerges from this work is that in order for contact to be effective, it needs to give rise to a sense of common identity, shared by members of both groups. This intuitive notion dates back to classic works of Allport (1954) and Sherif, Harvey, White, Hood and Sherif (1961), and was systematically investigated under the framework of processes associated with categorization (Dovidio & Gaertner, 2010). This chapter is devoted to this notion of commonality as means to create better intergroup relations.

In their classic studies on the basis of intergroup conflict, Sherif and colleagues (1961) have demonstrated that animosity between groups can be reverted by having members of both groups work together towards a common goal. This notion was later developed by Gaertner and Dovidio in their work on the common in-group identity model (2000, 2012). The principle behind the model is that inducing people to think of themselves as sharing a common, superordinate identity with members of another group can overcome fundamental intergroup bias. A superordinate identity may be, for example, a common school, organization or national identity, and can be also induced by providing people with goals, tasks or even only cues that emphasize common elements to both groups (Dovidio, Gaertner, & Saguy, 2015).

The mechanism behind the common identity effects is rooted in processes of categorization (Turner, Hogg, Oakes, Reicher, & Wetherell, 1987). To the extent that socially categorizing people into different groups automatically activates stereotypes and prejudice (Dovidio & Gartner, 2010), recategorizing the groups as sharing a superordinate, overarching identity can redirect those motivational and cognitive processes to increase positive orientations towards out-group members (Dovidio et al., 2015). Indeed, a focus on commonalities has consistently been shown to relate to more positive out-group attitudes (Gaertner & Dovidio, 2000), to foster more intimate cross-group interactions (Dovidio et al., 1997), and to promote prosocial behavior across group lines (Nier et al., 2001).

The development of a common in-group identity does not necessarily require each group to forsake its original, less inclusive group identity. Depending on their degree of identification with the different categories and contextual factors that make particular identities salient, individuals may activate two or more of their multiple social identities simultaneously (Roccas & Brewer, 2002) or sequentially (Turner et al., 1987). For example, people can conceive of two groups (e.g. science and art majors) as distinct units within the context of a superordinate social entity (e.g. university students). The mutual intergroup differentiation model (Brown & Hewstone, 2005) relatedly proposes that positive contact between members of different groups produces particularly robust improvements in intergroup attitudes when different groups maintain their separate identities but have cooperatively interdependent relations.

Although recategorization, both in terms of substituting separate group identities with a common in-group identity or creating dual identities, can produce more positive intergroup attitudes, in recent years scholars have begun to question the utility of a focus on commonalities. This line of critique links research on prejudice reduction to research on social change and collective action (Wright & Lubensky, 2009). While research on prejudice reduction has primarily focused on the psychology of members of advantaged groups, research on collective action has centered on psychological processes among the disadvantaged. This latter work has shown that in order for disadvantaged group members to engage in actions for promoting social change, they need to be strongly attached to their disadvantaged group (Stürmer & Simon, 2004), have negative views of the advantaged group (Simon & Klandermans, 2001) and be well aware of the existence of structural inequalities between the groups (van Zomeren, Spears, Fischer, & Leach, 2004). This observation has sparked criticism on optimal intergroup contact as an intervention that could, in practice, increase disadvantaged group members' acceptance of a biased system and weaken their motivation to act for equality (Dixon, Levine, Reicher, & Durrheim, 2012; Tausch, Saguy, & Bryson, 2015; Wright & Lubensky, 2009). As such, intergroup harmony might have ironic consequences by contributing to social stability rather than social change (Saguy, Tausch, Dovidio, & Pratto, 2009).

The goal of this chapter is to summarize research on the "irony of harmony" (Saguy et al., 2009) and to introduce new developments in this line of thinking. First, we review existing research on how members of disadvantaged groups respond to commonalities. This body of work demonstrates that among members of disadvantaged groups, a focus on commonalities (both via contact, but also independently of contact) can undermine attention to inequality and collective action tendencies. This section further describes the various mechanisms that were identified as responsible for such ironic effects. Second, we describe the documented effects of a commonality focus on members of advantaged groups, which reveal mixed evidence as for the existence of an irony of harmony effect. The third and final section in this chapter is devoted to new developments in the irony of harmony research, extending it to the realm of harmonious emotions (i.e. hope) and to gender relations, and identifies promising future directions for research in this area.

How do members of disadvantaged groups respond to commonalities?

In this section, we provide a chronological description of theorizing and research on the responses of disadvantaged group members to situations that emphasize cross-group commonalities. We begin by describing the early, and central, theorizing and findings that serve as the basis for subsequent developments on the irony of harmony phenomenon (2005–2009). We then move to describe more recent research from the years 2010 to the present day.

2005–2009: central theorizing and pioneering evidence

Up until 2005, most published work on intergroup contact was fairly optimistic (but see Forbes, 1997; Jackman & Crane, 1986; and Reicher, 1986; for notable exceptions), treating it as one of the greatest promises of social psychology to ameliorate social injustice, and even promote world peace (Hewstone, Cairns, Voci, Hamberger, & Niens, 2006). In 2005, Dixon, Durrheim and Tredoux published a paper in which they offered a "reality check" for the contact hypothesis. This paper introduced a set of challenges in (what was then) extant research on intergroup contact, among which was a rift between the ultimate aim of contact interventions, to transform social injustice at a broad social level, and the changes it was shown to produce, mainly reductions in individuals' prejudices. According to Dixon et al., an improvement in individuals' attitudes might not necessarily promote the political reforms that are essential for the reduction of racism. Furthermore, they added that positive contact might impact minority group members' political consciousness in ways that can lead them to become less concerned with current discriminatory practices.

At the time this paper was published, this notion did not have much empirical support (the sole paper cited to support this claim is by Ellison & Powers, 1994). In 2007, the authors published an empirical paper documenting correlations between contact and various outcomes that pertain to social change in South Africa (Dixon, Durrheim, & Tredoux, 2007). Consistent with their theoretical argument of the association between contact and political consciousness of minority groups, they found that Black South Africans who reported more positive contact with Whites were less supportive of compensatory policies promoting the interests of Blacks in education and employment.

A few years later, in 2009, a seminal chapter by Wright and Lubensky was devoted entirely to the rift between the theoretical individualism of prejudice reduction research, and the structural, system-related focus of research on social change. Being social psychological inquiries, both lines of research deal with individuals' perceptions, attitudes and emotions. However, while prejudice reduction research focuses on psychological orientations towards out-group members (emotions and attitudes towards them), collective action research examines psychological orientations towards the social system (to what extent it is fair, just, frustrating, etc.). In their chapter, Wright and Lubensky (2009) specified four specific contradictions between the intergroup contact approach and collective action approach—both of which are aimed at ameliorating social injustice.

As stated earlier, the first contradiction concerned the issue of identification and categorization. While collective action requires strong identification with one's subgroup, contact interventions for the most part are aimed at reducing the salience of intergroup boundaries, which can lead to reduction in in-group identification. The second, related issue involved recognition of disadvantage. While collective action requires the solid recognition of intergroup inequality (van Zomeren et al., 2004), contact interventions are designed to reduce the salience of status differences (so that those will not be reproduced in the encounter; see Saguy, Tropp, & Hawi, 2013). As such, contact interventions can direct attention away from the very recognition that is required in order for collective action to occur. The third contradiction between prejudice reduction research and collective action has to do with perceptions of boundary permeability. While collective action requires a perception of rather strict intergroup boundaries (Wright, 2001), contact interventions can serve to blur the boundaries between the groups (Rosenthal & Crisp, 2006), to the point of inducing a perception of permeability of group boundaries. Finally, the last contradiction between the two lines of thought concerns perceptions of the out-group. While collective action arises along with negativity towards the advantaged group (Simon & Klandermans, 2001), prejudice reduction efforts aim to produce the exact opposite effects by attempting to improve attitudes and emotions across group lines.

In the same year that this chapter was published, we published the first experimental evidence for the irony of harmony effects, supporting several of Dixon et al.'s and Wright and Lubensky's key claims (Saguy et al., 2009). Specifically, we created an intergroup dynamic in the laboratory by dividing students (who came to the laboratory in groups of six) into one of two 3-person groups. One group, the advantaged group, was assigned the power to allocate extra course credits to the two groups. The other, disadvantaged group, had no control over the allocation of credits. Before the advantaged group members allocated the credits, members of both groups interacted with instructions to focus on either intergroup commonalities or differences. Consistent with prior research, interactions focusing exclusively on commonalities (rather than differences) produced more positive intergroup attitudes for both advantaged and disadvantaged group members. In addition, for both groups, attention to inequality was lower when the interaction focused on commonalities. Moreover, in part because they had more positive feelings about the other group, members of the disadvantaged group expected the advantaged group to be fairer in allocating the resources and to distribute the credits in a more equitable fashion following discussions about commonalities, rather than about differences.

However, although disadvantaged group members expected a more equal distribution of credits after commonality-focused contact, advantaged group members were just as biased in this condition as in the difference-focused interaction—biasing in favor of their own group. Thus, this experiment demonstrated for the first time that for members of disadvantaged groups, commonality-focused contact resulted in false expectations for equality—an effect that reflects an inaccurate perception of one's social standing. These findings were corroborated in a field survey conducted among Arabs in Israel (Saguy et al., 2009, Study 2), in which we found that having more Jewish friends was associated with more positive attitudes towards Jews, and with reduced awareness to inequality between Jews and Arabs. These outcomes were associated with increased perceptions of Jews as fair and with reduced motivation for collective action to advance the status of Arabs in Israel.

Taken together, these studies provided initial support, both experimental and correlational, to the irony of harmony phenomenon among members of disadvantaged groups. Over the years, additional evidence, both correlational and experimental, has accumulated to further substantiate the findings as we elaborate below.

2010–2015: correlational and experimental evidence for the demobilizing effects of a focus on commonalities

Subsequent research, conducted in different parts of the world and employing various methods, further demonstrated that promoting common identity (e.g. via positive intergroup contact or via an emphasis on a one-group representation) can reduce minority group members' attention to structural inequality and motivation to engage in collective action to achieve equality.

Glasford and Dovidio (2011) experimentally induced either a superordinate representation of intergroup relations among minorities in the US or a dual-identity representation. In the common identity condition, participants read an alleged news report designed to increase salience of superordinate identity ("Recognizing that all of us are Americans can contribute to making America a better nation"). In the dual identity condition, both a common (American) and subordinate (racial/ethnic) identity were emphasized ("Recognizing that all of us are members of groups that have different traditions but also share a common American identity can contribute to making America a better nation"). Relative to the dual identity condition, promoting a common identity decreased social change motivation, an effect mediated by increased optimism about future relations. These results are much in line with Saguy et al. (2009), demonstrating that among disadvantaged group members a focus on commonalities gives rise to optimism (Study 1), which in turn can decrease motivation for social change (Study 2).

These findings are consistent with a correlational study conducted in South Africa around that same time (Cakal, Hewstone, Schwär, & Heath, 2011), in which a survey among 488 Black South African students revealed that intergroup contact negatively predicted collective action tendencies.

In a longitudinal analog, Tropp, Hawi, Van Laar and Levin (2012) examined the relationship between friendships with Whites and recognition of discrimination as well as support for ethnic activism. The study was conducted at the University of California (UCLA) between 1996–2001, involving 771 participants from three minority groups (African Americans, Latino and Asian Americans). Participants indicated how many of their closest friends at UCLA are Caucasian, whether they or other members of their ethnic group experienced discrimination at UCLA and whether they would consider partaking in different types of social change activities, such as signing petitions to advance the status of their group. The participants completed these measures at three different time points (end of first year in college, second/third year and end of college). More friendships with Whites at Time 1 predicted both lower perceptions of discrimination and less support for ethnic activism among African and Latino Americans at Time 2, but not among Asian Americans. In addition, a greater number of friendships with Whites and lower levels of perceived discrimination at Time 2 predicted marginally lower support for ethnic activism at Time 3 among African Americans, and significantly among Latino Americans, but not among Asian Americans—suggesting that for the latter there was less room for movement as a function of contact (given the already low levels of activism).

The association between contact and perceptions of discrimination was further corroborated in an experimental study conducted in Israel. Saguy and Chernyak-Hai (2012) had students from a low status academic institution (private college) engage in an interaction with an (alleged) member of a high status institution (highly prestigious public university). The colleges in Israel are unsubsidized and are associated with less academic prestige, often regardless of the actual level of the program. Thus, students who attend a private college often encounter challenges by having to "prove themselves" when applying for jobs. Participants were randomly assigned to one of three contact conditions. In one condition, the interaction emphasized commonalities between the institutions, in another condition the emphasis was on differences and in a third condition there was no contact involved.

After the interaction, participants were asked to judge a hypothetical scenario that described a student from their college who got rejected from a desirable position after successfully going through a long application process. Reasons for the rejection were purposefully left ambiguous, and participants then indicated whether they attributed the rejection to discrimination or to the applicant's abilities. Whereas after differences-focused contact participants were more likely to attribute rejection to discrimination rather than to internal attributes, after commonality-focused contact this tendency was reversed such that attributions to discrimination were less likely than attributions to lack of effort. In the control condition, the difference between attributions was not significant, but the patterns resembled the one in the differences condition.

Beyond the measure of attributions, Saguy and Chernyak-Hai (2012) assessed the extent to which the status relations between the institutions were considered to be legitimate. Results revealed that after the commonality-focused contact, legitimacy perceptions were significantly higher, both relative to the differences-focused condition and relative to the no-contact conditions. These findings were replicated in a field analog using Ethiopian Jews in Israel (Saguy & Chernyak-Hai, 2012, Study 2), providing additional evidence for the effects of contact on perceptions that can undermine participation in action for promoting social change. Consistent findings were obtained among members of the Maori ($N = 1,008$), a disadvantaged indigenous group in New Zealand, for whom having more friends from the dominant group (New Zealand Europeans) was associated with perceptions of inequality as arising from differences in individual merit, rather than from historical, group-based disparities (a meritocratic view; McCoy & Major, 2007). These views, in turn, predicted less support for reparative social policies (Sengupta & Sibley, 2013).

Additional studies, which were not centered on intergroup contact, attempted to illuminate the mechanisms underlining the association between harmonious intergroup dynamics and collective action orientations. Ufkes, Calcagno, Glasford and Dovidio (2016) experimentally varied whether participants focused on a common (US) identity with Whites, on their separate subgroup (racial/ethnic) identity or on their dual identity (Black-American or Latino-American identity). Emphasizing common identity led to low levels of anger and lower perceptions that collective action by their minority group would effectively accomplish change. Both of these perceptions, in turn, predicted lower motivation to engage in collective action to address structural inequality. These findings were supported in another study conducted in Europe among Kurds (Ufkes, Dovidio, & Tel, 2015) in which identification patterns were measured. Also in this study, stronger common in-group identity (i.e. identification as European) was negatively related to collective action to repair structural disadvantage, and strong Kurdish identity was positively related to collective action. Moreover, both effects were mediated by anger such that a common identity was associated with less anger regarding one's disadvantage, and strong sub-group identity was associated with more anger.

The role of identification in shaping the effects of commonalities on collective action is further evident in a field survey conducted among Latinos in the US (Tausch et al., 2015). Friendship contact with Whites was negatively associated with interest in collective action. This relation was due to both reduced identification with the disadvantaged group and positive attitudes towards the advantaged group, which predicted reduced anger about inequality. Interestingly, this study was the first to show that contact was also positively associated with an individual mobility orientation, a relationship that was explained through increased perceived permeability—providing further support for Wright and Lubensky's (2009) key formulations regarding the contradictions between prejudice reduction and collective action.

Taken together, the research on the responses of disadvantaged groups to a focus on commonalities suggests that despite its positive consequences when considering intergroup attitudes, it can have a sedative effect on disadvantaged group members, rendering them less concerned with their disadvantaged position and less motivated to repair their own situation. In the next section, we focus on advantaged group members, and on how their perceptions regarding the system and their orientations towards change are shaped by a focus on commonalities.

How do members of advantaged groups respond to commonalities?

The bulk of research on prejudice reduction, and particularly on intergroup contact, has focused on members of advantaged groups. For the most part, the outcomes that were considered in this line of research surrounded attitudes and emotions towards the disadvantaged group, which were shown to be more positive following contact (Pettigrew & Tropp, 2006). Little work has focused on the way members of advantaged groups conceive of social inequality following a focus on commonalities, and even less work has considered behavioral outcomes such as resource distribution. In this section, we review the research that did take this step by examining how a focus on commonalities, either via a superordinate identity or via positive contact, relates to outcomes pertaining to inequality and social change among members of advantaged groups. The section is organized around the two, somewhat inconsistent, conclusions that can be deduced from this research. First, one set of findings suggests that a focus on commonalities improves attitudes but does little to impact social change orientations of advantaged group members. Second, we move on to present the seemingly contradictory evidence showing that commonalities give rise to greater sensitivity to inequality, and even to egalitarian behavior. At the end of the section, we attempt to reconcile these sets of findings.

Paradoxical effects of contact on members of advantaged groups

Jackman and Crane published a paper in 1986 in which they analyzed data collected via a national probability survey ($N = 1,914$) in the US that included measures of interracial contact as well as measures of racial attitudes and support for policies that can benefit minorities. They found evidence for a positive association between contact and positive racial attitudes. In addition, though, they found that contact had little association with Whites' support for policies designed to redress racial inequalities (e.g. inequalities in housing and employment). This finding was echoed in work by Durrheim and Dixon (2004; see also Dixon et al., 2005), who argued for a general gap between advantaged group members' commitment to justice in principle, and their support for actual policies that can promote equality (e.g. affirmative action), a phenomenon they labelled "the principle-implementation gap" (Dixon et al., 2007).

Our experimental investigation in 2009 (Saguy et al., 2009), described earlier, offered an explanation for this gap. In that study, advantaged and disadvantaged group members engaged in either a commonality-focused or a differences-focused interaction. Members of the advantaged groups indeed came to like the disadvantaged group more after an interaction that centered on commonalities (rather than differences). However, in that condition, they also focused less on the inequality that was created in the study. Most importantly, members of advantaged groups discriminated against the disadvantaged group to the same extent after both types of contact. Thus, consistent with the notion of a rift between tolerant attitudes and egalitarian behavior, changes in attitudes across the contact conditions did not lead to changes in the allocation of resources, which were discriminatory regardless of the type of encounter.

In line with these ideas, Banfield and Dovidio (2013, Study 2) demonstrated paradoxical effects of commonalities on recognition of discrimination among majority group members. White participants in the US were exposed to a manipulation that emphasized common-group (American) identity of Blacks and Whites, separate racial-group memberships, or to a control condition that did not emphasize identities. Participants then read a hiring scenario that involved either subtle or blatant discrimination, in which a Black candidate was not offered a job. The outcomes of interest were perceptions of discrimination and expressions of willingness to protest on behalf of the applicant who was denied the job. Results revealed that when the bias witnessed was subtle, White participants for whom common identity was emphasized perceived lower levels of bias than those for whom separate identities were emphasized or those in a control condition, and these perceptions mediated less willingness to protest the negative outcome for the Black person who was rejected. No significant differences emerged when discrimination was blatant. In another study (Banfield & Dovidio, 2013, Study 3), the authors induced a common identity versus a dual identity (vs. an empty control). Although across conditions participants were equally likely to recognize racial bias, participants in the dual identity condition expressed greater willingness to protest the decision compared to participants in the common identity and control conditions.

Taken together, these findings suggest that a sole focus on commonalities can have the paradoxical outcome of reducing majority group members' sensitivity to inequality. Nevertheless, a focus that combines both commonalities and differences can more effectively promote willingness to take action on behalf of minority group members. In the next section, we move to describe somewhat inconsistent evidence, demonstrating that contact, and a focus on commonalities, can give rise to egalitarian tendencies among advantaged groups.

Contact, commonalities and commitment to equality among members of advantaged groups

Despite the evidence reviewed earlier, several correlational studies indicate a positive association between experiences of contact and social change orientations among majority groups. In the research by Dixon and colleagues described earlier (2007), White South Africans were surveyed regarding their contact with minorities and their support for a range of race-related policies. Results showed evidence for a principle-implementation gap, such that while only few Whites opposed the principle of equality, a much larger proportion of Whites opposed the *implementation* of justice-related polices. Nevertheless, friendships with Blacks was still positively associated with support for policies of restitution (in domains of education, land ownership and employment). Interpreting this finding, one needs to bear in mind that the effects of contact on such support were modest in size, and that overall, White's support for such policies was much lower than their support for justice as a principle. In a subsequent study, Dixon, Tropp, Durrheim and Tredoux (2010) attempted to further understand the type of egalitarian policies that are most likely to be supported as a function of intergroup contact. White South Africans ($N = 794$) indicated how much they experienced contact with Blacks and the degree to which contact was friendly, cooperative, close and equal in status. Respondents also evaluated government compensatory policies (e.g. scholarship for Black students), and race preferential policies (e.g. preferential tax breaks for Black businesses). Compensatory policies can be thought of as providing supplementary resources to Blacks (adjusting for historical barriers), whereas preferential policies give Blacks advantages over Whites in specified contexts—the latter, therefore, are more threatening to Whites' resources. Results revealed that the more contact Whites had with Blacks, and the better the quality of such contact, the less likely they were to oppose both types of policies. However, the effect of contact on support for compensatory policies tended to be stronger than its effect on attitudes for preferential policies—suggesting that contact exerts stronger effects on policies that encompass less immediate threat to Whites' resources.

Studies in Western Europe and the US further find that positive contact with immigrants is associated with pro-immigration attitudes. For example, Hayes and Dowds (2006) found that non-immigrants in the UK who had been exposed to immigrants, as friends, neighbors, or work colleagues were more likely to support the inclusion of immigrants in the UK, and to have close contact with immigrants (see also Pettigrew, Wagner, & Christ, 2007). Similar effects were found among advantaged group members in the study by Cakal and colleagues described earlier (2011) conducted among Whites ($N = 244$) in South Africa: they found that intergroup contact was significantly associated with support for policies favoring Blacks.

A recent experimental study with US participants supports this line of findings (Kunst, Thomsen, Sam, & Berry, 2015). These researchers examined how induced common identity impacts egalitarian behaviors of advantaged group members towards immigrants. Common identity was primed with an emphasis on shared fate and heritage to both White Americans and immigrants, whereas in the separate group condition the items emphasized the differences between the groups. In the common identity condition, participants were more willing to donate money to an organization dedicated to integrating immigrants and to volunteer to help support them—suggesting that the effects of common identity translated via tolerance into egalitarian behavior.

Reconciling the findings for advantaged group members

Taken together, the findings regarding the effects of a commonality focus on advantaged group members seem to be inconclusive. While some research shows that a commonality focus does little to impact advantaged group members' egalitarian behavior (e.g. Banfield & Dovidio, 2013; Saguy et al., 2009), other studies point to a positive association between contact and support for policies that can advance disadvantaged group members (e.g. Cakal et al., 2011; Hayes & Dowds, 2006). How can these seemingly contradictory lines of evidence be reconciled?

As far as we are aware, no study (except for Saguy et al., 2009, Study 1) has examined the effects of experimentally manipulated *contact* on majority group's actions aimed at advancing equality. To be sure, self-reported contact likely represents contact in its naturalistic form more than manipulated contact does. Nonetheless, we are still limited as for the *causal* claims that can be drawn regarding the effects of positive contact on egalitarian tendencies of majority groups. In the absence of this causal evidence, a plausible competing explanation for the correlational effects described above is that general tolerance, or tolerant norms, account for both increased contact and support for egalitarian policies. Moreover, although most of the studies described in the previous section have considered support for social policies that could benefit disadvantaged groups, they measure behavioral *intentions* rather than actual behavioral outcomes. Thus, the principle-implementation gap (Dixon et al., 2005) can be a valid conceptual lens via which these findings can be interpreted—suggesting that while contact may predict advantaged group members' support for minority rights in principle, their support for the practice of equality is less clearly predicted by a focus on commonalities.

The distinction between support for the principle of equality and for the implementation of equality, nevertheless, does not explain all of the inconsistency described earlier, particularly when considering Kunst et al.'s (2015) findings showing that emphasizing common connections produced more helpful behaviors towards immigrants. Given the strong emphasis on assimilation in American culture, it could be the case that priming commonalities in this context primes the values of individual freedom and equality, hence leading majority group members to endorse equality also for immigrants. However, this might not be the case in contexts that are marked by more enduring power dynamics, where most of the inequality is structural and often difficult to detect (Ufkes et al., 2016). In those dynamics, commonalities can still mask central differences in the power dynamics between the groups, and give rise to less support for egalitarian actions. Indeed, in the study by Banfield and Dovidio described earlier, an emphasis on commonalities undermined recognition of subtle disadvantage but not of blatant disadvantage. This calls for additional research, and particularly experimental research, that could potentially investigate the conditions under which a focus on commonalities (via contact or not) drives recognition to power inequalities and related action.

In the next section, we move to describe new developments within research on the irony of harmony. We briefly present two different lines of research. One takes the irony of harmony ideas to the realm of violent conflicts; it focuses on hope as a harmonious emotion in those contexts. The second line of work begins to apply the ideas of the irony of harmony to the contexts of gender relations. Even though scholars have theorized about gender relations as providing a fertile ground for ironic effects of harmony, no studies that we are aware of have considered such effects.

The irony of harmony: new developments and future directions

The theory and research we have reviewed earlier on the irony of harmony suggest that harmony created by contact between groups can distract attention away from inequality, and thereby weaken disadvantaged groups' commitment to social change. This line of research can be taken further to argue that certain emotions experienced by disadvantaged group members can reflect harmonious orientations towards the advantaged group, and therefore, experiencing such emotions can undermine engagement in collective action (even in the absence of actual harmony).

We are currently investigating this idea by focusing on hope in the contexts of violent intergroup conflicts (Hasan-Aslih, Pliskin, van Zomeren, Halperin, & Saguy, in press). Hope, when referring to the feasibility of social change, is considered an important basis for individuals' motivation to engage in collective action (Cohen-Chen, van Zomeren, & Halperin, 2015). However, this type of hope for change is not the only type of hope that can be experienced in situations of conflict. Hope can also refer to expectations for better future relationships between the disadvantaged and the advantaged group. We tested the idea that such hope for harmonious intergroup relations, even without the occurrence of actual harmony, could produce optimism about the prospects for equality between groups and hence undermine motivation for social change.

We conducted two field studies among Palestinian citizens of Israel during two different periods of mass protests against the Israeli government. The studies examined the association between two types of hope and collective action: hope regarding better future relations with the advantaged out-group (harmony-based hope), and hope for promoting the future status of the in-group (empowerment-based hope). As expected, across studies, harmony-based hope was associated with decreased intentions for collective action, while empowerment-based hope was unrelated to collective action. Moreover, the relationship between harmony-based hope and collective action was found mainly among Palestinians who were less identified with their group, whereas highly identified participants had relatively strong action tendencies regardless of their feelings of hope. This moderation likely reflects high identifiers' solid motivation for social change (Van Zomeren, Spears, & Leach, 2008), indicating that strong identification could work to protect against the demotivating effects of hope related to harmony.

This work extends insights from research on the irony of harmony to the realm of harmony-based *emotions*, suggesting that it is not only identity representations, or optimal contact, that can give rise to psychological tendencies that relax concerns about structural inequality. This line of thinking opens several directions for future research. One such direction involves the effects of *communicated* hope on members of advantaged groups. It could be the case that to the extent that disadvantaged group members communicate hope about the future relations (harmony-based hope), members of advantaged groups will become less threatened because the possibility of collective resistance might seem less plausible. One possible consequence of this process can be reduced commitment to equality on the part of advantaged groups, whose concerns about losing power and about appearing moral might be relaxed as a function of communicated hope by the disadvantaged. This notion would parallel some of the effects mentioned earlier, indicating that a focus on commonalities with the disadvantaged group can undermine commitment to equality among members of advantaged groups.

Along the same lines, members of advantaged groups might even become motivated to *induce* hope among the disadvantaged, so that the status quo would remain stable. Even though this idea was yet to be tested, it is in line with research on appeasement, showing that advantaged group members are motivated, particularly under threat, to render disadvantaged groups satisfied (Chow, Lowery, & Hogan, 2013).

Indeed, apart from hope, relations between groups can also generate other positive emotions such as satisfaction, which may function like hope and induce harmony between groups. Extending these ideas, we attempted to deepen our investigation of the role of positive emotions in unequal power dynamics by testing the irony of harmony ideas in the context of satisfactory and intimate heterosexual romantic relationships.

Even though women's status in Western society has improved considerably over the last 50 years, gender gaps remain significant and there is still undeniable evidence of gender inequality across various life domains (Ridgeway, 2011). At the same time, relations between men and women on an interpersonal level are characterized by intimacy and oftentimes manifest as close and meaningful relationships. This dynamic, involving enduring positive contact between members of the groups at the interpersonal level alongside pervasive inequality at a structural level calls for the question of whether one feeds the other. Namely, could it be the case that the very harmony that characterizes many relations between men and women serves to demotivate women from engaging in social change?

To test this possibility, we conducted an initial study aimed at testing whether the occurrence of optimal contact between men and women predicts women's lower recognition of inequality and less support for social change (Sobol, Shchori-Eyal, & Saguy, in preparation). Even though they are rarely considered as such, romantic relationships between men and women usually answer Allport's (1954) conditions necessary for optimal contact, particularly when relations in Western society are considered. First, the relationship partners often share mutual goals (e.g. child rearing), and they collaborate in order to achieve them. Personal familiarity between the partners is an integral part of romantic relationships. Moreover, even though status relations between the groups are evident, at an interpersonal level man and woman mostly enter the relationship as equal beings (at least at a stated level). Finally, in most romantic relationships, institutional support is present and accompanies the formalization of the relationships. If committed romantic relationships do indeed meet the conditions of optimal contact, then the demobilizing effects of optimal contact on disadvantaged groups may also apply to women.

In the initial study we run, sixty-seven women completed a measure assessing the degree to which the committed relationship in which they were engaged met the conditions of optimal contact (e.g. "I feel my partner and I have common goals"). They then completed measures of gender-related system justification, modern sexism, and perceptions and feelings about the power relations between men and women. Consistent with our reasoning, to the extent that women reported their relationship quality as high on dimensions reflecting optimal contact, the stronger were their justification of gender power relations. Supporting the irony of harmony effect, optimal contact was also positively correlated with satisfaction regarding gender relations in general.

As in many other contact studies, due to the correlative nature of the study we cannot draw conclusions about causality. It could certainly be the case that gender system justification drives satisfaction with romantic relationship, and not the other way around. Nevertheless, the initial evidence gathered sets the stage for future experimental work in which different elements pertaining to optimal contact can be manipulated in the context of close relationships.

Finally, perhaps the most fundamental and pressing question for future work is how harmony *can* be effectively produced, while not involving demobilizing effects on disadvantaged or advantaged groups. Vezzali, Andrighetto and Saguy (2016) have begun to address this question by proposing that direct contact would not undermine motivation for social change, and might even increase it, when the content of the contact is focused more on differences than commonalities between groups. In their work, they found that among native Italians (advantaged group members), cross-group friendships with immigrants were associated with increased social change motivation, but only when contact was focused more on differences than commonalities. Results were replicated with another sample of both advantaged (Italian) and disadvantaged (immigrant) group members.

In addition to being consistent with Brown and Hewstone's (2005) model, which advocates an emphasis on separate as well as on common identities, these results are also consistent with the "critical intergroup dialogue approach", advocating the explicit focus on power relations during a structured contact situation (Zúñiga, Nagda, & Sevig, 2002). Similarly, Becker, Wright, Lubenski and Zhou (2013) demonstrated that when the content of contact involved (versus did not involve) a focus on power differences as illegitimate, contact did not have a demobilizing effect among members of disadvantaged groups. Future research can productively develop a systematic model of contact that involves a focus on differences, and/or differences in power—such a model will be evidenced-based, and will enable critical theoretical and practical advancement in this field of intergroup contact, and harmony more generally.

When thinking of such a model of contact, a great challenge that arises is how to get members of advantaged and disadvantaged groups to be willing to openly address their differences, and particularly their differences in power. Extant research suggests that members of advantaged groups would avoid such discussions in order to protect their moral image (Knowles, Lowery, Chow, & Unzueta, 2014; Saguy & Kteily, 2014). Future work can advance this very avenue by investigating ways to promote advantaged group members' willingness to recognize their advantage and dismantle inequality. Such interventions should rely on relevant findings on the psychology of dominant groups. For example, one potential way of raising recognition to inequality can be to direct majority group members' attention to potential losses in their moral image, given a certain inequality. Such an intervention would consider advantaged group members' motive to sustain a sense of morality in the face of privilege (Knowles et al., 2014; Lickel, Schmader, & Barquissau, 2004) and could be potentially effective.

Closing remarks

Harmony-inducing strategies can have obvious and relatively immediate positive consequences for intergroup attitudes. Nevertheless, research on the irony of harmony effect clearly demonstrates that even though the consequences for the advantaged group are sometimes positive, members of disadvantaged groups are likely to become more supportive of the very system that disadvantaged them. This dynamic is first important to recognize because, without such recognition, many prejudice reduction interventions might reinforce the status quo even though they aim to achieve the opposite outcome. Second, it is critical to attempt and provide solutions to such contradiction. The little work that begins to provide solutions clearly points to the importance of having members of advantaged groups be willing to address differences during contact, and more importantly, be critical of their own power position. This can maintain pressures for social change by disadvantaged group members while providing an avenue for communication and exchange with advantaged group members. In addition, to the extent that recognizing both commonality and group-based differences and inequality helps people extend principles or morality across group lines, advantaged group members may become motivated to advance change themselves. Future research can focus on how to bring members of both advantaged and disadvantaged groups to be able to address such topics in a way that would promote sensitivity to inequality, while not undermining potential harmony between the groups.

References

Allport, G.W. (1954). *The nature of prejudice*. New York, NY: Addison-Wesley.

Banfield, J.C., & Dovidio, J.F. (2013). Whites' perceptions of discrimination against Blacks: The influence of common identity. *Journal of Experimental Social Psychology, 49,* 833–41. doi: 10.1016/j.jesp.2013.04.008

Becker, J.C., Wright, S.C., Lubensky, M.E., & Zhou, S. (2013). Friend or ally: Whether cross-group contact undermines collective action depends on what advantaged group members say (or don't say). *Personality and Social Psychology Bulletin, 39,* 442–55. doi: 10.1177/0146167213477155

Brown, R., & Hewstone, M. (2005). An integrative theory of intergroup contact. *Advances in Experimental Social Psychology, 37,* 255–343. doi: 10.1016/S0065-2601(05)37005-5

Cakal, H., Hewstone, M., Schwär, G., & Heath, A. (2011). An investigation of the social identity model of collective action and the "sedative" effect of intergroup contact among Black and White students in South Africa. *British Journal of Social Psychology, 50,* 606–27. doi: 10.1111/j.2044-8309.2011.02075.x

Chow, R.M., Lowery, B.S., & Hogan, C.M. (2013). Appeasement: Whites' strategic support for affirmative action. *Personality and Social Psychology Bulletin, 39,* 332–45. doi: 10.1177/0146167212475224

Cohen-Chen, S., van Zomeren, M., & Halperin, E. (2015). Hope(lessness) and collective (in)action in intractable intergroup conflict. In E. Halperin & K. Sharvit (Eds.), *The social psychology of intractable conflicts: Celebrating the legacy of Daniel Bar-Tal, vol. I.* (pp. 89–101). (Peace Psychology Book Series; Vol. 27). Springer. 10.1007/978–3-319–17861–5-7

Demoulin, S., Leyens, J.P., & Dovidio, J.F. (Eds.) (2009). *Intergroup misunderstandings: Impact of divergent social realities*. Philadelphia, PA: Psychology Press.

Dixon, J., Durrheim, K., & Tredoux, C. (2005). Beyond the optimal contact strategy: A reality check for the contact hypothesis. *American Psychologist, 60,* 697–711. doi: 10.1037/0003–066X.60.7.697

Dixon, J., Durrheim, K., & Tredoux, C. (2007). Intergroup contact and attitudes toward the principle and practice of racial equality. *Psychological Science, 18,* 867–72. doi: 10.1111/j.1467–9280.2007.01993.x

Dixon, J., Levine, M., Reicher, S., & Durrheim, K. (2012). Beyond prejudice: Are negative evaluations the problem and is getting us to like one another more the solution? *Behavioral and Brain Sciences, 35,* 411–25. doi: 10.1017/S0140525X11002214

Dixon, J., Tropp, L.R., Durrheim, K., & Tredoux, C.G. (2010). 'Let them eat harmony': Prejudice reduction and the political attitudes of historically disadvantaged groups. *Current Directions in Psychological Science, 19,* 76–80. doi: 10.1177/0963721410363366

Dovidio, J.F., & Gaertner, S.L. (2010). Intergroup bias. In S.T. Fiske, D. Gilbert, & G. Lindzey (Eds.), *Handbook of social psychology* (Vol. 2, pp. 1084–121). New York, NY: Wiley.

Dovidio, J.F., Gaertner, S.L., & Kawakami, K. (2003). Intergroup contact: The past, present, and the future. *Group Processes and Intergroup Relations, 6,* 5–21. doi: 10.1177/1368430203006001009

Dovidio, J.F., Gaertner, S., & Saguy, T. (2015). Color-blindness and commonality: Included but invisible? *American Behavioral Scientist, 59,* 1518–38. doi: 10.1177/0002764215580591

Dovidio, J.F., Gaertner, S.L., Validzic, A., Matoka, K., Johnson, B., & Frazier, S. (1997). Extending the benefits of recategorization: Evaluations, self-disclosure, and helping. *Journal of Experimental Social Psychology, 33*, 401–20. doi: 10.1006/jesp.1997.1327

Durrheim, K., & Dixon, J.A. (2004). Attitudes in the fiber of everyday life: The discourse of racial evaluation and the lived experience of desegregation. *American Psychologist, 59*, 626–36. doi: 10.1037/0003–066X.59.7.626

Ellison, C.G., & Powers, D.A. (1994). The contact hypothesis and racial attitudes among Black Americans. *Social Science Quarterly, 75*, 385–400.

Forbes, H. (1997). *Ethnic conflict: Commerce, culture and the contact hypothesis.* New Haven, CT: Yale University Press.

Gaertner, S.L., & Dovidio, J.F. (2000). *Reducing intergroup bias: The common ingroup identity model.* Philadelphia, PA: Psychology Press.

Gaertner, S.L., & Dovidio, J.F. (2012). Reducing intergroup bias: The common ingroup identity model. In P.A.M. Van Lange, A.W. Kruglanski, & E.T. Higgins (Eds.), *Handbook of theories of social psychology* (Vol. 2, pp. 439–57). Thousand Oaks, CA: Sage.

Glasford, D.E., & Dovidio, J.F. (2011). E pluribus unum: Dual identity and minority group members' motivation to engage in contact, as well as social change. *Journal of Experimental Social Psychology, 47*, 1021–4. doi: 10.1016/j.jesp.2011.03.021

Hasan-Aslih, S., Pliskin, R., van Zomeren, M., Halperin, E., & Saguy, T. (in press). A darker side of hope: Harmony-based hope ironically decreases collective action intentions among the disadvantaged. *European Journal of Social Psychology.*

Hayes, B., & Dowds, L. (2006). Social contact, cultural marginality, or economic self-interest? Attitudes towards immigrants in Northern Ireland. *Journal of Ethnic and Migration Studies, 32*, 455–76. doi: 10.1080/13691830600554890

Hewstone, M., Cairns, E., Voci, A., Hamberger, J., & Niens, U. (2006). Intergroup contact, forgiveness and experience of "The Troubles" in Northern Ireland. *Journal of Social Issues, 62*, 99–120. doi: 10.1111/j.1540–4560.2006.00441.x

Jackman, M.R., & Crane, M. (1986). "Some of my best friends are blacks": Interracial friendship and Whites' racial attitudes. *Public Opinion Quarterly, 50*, 459–86. doi: 10.1086/268998

Knowles, E.D., Lowery, B.S., Chow, R.M., & Unzueta, M.M. (2014). Deny, distance, or dismantle? How White Americans manage a privileged identity. *Perspectives on Psychological Science, 9*, 594–609. doi: 10.1177/1745691614554658

Kunst, J.R., Thomsen, L., Sam, D.L., & Berry, J.W. (2015). "We are in this together": Common group identity predicts majority members' active acculturation efforts to integrate immigrants. *Personality and Social Psychology Bulletin, 41*, 1438–53. doi: 10.1177/0146167215599349

Lickel, B., Schmader, T., & Barquissau, M. (2004). The evocation of moral emotions in intergroup contexts: The distinction between collective guilt and collective shame. In N. Branscombe & B. Doosje (Eds.), *Collective guilt: International perspectives* (pp. 35–55). Cambridge, UK: Cambridge University Press.

McCoy, S.K., & Major, B. (2007). Priming meritocracy and the psychological justification of inequality. *Journal of Experimental Social Psychology, 43*, 341–51. doi: 10.1016/j. jesp. 2006.04.009

Nier, J.A., Gaertner, S.L., Dovidio, J.F., Banker, B.S., Ward, C.M., & Rust, M.C. (2001). Changing interracial evaluations and behavior: The effects of a common group identity. *Group Processes and Intergroup Relations, 4*, 299–316. doi: 10.1177/1368430201004004001

Paluck, E.L., & Green, D.P. (2009). Prejudice reduction: What works? A review and assessment of research and practice. *Annual Review of Psychology, 60*, 339–67. doi: 10.1146/annurev.psych.60.110707.163607

Pettigrew, T.F. (1998). Intergroup contact theory. *Annual Review of Psychology*, *49*, 65–85. doi: 10.1146/annurev.psych.49.1.65

Pettigrew, T.F., & Tropp, L.R. (2006). A meta-analytic test of intergroup contact theory. *Journal of Personality and Social Psychology*, *90*, 751–83. doi: 10.1037/0022–3514.90.5.751

Pettigrew, T.F., Wagner, U., & Christ, O. (2007). Who opposes immigration? Comparing German with North American findings. *Du Bois Review*, *4*, 19–39.

Reicher, S. (1986). Contact, action and racialization: Some British evidence. In M. Hewstone & R. Brown (Eds.), *Contact and conflict in intergroup encounters* (pp. 152–68). Oxford, UK: Blackwell.

Ridgeway, C.L. (2011). *Framed by gender: How gender inequality persists in the modern world*. New York, NY: Oxford University Press.

Roccas, S., & Brewer, M.B. (2002). Social identity complexity. *Personality and Social Psychology Review*, *6*, 88–106. doi: 10.1207/S15327957PSPR0602–01

Rosenthal, H.E.S., & Crisp, R.J. (2006). Reducing stereotype threat by blurring intergroup boundaries. *Personality and Social Psychology Bulletin*, *32*, 501–11. doi: 10.1177/0146167 205281009

Saguy, T., & Chernyak-Hai, L. (2012). Intergroup contact can undermine disadvantaged group members' attributions to discrimination. *Journal of Experimental Social Psychology*, *48*, 714–20. doi: 10.1016/j.jesp.2012.01.003

Saguy, T., & Kteily, N. (2014). Power, negotiations, and the anticipation of intergroup encounters. *European Review of Social Psychology*, *25*, 107–41. doi: 10.1080/10463283. 2014.957579

Saguy, T., Tausch, N., Dovidio, J.F., & Pratto, F. (2009). The irony of harmony: Intergroup contact can produce false expectations for equality. *Psychological Science*, *20*, 114–21. doi: 10.1111/j.1467–9280.2008.02261.x

Saguy, T., Tropp, L.R., & Hawi, D.R. (2013). The role of group power in intergroup contact. In G. Hodson & M. Hewstone (Eds.), *Advances in intergroup contact* (pp. 113–32). New York, NY: Psychology Press.

Sengupta, N.K., & Sibley, C.G. (2013). Perpetuating one's own disadvantage: Intergroup contact enables the ideological legitimation of inequality. *Personality and Social Psychology Bulletin*, *39*, 1391–403. doi: 10.1177/0146167213497593

Sherif, M., Harvey, O.J., White, B.J., Hood, W., & Sherif, C.W. (1961). *Intergroup conflict and cooperation: The Robbers Cave experiment*. Norman, OK: The University Book Exchange.

Simon, B., & Klandermans, B. (2001). Politicized collective identity: A social psychological analysis. *American Psychologist*, *56*, 319–31. doi: 10.1037/0003-066X.56.4.319

Sobol, D., Shchori-Eyal, N., & Saguy, T. (in preparation). *Harmony in close-relationships contributes to the persistence of gender inequality*.

Stürmer, S., & Simon, B. (2004). The role of collective identification in social movement participation: A panel study in the context of the German gay movement. *Personality and Social Psychology Bulletin*, *30*, 263–77. doi: 10.1177/0146167203256690

Tausch, N., Saguy, T., & Bryson, J. (2015). How does intergroup contact affect social change?: Examining collective action and individual mobility intentions among members of disadvantaged groups. *Journal of Social Issue*, *71*, 536–53. doi: 10.1111/josi.12127

Tropp, L.R., Hawi, D., Van Laar, C., & Levin, S. (2012). Cross-ethnic friendship, perceived discrimination, and their effects on ethnic activism over time: A longitudinal investigation of three ethnic minority groups. *British Journal of Social Psychology*, *51*, 257–2. doi: 10.1111/ j.2044-8309.2011.02050.x

Turner, J.C., Hogg, M.A., Oakes, P.J., Reicher, S.D., & Wetherell, M.S. (1987). *Rediscovering the social group: A self-categorization theory*. Oxford, UK: Blackwell.

Ufkes, E.G., Calcagno, J., Glasford, D.E., & Dovidio, J.F. (2016). Understanding how common identity undermines collective action among disadvantaged group members. *Journal of Experimental Social Psychology, 63,* 26–35. doi: 10.1016/j.jesp.2015.11.006

Ufkes, E.G., Dovidio, J.F., & Tel, G. (2015). Identity and collective action among European Kurds. *British Journal of Social Psychology, 54,* 176–86. doi: 10.1111/bjso.12084

van Zomeren, M., Spears, R., Fischer, A.H., & Leach, C.W. (2004). Put your money where your mouth is! Explaining collective action tendencies through group-based anger and group efficacy. *Journal of Personality and Social Psychology, 87,* 649–64. doi: 10.1037/0022-3514.87.5.649

van Zomeren, M., Spears, R., & Leach, C.W. (2008). Exploring psychological mechanisms of collective action: Does relevance of group identity influence how people cope with collective disadvantage? *British Journal of Social Psychology, 47,* 353–72. doi: 10.1348/014466607X231091

Vezzali, L., Andrighetto, L., & Saguy, T. (2016). *When intergroup contact can backfire: The content of intergroup encounters and desire for equality.* Under review.

Wright, S.C. (2001). Strategic collective action: Social psychology and social change. In R. Brown & S.L. Gaertner (Eds.), *Intergroup processes: Blackwell handbook of social psychology* (Vol. 4, pp. 409–30). Oxford, UK: Blackwell.

Wright, S.C., & Lubensky, M. (2009). The struggle for social equality: Collective action vs. prejudice reduction. In S. Demoulin, J.P. Leyens, & J.F. Dovidio (Eds.), *Intergroup misunderstandings: Impact of divergent social realities* (pp. 291–310). New York, NY: Psychology Press.

Zúñiga, X., Nagda, B.R.A., & Sevig, T.D. (2002). Intergroup dialogues: An educational model for cultivating engagement across differences. *Equity and Excellence in Education, 35,* 7–17. doi: 10.1080/713845248

5

A TEMPORALLY INTEGRATED MODEL OF INTERGROUP CONTACT AND THREAT (TIMICAT)

Dominic Abrams and Anja Eller

Key words: intergroup contact, threat, longitudinal, prejudice

This chapter focuses on the issue of how intergroup contact and intergroup threat may combine, temporally, to influence prejudice. We propose a conceptual framework for moving towards new research questions, and draw on illustrative evidence from our own and other research in order to set the scene for the development of future theory and research.

Intergroup contact theory has long proposed that high-quality contact as friends can be sufficient to promote more positive intergroup relations (Allport, 1954; Pettigrew, 1998). From a different starting point, integrated threat theory (ITT; Stephan & Stephan, 2000) holds that higher levels of various types of threat can result in deteriorating intergroup relations or can prevent relations from becoming positive. Surprisingly, little research or theory has explicitly addressed the *temporal* roles of threat and contact in relation to prejudice. We propose that threat can play different roles at different stages of the contact–prejudice relationship and contact can play different roles at different stages of the threat–prejudice relationship.

Our framework builds on a proposed taxonomy of contact and threat contexts. First, contact has a temporal component, which provides a context for prejudice (no contact, past contact only, discrete single contact, multiple contact, continuous contact, future contact only). Much research on direct intergroup contact focuses on continuous contact contexts or on discrete contact contexts. In contrast, research on indirect contact often focuses on no contact or potential future contact. Yet there is no particular reason to distinguish direct and indirect contact on these lines. Both are forms of contact, which could be pertinent in each of the contexts.

There has also been little effort to distinguish whether the role of intergroup threat differs across these different contact contexts, yet there is good reason to believe that threat might operate very differently in each. Moreover, like contact, threat and its various dimensions have a temporal dimension. It is possible to think of prejudice that arises in a no-threat context (e.g. anti-Semitism that exists in various countries worldwide despite there being very few or no Jewish people in those countries), a discrete threat context, a continuous threat context, or a post-threat context.

We also argue that the threat context and the contact context can be completely orthogonal. For example, one can readily envisage a situation of a discrete threat but continuous contact (e.g. a terrorist bombing incident in a multicultural city), or continuous threat but a discrete contact (e.g. a single encounter between a North and South Korean person), or any other combination. It would seem odd, then, to assume that the contact–threat–prejudice triangle would necessarily have causal arrows in only one direction, or that the weight of each causal arrow would be constant across these different combinations of threat and contact contexts. Moreover, if we conceptualize contact and threat as operating in distinct temporal pathways, we then need to consider whether different *types* of contact and different *types* of threat may play stronger or weaker roles in each of these situations. Space does not permit us to delve extensively into these specific subtypes of threat and contact, but clearly there is much complexity to be captured. Our goal here is to use a single dimension (the temporal frame) to organize our thinking about both of these two important factors in intergroup prejudice.

We review some relevant evidence from the contact literature and the threat literature, then focus on specific contexts and illustrate how threat can be differentiated according to the type of context. We argue that threat and contact can have independent, additive, sequential, and interactive effects on prejudice depending on the particular contact/threat contexts. We conclude the chapter with a proposed set of hypotheses for future research.

A sequential approach to intergroup contact

Pettigrew (1998) drew on three influential models of social categorization to argue that different types of categorization were likely to be most beneficial at different stages of contact. Specifically, initial contact should ideally be *decategorized* (i.e. taking place on an interpersonal level of categorization), because decategorization weakens intergroup distinctions and should also therefore weaken category-based stereotypes (Brewer & Miller, 1984). At a later stage, contact should be *categorized* (i.e. interactants are strongly aware of their different group memberships) because learning positive things about a particular group member will only generalize to attitudes to the group as a whole if that member's group membership is salient during contact (Hewstone & Brown, 1986). Finally, contact should occur in a *recategorized* context (one in which superordinate shared group membership is made salient [Gaertner, Dovidio, Anastasio, Bachman, & Rust, 1993]), because this "unified group" level should achieve the maximum reduction in prejudice. Pettigrew (1998) also cautioned that groups may break off contact at any point and that these stages might overlap.

This last point is rather important. Indeed, it is easy to imagine or recall situations in which the sequence of categorization has been different or reversed from Pettigrew's ideal model. For example, it is not uncommon that a single group has suffered schism (cf. Sani, 2005), and the split groups have ultimately dissolved altogether or only one has survived. The transition of some Western countries from being mono-cultural and mono-racial to experiencing substantial immigration from one particular group or region, and then gradually becoming multi-ethnic and/or highly individualized, tracks exactly that transition. Moreover, a danger of superordinate categorization is that it immediately raises the prospect of prejudice against a larger superordinate out-group. Therefore, it would be useful to complement Pettigrew's idealized fixed-sequence causal model with a focus on the dynamic interconnecting and interlocking effects of variables on intergroup prejudice over time. For example, determining the type of categorization that might be most beneficial requires attention to the context and external factors that frame the relationship, and that affect why contact is occurring at all.

Integrated threat theory (ITT)

Threat theories propose that attitudes towards out-groups are affected by the presence of minority members (Blalock, 1967), in large part, because of perceived competition for resources (cf. Sherif, 1966). Consequently, the larger this subgroup becomes, the more threatening is the presence of its members and the greater are the chances of intergroup prejudice and conflict. In fact, this proposition is quite contentious and is contradicted by various sources of evidence (e.g. Leader, Mullen, & Abrams, 2007).

Researchers have also focused on the *psychological* aspects of threat, most comprehensively in work based around ITT (Stephan & Stephan, 2000). This well-supported theory specifies various types of psychological threats as primary drivers of prejudice: "realistic" threats to the well-being, survival or economic situation of the in-group; "symbolic" threats to the values, principles, culture and way of life held dear by the in-group; intergroup anxiety, which is the worry or fear of unpleasant experiences or personal risk during an interaction with an out-group member; and negative stereotypes about the out-group. A meta-analytic summary of the effects of threat (Riek, Mania, & Gaertner, 2006) concluded that these various types of threats are indeed associated with more negative stereotypes and attitudes towards out-groups. Moreover, these effects are stronger among majority than minority group members, supporting the idea that relative in-group status is an important moderating factor (Stephan & Renfro, 2002; Tausch, Hewstone, Kenworthy, Cairns, & Christ, 2007). Different theories also suggest that stereotypes could either be a precursor of the other threats (Stephan et al., 2002), or be a consequence of threats (Sherif, 1966) or possibly a consequence of prejudice (Myers, Abrams, Rosenthal, & Christian, 2013). More generally however, Riek et al.'s analysis points to a question mark over where, in a causal sequence, the different threats might sit.

Threat as a mediator

ITT holds that, along with variables such as prior in-group identification and personal relevance of the out-group, negative intergroup contact is a key antecedent of intergroup anxiety (Stephan et al., 2002), and thus, researchers have generally focused on contact as an important *cause* of threat (e.g., Stephan, Diaz-Loving, & Duran, 2000) with threat posited as a critical mediator between contact and prejudice. Indeed, this has been the predominant assumption tested in empirical research. However, evidence suggests that the contact-threat relationship is likely to be bi-directional and that threat does not function as an integrated construct. Tausch, Hewstone and Roy (2009) found that, whereas realistic threat mediated between Hindu–Muslim contact and prejudice more strongly among Hindus, symbolic threat mediated more strongly among Muslims. Moreover, Levin, van Laar and Sidanius' (2003) 4-year longitudinal study of college students in California revealed approximately equivalent causal paths from intergroup friendships to bias and anxiety as from bias and anxiety to friendships. Finally, J. Binder et al.'s (2009) longitudinal analysis tested the role of anxiety as a mediator between contact and social distance, but attended less closely to the fact that the T1 contact to T2 anxiety correlation (−.20) was almost equal to the T1 anxiety to T2 contact relationship (−.18) (see J. Binder et al., 2009, Table 5).

Instead of regarding such findings as problematic, we consider them to be highly illuminating because they shift the question from "does threat mediate between contact and prejudice?" to "when do threat, contact and prejudice each exert an influence on one another?" The latter question calls for a framework that either brings in extra variables as moderators (e.g. objective threats, group size, salience, etc.) or, perhaps more usefully, demands attention to the temporal issues that frame an intergroup relationship.

Al Ramiah, Hewstone, Little and Lang (2013) examined effects of interethnic contact between a majority (Malay) and two minority (Chinese and Indian) groups within National Service trainees in Malaysia following a nation-building inter-vention. They found that effects of contact on prejudice were mediated by sym-bolic and realistic threat, but only among the minority groups. Yet contact was related to at least two forms of threat (from symbolic and realistic threats and anxiety) in all three subgroups. Thus, we infer that threat could plausibly be either a precursor or an outcome of contact

Pettigrew, Wagner and Christ's (2010) review concluded that objective threat (defined as a higher number and density of minority group members) does not equate to perceived threat (perceived proportions), and that it is perceived threat that predicts prejudice (Semyonov, Rajman, Tov, & Schmidt, 2004). Pettigrew et al. (2010) proposed that contact and (objective) threat interact because the higher out-group proportions create perceived threat but also provide more opportunities for contact. Among people who are politically, ideologically or normatively inclined to engage with the out-group, prejudice is lowered (cf. Eller, Gómez, Vazquez, & Fernández, 2015). Among those less so inclined, prejudice seems to increase. A comparable point comes from Schmid, Hewstone and Al Ramiah's

(2013) finding that higher neighbourhood diversity directly led to lower trust but indirectly led to higher trust via greater contact and reduced sense of threat.

Only a few studies illuminate the effects of contact in situations of violent conflict (Al Ramiah & Hewstone, 2013; cf. Paluck, 2009), and there is a relative dearth of longitudinal evidence. This is important because psychological threat itself provides a context within which contact is interpreted. Indeed, salient negative intergroup contact results in increased prejudice (Vorauer & Sasaki, 2011, see also Graf & Paolini, this volume). Yet it may also be highly prejudiced individuals whose attitudes change most following contact (Dhont & Van Hiel, 2009; Hodson, Harry, & Mitchell, 2009), consistent with the idea that it is those who feel most threatened who may be the ones that are most likely to reconsider their position in the light of positive contact. Conversely, earlier and cumulatively more positive contact in a context of an extended conflict seems to weaken the effect of recent contact (Al Ramiah, Hewstone, Voci, Cairns, & Hughes, 2013). Interpreted differently, if the shared threat remains relatively constant, repeated contact experiences do not make much inroads on prejudice.

Intergroup contact research has generated an impressive array of "relevant variables", other than threat, that are involved in the contact–prejudice relationship. These include a host of potential moderators and mediators, such as trust, empathy and perspective-taking (e.g. Cehajic, Brown, & Castano, 2008; Tam, Hewstone, Kenworthy, & Cairns, 2009). But it is hard to imagine that the ideal set of conditions for contact and these mediating processes ever actually occurs—a situation of equal status, cooperation, common goals, institutional support, a balanced majority-minority ratio, friendship and self-disclosure with typical members followed by perspective-taking, empathy, intergroup learning, aided by supportive in-group norms, all following in sequence from decategorized to categorized to recategorized relationships. We can think of no experimental study that has ever demonstrated the combined effects of all these elements. Even if such situations can be created, or arise in well-constrained contexts, such as schools or special training sessions (Wagner & Hewstone, 2012), they could also be overridden by events and other factors. In practical terms, the aspiring social psychological interventionist is likely to be in the situation of a chef who is expected to produce a gourmet dish but whose Michelin star capabilities remain thwarted by being unsure of which or how many guests are coming for dinner, being equipped only with a single camping gas, a small aluminum pan and a maximum of three ingredients.

We note that positive friendship contact does entail that, at the individual level, people are less likely to sustain inaccurate generalizations or unwarranted negative attitudes towards out-groups. Establishing a favorable environment for positive contact (e.g. to extend our analogy, a dry, draft-proof cooking area and a good supply of gas and ingredients) is likely to make an important contribution. In principle, situations in which contact is generally promoted or is structurally inevitable should help to reduce the likelihood that intergroup differences will spiral into conflicts (see Abrams, Vasiljevic, & Wardrop, 2012; Varshney, 2002). Opportunity for contact alone, however, is insufficient to guarantee actual contact of the necessary kind. There are certainly situations in which contact is likely to be negative (this is more likely to be the experience of a minority member than a majority member), and situations in which antagonistic contact is deliberately sought (e.g. when minority members actively seek to confront majority members, cf. Dixon, Levine, Reicher, & Durrheim, 2012). Thus, even the expert chef may be thwarted as the ingredients and utensils for the perfect recipe are never available at the same place and time, and we cannot assert that contact per se will always generate positive results or the same results in times of peace versus conflict (Al Ramiah & Hewstone, 2013).

Threat and the intergroup context

Let us now reconsider the question of what factors will affect the relationships between perceived threat, intergroup contact, and prejudice. We noted earlier that contact can affect the "mediating" role of particular threats differently for different groups. This suggests that certain threats can be more "in the air", or embedded in the context in different ways. We think the temporal perspective helps because contact and threats both arise in *particular* times and places—they are not the abstract processes in the way often depicted by social psychologists. We should not be surprised if findings from studies on the Israeli–Palestinian conflict might generate different findings depending on the events that immediately preceded the period of data collection. Similarly, contemporary studies of the conflict in Northern Ireland are liable to be sensitive to ebbs and flows of political influence and power struggles in the Northern Ireland Assembly, whereas 20 years ago it was the occurrence of regular bombings and shootings that provided the context.

We therefore advocate moving away from idealized models in which contact and threat are treated as if one is the mediator of the other and towards an approach that views them as continually interacting and mutually influential variables. Statistically, each will influence the other at various points, an interdependence that enables researchers to characterize one as a mediator and the other as an independent variable. However, when considering their impact over time, it may make more sense to think of them as if they were click-clack balls, each with the potential to be set off from its own side of the apparatus. Regardless of which side the rhythm is started from, it will continue to repeat until energy is lost from the system. The more balls there are between the two (i.e. mediators), and the more the external sources of energy impinge from other directions (such as, a person or object pushing, suspending, impeding or deflecting—moderators), the weaker will be the overall strength of the impact of one ball on the other.

Following this analogy, we can readily see that the critical issue becomes the external environment—the hand that stays, lifts or swings the ball on either side.

The Temporally Integrated Model of Intergroup Contact and Threat (TIMICAT)

In the remainder of this chapter, we propose a model that addresses the temporal perspective on the connection between threat and contact. The model essentially holds that contact and threat can both vary over time and in relation to one another. We illustrate the model using some of our own research. Table 5.1 depicts the framework and provides one or two examples of how it might apply to different intergroup relationships.

The first principle in the model is that each temporal component of threat or contact exerts an impact on prejudice. Each element has its own mass and momentum. These can be cumulative and additive. As shown in Table 5.1, moving from left to right, a tick in any column adds to the total impact of threat. Similarly, a tick in any row adds to the total impact of contact. The situation is complicated by the fact that contact can have both positive and negative valence. If every type of contact that is experienced is positive then the more temporal boxes that are ticked the better. If every type is negative, then the more boxes that are ticked, the worse. But it is therefore quite conceivable that every row might be ticked and that the negatives cancel out the positives.

The second principle, using the notion of a rudderless ship as an example, is that the overall impact of contact and threat on prejudice can be disrupted by salient changes in any temporal element. We assume that, owing to multiple random forces, the impact of relatively stable historic levels of contact and threat gradually begin to weaken and dissipate. A high-intensity or focused instance of a new threat or new contact experience might be sufficient to dramatically slow, accelerate or rock the boat or to change its direction.

For example, in some settings, contact (e.g. through segregation or other factors) might be quite stable and predictable over time. It might occur routinely, or not at all. In these settings, fluctuations and variations in threat might be expected to play a larger role in variations in prejudice, and indeed in intentions to seek future contact. In other situations, threats might be quite stable (e.g. consider the entire period of the cold war), but actual contact and contact opportunities may vary and fluctuate. In that case, we would expect variations in contact to have a stronger direct effect on prejudice.

This depiction is further nuanced by the different types of threats and types of contact that are in play. For example, if positive contact remains at a low but stable level, single unusual instances of negative contact could elevate threats and prejudice. Alternatively, if symbolic threat remains at a low but stable level, both new objective threats and subjective realistic threats might inhibit contact or might directly affect prejudice. Less or more complexity enters the situation to the extent that one or both factors (contact and threat) are very stable or very variable.

To organize these ideas systematically, we structure the context in terms of the *temporal frame* for contact and for threats (none, past, continuous, discrete, multiple, future). We do not assume that contact and threats necessarily operate in identical time frames. Nor do we assume that only one time frame is relevant. The ordering of the sequence is deliberate. We assume that each temporal level provides the potential context of the next. Thus, one moves from the most minimal zero state (no contact, no threat) to one in which there is some history, to a context in which there is a continuous presence, and/or a single event, or multiple events and/or the prospect of a future event.

Taking contact as an example, there may be no prior contact or there may be a history of past contact (e.g. different ethnic groups that shared communities in former Yugoslavia), which would provide a context for contemporary contact. The contemporary contact might involve either a single instance or multiple instances (either with a lot of people in the same situation or the same person across multiple situations). There are also cases in which contact is effectively continuous (e.g. routine contact as part of a shared environment, such as might arise in a multicultural capital city), but some newly salient contact event could change the implications of such contact. An example might be the spread of the HIV epidemic in the early 1980s when particular subgroups were labelled as "risk groups", and thus public health campaigns implied that current and future contact with members of those groups raised the prospect of a realistic (health) threat. In addition to any prior or present contact, people may also imagine situations of future contact. The same approach would be applied to the temporal perspective on threats.

Depending on their relative force, velocity and direction, different elements of contact and threat could be expected to have varying impacts on the levels and targets of prejudice. If the oil tanker of historical conflict, now with no captain steering the ship, is already on course to crash into the harbor wall, diverting the catastrophe will take a very large number of tugboats pulling in a different direction (e.g. positive current or anticipated contact), or the insertion of some very large buffers and a way to empty the oil (reductions in threats) before the crash happens. Thus, when considering the likely magnitude of the contact–prejudice relationship and the threat–prejudice relationship, as well as their valence, we are trying to capture the total amount of energy entering the system and the direction of the force. Different temporal combinations might have the potential to yield different magnitudes and valences of impact.

Research typically focuses on how positive contact can help to dissolve intergroup antipathy and tensions. However, the reverse scenario is also conceivable. For example, in the context of otherwise low threat and positive continuous contact, a salient direct or indirect negative contact experience could evoke a re-evaluation of the out-group that produces a spike in prejudice (cf. Paolini et al., 2014). Moreover, contemporary events might change the interpretation of past contact or past threats. Negative re-evaluations of cherished accounts of colonial and imperial history are one example. Other examples might include the exposure of former celebrities, ministers of state or senior bishops whose perpetration of serial sexual or physical abuses may generate growing mistrust of the formerly venerated institutions that they represent.

Beyond these more general effects and interconnections, the mutual influences of contact and threat within these time frames can be differentiated further in terms of their *specificity*. As well as considering the quality, frequency and valence of contact, it seems meaningful to characterize contact as personal (e.g. one's own experience), intergroup (e.g. experienced or viewed as arising between prototypical

TABLE 5.1 Temporally integrated model of intergroup contact and threat (TIMICAT)—Examples

Temporal context	Threats	*No threat*	*Past threat*	*Continuous threat*	*Discrete single threat*	*Multiple threat*	*Future threat only*
	Positive or negative contact *(e.g. segregation, isolation, ignorance)*	⇧	⇧ *(e.g. historical)*	⇧ *(e.g. long term vulnerable legal status, increasing geographical encroachment, exposure to foreign language)*	⇧ *(e.g. new financial sanction, physical attack, demonstration)*	⇧ *(e.g. series of terrorist attacks)*	*(e.g. prospect of change in immigration rules)*
⇨	**No contact** *(e.g. past wars, likely just intergroup)*	Two geographically separate nations, e.g. Papua New Guinea and Mexico	Formerly warring tribes in the Amazon region	Settlers arriving in North America from seventeenth century onwards, encroaching on native people's land	One-off fight between members of different drug gangs	Violent attacks on Planned Parenthood clinics in the US	Little village in Northern Europe that might (or not) receive number of refugees
⇨	**Past contact**	Countries during Communist era, e.g. Eastern Germany and Cuba	Jews and Christians in Hungary during WWII	North and South Korea	Former classmates in sports competition	Israel and Egypt pre-1977	Boys at the beginning of Sherif's summer camp studies
⇨	**Continuous contact** *(e.g. living in the same area, working in the same space)*	Colleagues in a peaceful company	Colleagues in a seamless merger between two	Mestizos and indigenous people in Latin America	International students in university	Israelis and Palestinians in the Gaza Strip	University staff in two departments

⇨ *Discrete single contact* *(one person or one event, possibly intergroup)*	Visit of foreign dignitary (e.g. Nelson Mandela) to other country	First contacts between West and East Germans after the fall of the wall	previously competing companies West Germans visiting East Germany during communism	residence; one-off fight between students of different nationalities Anthropologists studying indigenous tribes	Demonstrations of Zapatistas in Mexico	in the process of merging Columbus and his crew first arriving in Latin America
⇨ *Multiple contact* *(e.g. one over time or many at one time, potentially intergroup)*	Weekly joint classes of students of all-girls school and all-boys school	Christians and Jews in Germany	Employees in Mexican multinational company and their US counterparts	Christians and Jews in Germany; attack on synagogue	Rapes of women in India	Low status and high status university; future ranking shows near equality in status
⇨ *Future contact only* *(potentially intergroup)*	International exchange students waiting to travel to their country of destination	Japanese people travelling to the US	(Until recently) Cubans moving to the US	Future contact among students of all-girls and all-boys schools, after sexist remarks from one of the schools	North and South Korea Little village in Northern Europe that will receive number of refugees	

Note: Arrows denote potentially cumulative impact of threats and of positive and negative contact.

in-group member(s) and the out-group), or both. Likewise, threats can be personal or group-based, but it is also necessary to consider whether they are specific (e.g. just one aspect of threat) or more general (likely to affect a combination of threats). If we are to predict what forms of contact and threat might be most influential in preventing or reducing prejudice, it will be necessary to account explicitly for the role of these specific elements.

Illustrative evidence

Turning to some of our own research, we can partially populate our conceptual framework.

A large study investigated school inter-class relations among 708 German high school students (Eller, 2002). The temporal context was one of no or low past contact that had been followed by continuous contact. Most high schools (*Gymnasium*) in Germany divide their students into three to five different parallel classes within each grade. These categorizations are sometimes based upon pupils' foreign language preferences (e.g. to start learning English vs. Latin in Grade 5, the lowest grade), or other curricular choices. Despite the relative arbitrariness of these selections (and lack of any predictability as to which other pupils will share their classroom), students tend to identify rather strongly with their respective classes and there is often a certain level of inter-class antipathy that has occasionally required intervention. Indeed the situation in one of the participant schools several years prior to the study had been sufficiently bad that it had to implement a conflict resolution program to tackle inter-class conflict (something our study participants were unaware of).

Therefore, in our matrix, this initial situation was akin to a low-contact, low-threat context. This would suggest that group-level threats were not very pertinent but that salient categorization would promote negative out-group stereotypes and intergroup anxiety. We examined the mediating role of those forms of threat and found that high-quality (positive) contact was indeed associated with less negative stereotypes and less intergroup anxiety and with more positive general out-group evaluation. Moreover, perceived intergroup conflict (which we interpret as historical threat) was related to more negative stereotypes and more negative out-group evaluation. Intergroup anxiety and negative stereotypes both related negatively to out-group evaluation, and both anxiety and stereotypes showed significant statistical mediation of the effects of contact and historic conflict.

Eller and Abrams (2004, Study 1) examined Anglo-French contact among a sample of seventythree British university students. Relations between the French and the British have historically been marked by antagonism, distrust and isolationism—despite, or perhaps, precisely *because* of their geographical proximity—continuing into the present time. The temporal context was thus one of two similarly powerful countries with a long history of tension, mutual mistrust, but also economic cooperation. Moreover, for British students, a significant (continuous) threat arises from their (generally) poor second (French) language skills and their relative disadvantage in terms of intergroup communication and familiarity with out-group culture. The time frame of contact is that of multiple contact (e.g. as tourists). For most individuals, contact is not particularly intensive or continuous, but for others it might be more personalized if they had spent extended periods in France on exchanges or visits, or if they had a close friend who was French.

In terms of the TIMICAT, we can see that enduring and historic intergroup conflict (a general form of threat) provided the backdrop to the effects of single or multiple contact. Path analyzes confirmed that perceived intergroup conflict had a direct relationship with out-group evaluation, but this was *not* mediated by variations in threats or anxiety. Conversely, variations in high quality contact most strongly affected intergroup anxiety, which partially mediated the relationship between contact and out-group evaluation. Given the temporal stability of in-group identification and knowledge of the out-group, it was not too surprising that these had no significant associations with other variables. One other relationship was notable. Intergroup contact was associated with realistic threat (but this was not associated with out-group evaluations). This related to two single salient economic threats at the time of the study. France had banned the import of British beef and the relative strength of the Pound versus the Euro changed—both objective, economic, realistic threats. It is plausible that having an out-group friend meant that this threat, emanating from out-group government policy, was less likely to be regarded as reflecting overall hostility from the out-group.

A third study was conducted in a Mexican-American intergroup context (Eller & Abrams, 2003). Participants were 100 US American language school students who spent a few weeks in Cuernavaca, Mexico, to learn Spanish and immerse themselves into Mexican culture. We measured contact quality and all four threats from ITT. The TIMICAT requires close attention to the context. The history and context of Mexican-American relations involves major conflicts and differences of history, religion, ethnic origin, and language. Mexico lost half of its territory to the US after their 1846–1848 war, and there is a substantial asymmetry of power and status. However, relations between the two countries are also framed by positive international relations, particularly in the politico-economic realm through the 1994 North American Free Trade Agreement (NAFTA) between Mexico, the US and Canada, which opened the US-Mexico border to trade in services in the areas of finance, transportation and telecommunications and has greatly increased bilateral trade.

Thus, the temporal context involved multiple or even continuous contacts, historic and continuous threats and also more favorable contemporary conditions. The language-school context constituted an ideal setting in which to test the effect of continuous or multiple contact on intergroup threat. The American participants in the study were likely to have relatively positive baseline attitudes towards Mexicans, as they voluntarily travelled to Mexico to learn the language and engage with the culture. They had little prior intergroup contact at the outset of the study but, because participants were staying with Mexican families, meeting locals, and were highly motivated to learn Spanish, the situation created high potential for contact and for intergroup friendship.

This study was also rather unique in that it assessed Americans' attitudes towards Mexicans *in* Mexico. The TIMICAT framework suggests that the primary impact of contact should be a reduction in intergroup anxiety, whereas contact would not bear greatly on historical levels of symbolic or realistic threats experienced by Americans—symbolic threats might be more relevant when investigating attitudes towards Mexican immigrants in the US. Moreover, at the time of the study, there were no specific realistic threats that could have been reduced via contact. Thus, although the historic intergroup structure did involve contact, the particular form of contact that was introduced in the situation had the potential to have a strong effect on just one form of threat. Path analyzes showed that high-quality intergroup contact affected threat and threat affected positive general out-group evaluation. But, as in the Anglo-French study, the mediated paths were quite specific. Symbolic threat was not significantly related to any other variable. In contrast, intergroup anxiety was associated with four different variables and mediated between contact and out-group evaluations. The findings were consistent with the effects of intense personal intergroup contact, because that type of contact involves potential to influence numerous elements of intergroup anxiety, such as deciding how to act, avoiding being misunderstood, and the risk of being perceived as being racist, etc.

What happens when the contact is looked at from a minority-group perspective? Still in the Mexican-American context, we examined the experience of 206 Mexican employees of international companies in a 2-year longitudinal study (Eller & Abrams, 2004, Study 2). In contrast to the previous study, which investigated the effect of a dramatic increase in sustained intergroup contact, the participants in this study had more varied prior contact with Americans. All were engaged in international work, so we expected that most would experience multiple contacts over the course of the study. Mexicans' attitudes towards the US have been characterized as deeply ambivalent, distrustful, resentful and even xenophobic (Shabat, 1993), but also as including enthusiastic adoption of American consumerism and materialism (e.g. N.E. Binder, Polinard, & Wrinkle, 1997), and given the business-focused nature of the contact, and the minority status perspective of our participants, contact would be expected to ameliorate symbolic and realistic threats even if not sufficient to reduce intergroup anxiety.

Largely consistent with the TIMICAT, cross-sectional path analysis at Time 1 showed that high-quality intergroup contact was associated with lower symbolic and realistic threat, and also with lower intergroup anxiety and more positive out-group evaluation. Symbolic threat and intergroup anxiety mediated between contact and general out-group evaluation. Speaking to the longer-term threat issues, higher perceived intergroup conflict (an index of historic and continuous threats) related to higher symbolic threat and negative stereotypes and more negative out-group evaluation, while symbolic threat and negative stereotypes mediated between perceived intergroup conflict and out-group evaluation.

Equally interesting are the (admittedly marginal) effects of the supposed mediator variables at Time 1 on the supposed independent variables (contact) at Time 2. Specifically, higher realistic threat at T1 predicted lower-quality contact at T2; symbolic threat at T1 predicted lower-quality contact despite higher out-group knowledge at T2; and higher intergroup anxiety at T1 predicted lower-quality contact and greater perceived intergroup conflict at T2.

One can readily envisage such influences. A person trying to do business with out-group members feels that the out-group poses a real competitive threat and this shapes the quality of subsequent interactions with out-group members. Such interactions are also degraded by situational anxiety about the relationship. The enduring sense of cultural threat from the out-group casts a shadow over subsequent interactions, while also prompting vigilance about the out-group's actions and likely intentions. In terms of the TIMICAT, the sense of continuous as well as situational threats from the out-group inhibits the possibility of favorable intergroup contact in multiple encounters.

Together, these four studies illustrate some important points. First, we believe that the temporal aspects of the threats may have determined the impact of contact. Intergroup anxiety, but not symbolic threat predicted American language students' out-group evaluations following contact with Mexicans whereas symbolic, but not realistic threat predicted Mexican employee's evaluations following contact with Americans. In both cases, the relationship emerged in the zone in which variability could be introduced as a result of a contact experience. The different relative status of the in-group vis-à-vis the out-group seems likely to be an important determinant of which types of threats constitute the long-term (or stable), and which constitute the shorter-term (or variable) elements in each case. Moreover, the evidence is consistent with our argument that the causal direction proposed by the ITT, which is largely accepted by intergroup contact theorists, is by no means inevitable. Consistent with the TIMICAT framework we observed that realistic threat, symbolic threat and intergroup anxiety are plausible potential precursors that shape the quality of intergroup contact at later time points.

The independent role of threat

Recently, we were able to report historical primary data on British population attitudes towards Muslims before and after the London 7/7 bombings—a case in which threat could or should operate as an independent variable rather than a mediator (Abrams, Van de Vyver, Houston, & Vasiljevic, 2016). The implication of this approach is that the threat–prejudice relationship could be independent and additive to those of the contact–prejudice relationship. Threat could also plausibly interact with contact, and threat could be either a precursor or consequence of contact. In other words, any and all moderating and mediating links could be tenable.

The research followed Abrams and Houston's (2006) nationally representative survey of approximately 1,000 people, and measured intergroup contact, perceived threats and social distance from Muslims. This study was first conducted just a few weeks prior to the 7/7 London bombings unleashed by Islamic fundamentalist terrorists. Funders sponsored a follow-up survey a few weeks after the bombing, providing matched samples that enabled Abrams et al. (2016) to test the impact of both threat and contact at the two time points. Because both samples were representative and thus matched, this provided us with a quasi-longitudinal study that helps to illuminate the TIMICAT.

At Time 1 (pre 7/7), Muslims posed some degree of symbolic threat, some degree of economic threat and very little realistic or direct threat to the majority population. Moreover, contact levels could be characterized as quite stable from the majority perspective (mostly infrequent and not very close), albeit framed by some historic conflict and differences. By Time 2 (post 7/7), the context was radically different. The 7/7 bombings presented a highly salient act of direct aggression against the majority population, government terror alert levels were very high, and those in contact with Muslims were being entreated to be vigilant for suspicious activity.

How might this dramatic increase in objective threat levels (a single instance event) change the role of contact and subjective threats as predictors of prejudice? Contact theory did not embrace events such as terrorist attacks, but these and other rapid changes in the intergroup context do arise (e.g. a sudden influx of refugees from Syria to Turkey and Europe precipitated by catastrophic levels of suffering in their homeland). Moreover, knowledge and awareness of such events spread extremely rapidly, and so in that sense, a change in threat levels may change the collective meaning or impact of intergroup contact on prejudice levels.

Although research had shown that contact can reduce prejudice even when Allport's essential conditions are not met (Pettigrew & Tropp, 2006) and even in the context of enduring intergroup conflict (Hewstone, Tausch, Hughers, & Cairns, 2008), research had not addressed whether it continues to have such positive effects following acts of terror. Abrams et al. (2016) labelled the assumption that it would do the "contact prevails hypothesis". Alternatively, given that terror acts do increase prejudice towards perpetrator groups (Coryn, Beale, & Myers, 2004; Echebarria-Echabe & Fernández-Guede, 2006), it seemed plausible that this is because effects of prior contact are neutralized. This was labelled the "threat inhibits hypothesis".

We also considered the specificity in how threats bear on prejudice. Defining the 7/7 bombings as an objective realistic threat, subjective threats were measured as symbolic threat (to culture and values) and two types of realistic threat: economic threat and safety threat. Objective threat should elevate safety threat and symbolic threat, but should not affect economic threat. Therefore, the impact of objective threat on prejudice should be mediated by safety and symbolic threat only. The research measured non-Muslims' quality of prior contact with Muslims. High-quality prior contact should have a *general* neutralizing effect on all types of threat to the extent that greater knowledge and familiarity with the out-group should assuage fears on all three grounds. The TIMICAT framework therefore predicts general effects of this more embedded contact, but specific effects of the immediate objective threat.

Multigroup mediation analysis confirmed these expectations. Regardless of the objective threat level, contact positively predicted lower levels of the three subjective threats, and these mediated the relationship between contact and prejudice. Moreover, the increased objective threat from Time 1 to Time 2 was associated with increased levels of subjective safety and symbolic threat, but not increased economic threats. In turn, the impact of the objective threat on prejudice was mediated only by safety and symbolic threat. Equally important is that both the objective threat and prior contact continued to have a direct effect on prejudice. What this evidence tells us is that the role of threat as a "mediator" is only part of the story. Threat and contact can operate in parallel as independent influences on prejudice. Particular types of threat can become more or less predictive of prejudice in response to new circumstances even when there are stable effects of contact, which might arise through influences on other types of threat.

Further implications for future research

The TIMICAT is at an early stage of development and raises a wider issue for contact research, namely, the role of different types of research design and measurement, and how far we should generalize across these. In particular, the use of different time frames has implications for when and how longitudinal and prospective studies might be useful, how to dovetail salient instances with more continuous and gradually developing states of contact and threat, and how much specificity of measurement is ideal or practical. Given advances in statistical and research methods (e.g. longitudinal and multilevel structural equation modelling, use of virtual reality and other simulation and modelling methods), there is much scope for innovative work and meta-analytic testing of how different temporal elements interconnect.

For the moment, we offer the TIMICAT framework as a different way to conceptualize contact–threat–prejudice links. We hope that a stronger focus on temporal factors, and disaggregation of the temporal elements of threat and contact can generate new hypotheses and new research questions for the future, while also providing more sensitivity and nuance in social psychological predictions, explanations and interventions for reducing intergroup prejudice.

Closing remarks

In this article, we presented a small selection of evidence to highlight the potential utility of the TIMICAT model. However, research has not generally set out to capture the temporal framing of threat and contact independently of one another. Therefore, we invite others to locate their research studies using the framework in order to test out its usefulness in the hope that the framework might prove useful for future work.

In developing the TIMICAT, we wanted to ensure that it really would be capable of capturing a wealth of intergroup scenarios. Table 5.1 offers potential instances that fit the various temporal combinations of threat and contact. This was made a little more complex by the fact that many intergroup relationships involve layerings of multiple temporal components. For example, the magnitude of effects of a salient contemporary contact (or threat) event that implies a positive or negative bearing on prejudice could depend on whether it is just "more of the same" or the first meaningful instance, or if it reignites feelings associated with a dormant past history of intergroup conflict (e.g. a genocidal episode). Indeed, it may be the confirmation or *contrast* against relatively stable background levels of threat or contact that is the key determinant of changes in prejudice. These are questions for future research.

References

Abrams, D., & Houston, D.M. (2006). *A profile of prejudice in Britain: Report of the National Survey*. The Equalities Review. Cabinet Office. Retrieved from http://webarchive.nationalarchives.gov.uk/20100807034701/http://archive.cabinetoffice.gov.uk/equalitiesreview/upload/assets/www.theequalitiesreview.org.uk/kentequality.pdf

Abrams, D., Van de Vyver, J., Houston, D.M., & Vasiljevic, M.D. (2016). Does terror defeat contact? Intergroup contact and prejudice toward Muslims before and after the London bombings. *Peace and Conflict Research*. doi: 10.1037/pac000167

Abrams, D., Vasiljevic, M.D., & Wardrop, H. (2012). Prejudice reduction, collective action, and then what? *Behavioral and Brain Sciences, 35*, 425–6. doi: 10.1017/S0140525X12001136

Al Ramiah, A., & Hewstone, M. (2013). Intergroup contact as a tool for reducing, resolving, and preventing intergroup conflict: Evidence, limitations, and potential. *American Psychologist, 68*, 527–42. doi: 10.1037/A0032603

Al Ramiah, A., Hewstone, M., Little, T., & Lang, K. (2013). The influence of status on the relationship between intergroup contact, threat, and prejudice in the context of a nation-building intervention in Malaysia. *Journal of Conflict Resolution, 58*, 1202–29. doi: 10.1177/0022002713492634

Al Ramiah, A., Hewstone, M., Voci, A., Cairns, E., & Hughes, J. (2013), It's never too late for "us" to meet "them": Prior intergroup friendships moderate the impact of later intergroup friendships in educational settings. *British Journal of Educational Psychology, 83*, 57–75. doi: 10.1111/j.2044–8279.2011.02054.x

Allport, G.W. (1954). *The nature of prejudice*. New York, NY: Addison-Wesley.

Binder, J., Zagefka, H., Brown, R., Funke, F., Kessler, T., Mummendey, A., . . . & Leyens, J.P. (2009). Does contact reduce prejudice or does prejudice reduce contact? A longitudinal test of the contact hypothesis amongst majority and minority groups in three European countries. *Journal of Personality and Social Psychology, 96*, 843–56. doi: 10.1037/a0013470

Binder, N.E., Polinard, J.L., & Wrinkle, R.D. (1997). Mexican American and Anglo attitudes toward immigration reform: A view from the border. *Social Science Quarterly, 78*, 324–37. doi: 10.1037/pac0000167

Blalock, H.M. (1967). Percent non-white and discrimination in the South. *American Sociological Review, 22*, 677–82.

Brewer, M.B., & Miller, N. (1984). Beyond the contact hypothesis: Theoretical perspectives on desegregation. In N. Miller & M.B. Brewer (Eds.), *Groups in contact: The psychology of desegregation* (pp. 281–302). Orlando, FL: Academic Press.

Cehajic, S., Brown, R., & Castano, E. (2008). Forgive and forget? Antecedents and consequences of intergroup forgiveness in Bosnia and Herzegovina. *Political Psychology, 29*, 351–67. doi: 10.1111/j.1467-9221.2008.00634.x

Coryn, C.L., Beale, J.M., & Myers, K.M. (2004). Response to September 11: Anxiety, patriotism, and prejudice in the aftermath of terror. *Current Research in Social Psychology*, *9*, 165–84.

Dhont, K., & Van Hiel, A. (2009). We must not be enemies: Interracial contact and the reduction of prejudice among authoritarians. *Personality and Individual Differences*, *46*, 172–7. doi: 10.1016/j.paid.2008.09.022

Dixon, J., Levine, M., Reicher, S., & Durrheim, K. (2012). Beyond prejudice: Are negative evaluations the problem and is getting us to like one another more the solution? *Behavioral and Brain Sciences*, *35*, 411–25. doi: 10.1017/S0140525X11002214

Echebarria-Echabe, A., & Fernández-Guede, E. (2006). Effect of terrorism on attitudes and ideological orientation. *European Journal of Social Psychology*, *36*, 259–65. doi: 10.1002/ejsp.294

Eller, A. (2002). Putting Pettigrew's reformulated model to the test: The intergroup contact theory in transition. Ph.D. thesis. University of Kent, UK, 29 November.

Eller, A., & Abrams, D. (2003). "Gringos" in Mexico: Cross-sectional and longitudinal effects of language school-promoted contact on intergroup bias. *Group Processes and Intergroup Relations*, *6*, 55–75. doi: 10.1177/1368430203006001012

Eller, A., & Abrams, D. (2004). Come together: Longitudinal comparisons of Pettigrew's reformulated intergroup contact model and the Common Ingroup Identity Model in Anglo-French and Mexican-American contexts. *European Journal of Social Psychology*, *34*, 229–56. doi: 10.1002/ejsp.194

Eller, A., Gómez, A., Vazquez, A., & Fernández, S. (2015). Collateral damage for ingroup members having outgroup friends: Effects of normative vs. counter-normative interactions with an outgroup. *Group Processes and Intergroup Relations*. doi: 10.1177/1368430 215612222

Gaertner, S.L., Dovidio, J.F., Anastasio, P.A., Bachman, B.A., & Rust, M.C. (1993). The common ingroup identity model: Recategorization and the reduction of intergroup bias. *European Review of Social Psychology*, *4*, 1–26. doi: 10.1080/14792779343000004

Hewstone, M., & Brown, R. (1986). Contact is not enough: An intergroup perspective on the "contact hypothesis". In M. Hewstone & R. Brown (Eds.), *Contact and conflict in intergroup encounters* (pp. 1–44). Oxford, UK: Basil Blackwell.

Hewstone, M., Tausch, N., Hughes, J., & Cairns, E. (2008). *Can contact promote better relations? Evidence from mixed and segregated areas of Belfast*. Report to the Community Relations Unit, Northern Ireland. Retrieved from www.ofmdfmni.gov.uk/grpubs

Hodson, G., Harry, H., & Mitchell, A. (2009). Independent benefits of contact and friendship on attitudes toward homosexuals among authoritarians and highly identified heterosexuals. *European Journal of Social Psychology*, *39*, 509–25. doi: 10.1002/ejsp.558

Leader, T., Mullen, B., & Abrams, D. (2007). Without mercy: The immediate impact of group size on lynch mob atrocity. *Personality and Social Psychology Bulletin*, *33*, 1340–52. doi: 10.1177/0146167207303951

Levin, S., van Laar, C., & Sidanius, J. (2003). The effects of ingroup and outgroup friendships on ethnic attitudes in college: A longitudinal study. *Group Processes and Intergroup Relations*, *6*, 76–92. doi: 10.1177/1368430203006001013

Myers, C., Abrams, D., Rosenthal, H.E.S., & Christian, J. (2013). Threat, prejudice and stereotyping in the context of Japanese, North Korean, and South Korean intergroup relations. *Current Research in Social Psychology*, *20*, 76–85.

Paluck, E.L. (2009). Reducing intergroup prejudice and conflict using the media: A field experiment in Rwanda. *Journal of Personality and Social Psychology*, *96*, 574–87. doi: 10.1037/a0011989

Paolini, S., Harwood, J., Rubin, M., Husnu, S., Joyce, N., & Hewstone, M. (2014). Positive and extensive intergroup contact in the past buffers against the disproportionate impact of negative contact in the present. *European Journal of Social Psychology, 44*, 548–62. doi: 10.1002/ejsp.2029

Pettigrew, T.F. (1998). Intergroup contact theory. *Annual Review of Psychology, 49*, 65–85. doi: 10.1037/0022-3514.90.5.751

Pettigrew, T.F., & Tropp, L. (2006). A meta-analytic test of intergroup contact theory. *Journal of Personality and Social Psychology, 90*, 751–83. doi: 10.1037/0022-3514.90.5.751

Pettigrew, T.F., Wagner, U., & Christ, O. (2010). Population ratios and prejudice: Modeling both contact and threat effects. *Journal of Ethnic Migration Studies, 36*, 635–50. doi: 10.1080/13691830903516034

Riek, B.M., Mania, E.W., & Gaertner, S.L. (2006). Intergroup threat and outgroup attitudes: A meta-analytic review. *Personality and Social Psychology Review, 10*, 336–63. doi: 10.1207/s15327957pspr1004-4

Sani, F. (2005). When subgroups secede: Extending and refining the social psychological model of schism in groups. *Personality and Social Psychology Bulletin, 31*, 1074–86. doi: 10.1177/0146167204274092

Schmid, K., Hewstone, M., & Al Ramiah, A. (2013). Neighborhood diversity and social identity complexity: Implications for intergroup relations. *Social Psychological and Personality Psychology Science, 4*, 135–42. doi: 10.1177/1948550612446972

Semyonov, M., Rajman, R., Tov, A.Y., & Schmidt, P. (2004). Population size, perceived threat and exclusion: A multiple indicators analysis of attitudes toward foreigners in Germany. *Social Science Research, 33*, 681–701. doi: 10.1016/j.ssresearch.2003.11.003

Shabat, M.C. (1993). Prejuicio etnico en estudiantes universitarios [Ethnic prejudice in university students]. *Revista Mexicana de Psicologia, 10*, 183–8.

Sherif, M. (1966). *In common predicament: Social psychology of intergroup conflict and cooperation.* Boston, MA: Houghton Mifflin.

Stephan, W.G., Boniecki, K.A., Ybarra, O., Bettencourt, A., Ervin, K.S., Jackson, L.A., . . . & Renfro, C.L. (2002). The role of threats in the racial attitudes of Blacks and Whites. *Personality and Social Psychology Bulletin, 28*, 1242–54. doi: 10.1177/01461672022812009

Stephan, W.G., Diaz-Loving, R., & Duran, A. (2000). Integrated threat theory and intercultural attitudes: Mexico and the United States. *Journal of Cross-Cultural Psychology, 31*, 240–49. doi: 10.1177/0022022100031002006

Stephan, W.G., & Renfro, C.L. (2002). The role of threat in intergroup relations. In D.M. Mackie & E.R. Smith (Eds.), *From prejudice to intergroup emotions* (pp. 191–207). New York, NY: Psychology Press.

Stephan, W.G., & Stephan, C.W. (2000). An integrated threat theory of prejudice. In S. Oskamp (Ed.), *Reducing prejudice and discrimination: Social psychological perspectives* (pp. 23–45). Mahwah, NJ: Erlbaum.

Tam, T., Hewstone, M., Kenworthy, J., & Cairns, E. (2009). Intergroup trust in Northern Ireland. *Personality and Social Psychology Bulletin, 35*, 45–59. doi: 10.1177/0146167208325004

Tausch, N., Hewstone, M., Kenworthy, J.B., Cairns, E., & Christ, O. (2007). Cross-community contact, perceived status differences, and intergroup attitudes in Northern Ireland: The mediating roles of individual-level versus group-level threats and the moderating role of social identification. *Political Psychology, 28*, 53–68. doi: 10.1111/j.1467-9221.2007.00551.x

Tausch, N., Hewstone, M., & Roy, R. (2009). The relationships between contact, status and prejudice: An integrated threat theory analysis of Hindu-Muslim relations in India. *Journal of Community and Applied Social Psychology, 19*, 83–94. doi: 10.1002/casp.984

Varshney, A. (2002). *Ethnic conflict and civic life: Hindus and Muslims in India*. New Haven, CT: Yale University Press.

Vorauer, J.D., & Sasaki, S.J. (2011). In the worst rather than the best of times: Effects of salient intergroup ideology in threatening intergroup interactions. *Journal of Personality and Social Psychology, 101*, 307–20. doi: 10.1037/a0023152

Wagner, U., & Hewstone, M. (2012). Intergroup contact. In L.R. Tropp (Ed.), *The Oxford handbook of intergroup conflict* (pp. 193–209). New York, NY: Oxford University Press.

6

INVESTIGATING POSITIVE AND NEGATIVE INTERGROUP CONTACT

Rectifying a long-standing positivity bias in the literature

Sylvie Graf and Stefania Paolini

Key words: intergroup contact, negative contact, intergroup relations, prejudice

Prejudice and ways to challenge it are a prominent topic in social psychology. There has been a long discussion about whether contact with members of groups that are prejudiced against is likely to ameliorate or deteriorate intergroup relations (e.g. Amir, 1976; Jackson, 1993). In the seminal work *The Nature of Prejudice*, Allport (1954) defined conditions under which contact with out-group members was likely to decrease prejudice. Fifty years later, a large meta-analysis by Pettigrew and Tropp (2006) brought convincing evidence that intergroup contact typically reduces prejudice, to some extent independently of the conditions present in the contact situation. Pettigrew and Tropp's meta-analysis not only summarized key findings from past research but also identified gaps in the existing literature (see also Hewstone & Swart, 2011). The most serious limitation of all is the predominant focus on the effects of positive contact—at the expense of negative intergroup contact. This means that contemporary understanding of the role of intergroup contact in intergroup relations has long been biased towards its positive factors and its positive consequences.

This chapter invites fuller investigations on the effects of positive *and negative intergroup contact*. We will start with an analysis of the reasons for an omission of negative intergroup contact in past research and the reasons to rectify this literature bias. An outline of research on the effects of positivity and negativity in psychology will follow and provide a larger context to very recent investigations on the valence of contact experiences with the out-group. The central section of the chapter will discuss a model of intergroup valence asymmetry and then summarize research that has tested key components of this model, employing a variety of methodologies in several intergroup contexts. Lastly, we will suggest avenues for future research on the effects of positive and negative intergroup contact that extends its reach to novel intergroup processes such as collective action and has the potential to challenge current views on contact positivity and negativity (e.g. through a more detailed focus on attributional processes).

Legitimate reasons to neglect and now reconsider negative contact

The noble aim of challenging prejudice in society underpins intergroup contact researchers' enduring passion for positive intergroup contact and their related neglect of contact's darker side. The reasons for the prevailing interest in positive contact can be traced back to the history of intergroup contact theory: the 1950s in the US were far from being egalitarian. That society was marked by strong racial segregation reflecting conjectures that contact between different racial groups would lead to suspicion, fear, resentment, disturbance and even open conflict (Baker, 1934). In that context, Allport (1954) did not assume that *mere* contact between people from different social groups would be enough to bring about social harmony. Rather, drawing from evidence available then (e.g. Brophy, 1946; Singer, 1948), he argued for *optimal* contact conditions to ensure greater liking between the contact partners and ultimately greater liking of the out-group as a whole—aka reduced out-group prejudice through individual-to-group generalization. Allport's view has inspired and shaped a long and extensive research tradition on the most auspicious conditions for prejudice reduction through contact (for a historical overview, see Pettigrew & Tropp, 2011)—a research tradition that legitimately continues nowadays because the need to see more harmonious societies in the world has not diminished.

Positive contact, however, represents only one end of the full evaluative spectrum of possible intergroup contact experiences—or "contact valence". The other end has negative intergroup contact. Failing to consider the effects of negative contact restricts the knowledge gained from intergroup contact research and, as a consequence, limits its effective applicability to interventions in complex real life settings.

Research on the negative dimensions of intergroup contact was set as an immediate priority by Pettigrew and Tropp (2006) in their agenda for future research directions. Pettigrew and Tropp advised that "social psychologists must grant greater attention to the negative factors that deter intergroup contact from diminishing prejudice" (p. 767). Interestingly, this stance implies that negative factors exist *outside* of contact itself and from there interfere with contact's typically beneficial effects. Such factors might be intergroup anxiety, authoritarianism or normative forces; these factors would typically mediate or moderate the otherwise inverse contact–prejudice relationship.

However, recent investigations have started exploring negativity as an *integral* part of intergroup encounters (e.g. Dhont & Van Hiel, 2009; Paolini, Harwood, & Rubin, 2010) and thus have addressed dimensions of intergroup contact that can exacerbate prejudice, rather than simply failing to produce contact's typically positive outcomes. When considering negativity in intergroup contact, we can identify two distinguishable positions: one is centered around potential *negative effects* of intergroup contact; this implies that intergroup encounters can produce outcomes other than the beneficial ones established in the meta-analysis by Pettigrew and Tropp (2006). We see this position as the most consistent with Allport's original view (1954) that intergroup contact *without* optimal conditions can exacerbate rather than reduce prejudice.

A second position embedded in recent studies on intergroup contact valence— including our own within this chapter—deals with the effects of *negative intergroup contact*. Hence, rather than looking at negativity as a result of intergroup contact (i.e. an output or a mediator variable), this approach treats negativity as an input variable, and from this platform directly compares the social psychological consequences of different contact valences. Operatively, this is achieved in a variety of ways: in experimental tests, for example, participants are engaged to either a pleasant or unpleasant interaction with an out-group member (see Paolini et al., 2010, Study 1 for first-hand exposure through direct contact; Paolini et al., 2014, Study 2, for example of second-hand exposure through television mediated contact). Some correlational studies have allowed participants to freely describe the nature of their past intergroup encounters and then employed independent judges to rate the positivity and negativity of participants' contact descriptions (Graf, Paolini, & Rubin, 2014). Others have inquired about specific instances of positive and negative behaviors during contact (Aberson & Gaffney, 2009; Pettigrew, 2008) or surveyed global positivity and negativity of individuals' past contact experiences in general (Barlow et al., 2012; Dhont & Van Hiel, 2009).

While intergroup contact research has failed to systematically and program-matically investigate positive and negative intergroup contact in a single research design until very recently, we found extensive research comparing the psychological consequences of positivity and negativity in other domains of psychology. As we regard such body of evidence as a relatively untapped inspiration for future research, we start by briefly reviewing these contributions so to provide a broader context to contemporary research on the positivity and negativity of intergroup contact.

Positivity and negativity in psychology

Several domains of psychology have accumulated a significant body of evidence about the differential effects of positivity and negativity. Baumeister, Bratslavsky, Finkenauer and Vohs (2001) summarized evidence from independent research traditions consistently showing the superiority of negative events over positive ones in impacting a wide range of key psychological outcomes, including those in research on life events, interpersonal relationships, social support, child development, emotions, information processing, impression formation, self and health. Negative information, for instance, attracts more attention and receives more thorough cognitive processing than positive information (e.g. Fiske, 1980). Interpersonal relationships are more profoundly influenced by negative actions and conflict than by positive actions and harmony (e.g. Huston, Caughlin, Houts, Smith, & George, 2001). Negative, aversive interactions in one's social network generate stronger effects than positive, supportive behaviors (Rook, 1984). In the intergroup domain, negative stereotypes are quicker to form and more resistant to discon-firmation than more positive ones (Rothbart & Park, 1986). Consistent with Baumeister and colleagues, an independent review by Rozin and Royzman (2001), contrasting good and bad factors competing for influence against each other in the same situation, also found pervasive evidence of greater impact—or greater *prominence* of the effect—of negative as compared to positive entities (e.g. events, objects, personal traits, etc.).

The widespread nature of evidence that negativity is psychologically more consequential than positivity is ultimately explained, in both reviews, through the lens of evolutionary psychology as reflecting a testimony to the biological supremacy of the organism's drives for survival (i.e. avoidance of threats), over its drives for thriving (i.e. acquiring desired states). Greater readiness to negativity, at the expense of positivity, would guarantee that the organism survives when faced by threats to its physical and psychological integrity; missing out on experiencing positive things in life or achieving positive states and goals—while disappointing—would be less essential to preserve the individual's survival and reproductive chances and therefore would take a back seat in biologically defined processes.

While we do not necessarily agree with this biological explanation of valence asymmetries (Paolini et al., 2010, 2014; Paolini & McIntyre, 2016), we cannot help but recognize that the prominence of negativity has some obvious poignant implications for intergroup psychology in general and intergroup contact research in particular. In today's diverse societies, people have varied, at times possibly contrasting, experiences with members of different groups: positive and negative features can be present either within one, ambivalent, intergroup encounter, as well as coexist within one's accumulated history of past experiences with the out-group. Drawing from Baumeister and colleagues (2001) and Rozin and Royzman (2001), one would therefore predict that when positive and negative features (of comparable magnitude) co-occur to constitute a single whole, the negative component should be disproportionately more influential in determining the overall appraisal, and as a result in shaping downstream psychological processes than the positive component.

The gloomy superiority of negativity, however, can be reversed by an opposite *positive* bias in the frequency or *prevalence* of positive events. There is evidence, for instance, of higher frequency of positive words, positive experiences and positive views (Matlin & Stang, 1978). Similarly, there seems to be relatively higher prevalence of positive (vs. negative) direct contact experiences in both peaceful (Graf et al., 2014) and conflict-ridden settings (Husnu & Paolini, 2016). According to Peeters (1971), it is the simultaneous dominance or urgency of negativity and the frequency or ubiquity of positivity that form the fuller phenomenon of *positive-negative asymmetry*. On the positive side of valence asymmetries, there would be a fundamental human tendency to generate positive expectations and to experience positive events and positive emotions; on the negative side of the asymmetry, there would be the higher impact of negative over positive stimuli of the same intensity on behaviors, emotions and cognitions (Lewicka, Czapinski, & Peeters, 1992). As negative events signal a need for change and action, individuals attuned to negativity would have evolutionary advantage (Baumeister et al., 2001); positive events would not need to mobilize complex cognitive, affective and behavioral reactions to guide individuals' responses (Taylor, 1991). Ultimately, exactly because positive events are much more frequent, people would have adaptively developed expectations based on most likely occurrence of positive events along with alertness for rarer but more impactful negative events.

Systematic investigations on the effects of positive and negative intergroup contact in our research laboratories date as recently as 2010. We began with a focus on the greater prominence of negative contact (Paolini et al., 2010) and, more recently, moved onto an integrated analysis of both differential prominence and differential prevalence of positive and negative contact (Graf et al., 2014). In the pages that follow, we recount this still brief but exciting research journey we have embarked on; we start by describing the theoretical model that has guided our empirical efforts in this area.

Valence asymmetries in intergroup relations

As noted at the very start, most intergroup contact scholars now acknowledge that intergroup contact can improve, have limited impact, and possibly even worsen intergroup relations depending on the quality of the contact (cf. Allport, 1954; Paolini et al., 2010; Pettigrew & Tropp, 2011). In other words, positive intergroup contact should result in positive outcomes (i.e. have positive effects) and negative intergroup contact in negative outcomes (i.e. have negative effects). Predictions for these relatively uncontroversial effects of contact of varied valences are the basis of a model of intergroup valence asymmetries in intergroup relations

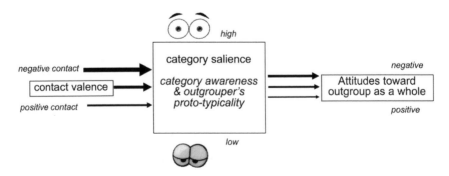

FIGURE 6.1 Model of intergroup valence asymmetry on social categorization and outgroup evaluations.

recently advanced by Paolini et al. (2010)—see arrows stemming from both positive and negative contact in Figure 6.1. This theoretical model has guided our early empirical efforts in this area and underpins most of the research summarized in this chapter.

The innovative and equally controversial side to this model at the time of its first inception rests in its predictions for a greater prominence, or impact, of negative contact, over positive contact (see Figure 6.1's bolder/thinner arrows). Drawing from the intergroup contact evidence available at that point in time (e.g. Brown & Hewstone, 2005; Pettigrew & Tropp, 2006) and self-categorization theory (Turner, Hogg, Oakes, Reicher, & Wetherell, 1987), we predicted a relative advantage of negative contact, over positive contact, in shaping important inter-group cognitions and evaluations. There are three building blocks to their model: (1) contact valence, (2) category salience and (3) out-group evaluations.

The first building block, in the role of predictor variable, is the valence of contact with individual members of the out-group; this valence can be either positive or negative depending on whether the intergroup exchange goes well or not; it is experienced as pleasant (or not), as successful (or not). Accounting for recent expansions in the conceptualization of intergroup contact beyond direct face-to-face exchanges, "contact" in this model refers broadly to *any* experience with individual out-group members, be it face-to-face, imagined or socially mediated (Crisp & Turner, 2012; Mazziotta, Mummendey, & Wright, 2011; Schiappa, Gregg, & Hewes, 2005; Vezzali, Hewstone, Capozza, Giovannini, & Wölfer, 2014; Wright, Aron, McLaughlin-Volpe, & Ropp, 1997).

The second building block, in the role of proximal outcome variable, is category salience. In the contact literature, the term "category salience" is used to refer broadly to the extent to which a social category is cognitively activated (i.e. salient) or dormant (i.e. non-salient) during contact (Brown & Hewstone, 2005). In line with classic models of categorization (Turner et al., 1987), this construct is generally assessed using global measures of category awareness, perceived group differences, perceived typicality of out-group members or any combination of these (see Paolini et al., 2014 for a broader discussion). The last building block in the model, in the role of distal outcome variable, is that of group-level judgments or evaluations. The model started with a focus on group-level or generalized out-group attitudes (or out-group prejudice; Paolini et al., 2010), and recently extended to encompass generalized changes in out-group stereotyping (Paolini & McIntyre, 2016). Later in the chapter, with prominent scholars in this area, we will recom-mend extending our reach even further to other group-relevant outcomes.

But how do the three building blocks of the model hold together exactly to predict greater impact of negative (vs. positive) contact on category salience and group evaluations? This is where analyzes of valence asymmetry in other psychology domains fell short and where we drew directly from the knowledge base of intergroup psychology to advance these predictions.

The causal links that Paolini et al.'s (2010) model introduces between contact valence and category salience are derived from self-categorization theory's perceived fit principle (Turner et al., 1987). According to this principle, experiences of negative contact with out-group members should increase category salience situationally because negative contact is more consistent—it has better *perceived fit* (Reynolds, Turner, & Haslam, 2000)—with people's generally negative expectations about out-groups and interactions with out-group members (Oakes, Haslam, & Turner, 1994). Therefore, measures of category salience should display evidence of negative contact's prominence—i.e. higher category salience under negative, than positive, contact—*because of* the evaluative fit mechanism.

Moving to the connections between the second and third blocks in the model, there are theoretical and empirical reasons to predict that the relative advantage of negative (vs. positive) contact on social categorizations should result in a relative advantage of negative (vs. positive) contact on out-group judgments—the causal relationships between category salience and out-group evaluation in Figure 6.1. Theoretically, these links draw from Rothbart and John's (1985) early cognitive analysis of intergroup contact: when people acquire new information about an out-group, the typicality of the contact partner and of the contact experience would determine which social category is activated among possible alternatives (see Turner et al.'s, 1987, "meta-contrast" principle). Extensive evidence synthesized in an influential review of intergroup contact and stereotype change effects by Brown and Hewstone (2005) showed that discrete experiences with out-group members are more likely to influence attitudes towards the out-group as a whole and group-level judgments more broadly when category salience (e.g. the typicality of contact partners) is high, rather than low.

In a nutshell, Paolini et al.'s (2010) model proposes that, in most intergroup stigmatizing contexts (i.e. contexts with prevailing negative views on an out-group), negative contact will have greater impact on social categorization than positive contact, and as a result, greater impact on generalized changes in out-group evaluations after contact (e.g. out-group attitudes, stereotyping). Hence, other things equal, when intergroup relations are marked by strong prejudices and negative stereotypes about the out-group, negative intergroup contact should be more influential than positive contact.

We should stress that predictions of negative intergroup asymmetries are *not* at odds with the optimistic conclusions of Pettigrew and Tropp's (2006) meta-analysis and are *not* a call for group segregation. Evidence of negative contact's prominence does not dispute the obvious merits and benefits of positive intergroup contact (see the arrows stemming from positive contact in Figure 6.1) or the benefits of intergroup contact that does not fully meet Allportian conditions for optimal contact (e.g. mildly positive or neutrally toned; Pettigrew & Tropp, 2006). We have and continue investigating the positive consequences of these types of contact in our research (see e.g. Harwood, Paolini, Joyce, Rubin, & Arroyo, 2011; Paolini et al., 2014) and very much encourage more structured interventions of positive intergroup contact in the future.

Predictions of negative intergroup valence asymmetries rather warn about the relative advantage—the prominence of—negative contact over positive contact in shaping intergroup processes and intergroup relations. They imply that, when people hold relatively negative out-group attitudes and stereotypes, the beneficial effects of positive contact will be most likely relatively small and unstable (but still there), whereas the detrimental effects of negative contact should be relatively larger and stabler over time.

A methodological precondition to appreciate any valence asymmetry in prominence is to assess the impact of both positive *and* negative intergroup contact. The next section provides an overview of recent research with designs that allow exactly this appraisal.

Returning evidence of negative contact's prominence

Our research on negative valence asymmetry started with a focus on social categorization as outcome variable—Paolini et al.'s proximal outcome in their intergroup valence asymmetry model in Figure 6.1. In a first study of prospective face-to-face interethnic contact (Paolini et al., 2010, Study 1), White Australians from the Anglosaxon majority engaged dyadically with a research confederate who was visibly from another ethnic background, as part of a study on "first impressions". We experimentally varied the ethnic confederate's non-verbal behaviors (posture and voice) to either be warm and welcoming (*positive* contact condition) or cold and detached (*negative* contact condition). Soon after the exchange, we measured the psychological salience of the ethnicity category using an established open-ended measure of person's construal (Kuhn & McPartland, 1954). We found that the White participants reported more frequent and earlier reference to the White-ethnic distinction in their open-ended descriptions of the ethnic partner when they were in the negative, than when they were in the positive contact condition. In other words, participants showed stronger signs of distinguishing between the in-group-out-group categories when the intergroup exchange was unpleasant, than when it was pleasant.

Since this founding first study, we have accumulated more experimental and longitudinal evidence (Paolini et al., 2010, 2014; see also Greenland & Brown, 1999) and thus proved that negative contact does not simply *go together* (or co-vary) with increased category salience, as we already knew from past correlational evidence (see review in introduction of Paolini et al., 2010). These data tell us that negative contact indeed *causes* heightened category salience as compared to positive contact.

Incisive experimental and longitudinal evidence of negative valence asymmetry in categorization now is available from peaceful (Greenland & Brown, 1999; Paolini et al., 2010), as well as from conflict-ridden societies (Paolini et al., 2014). This evidence spans across a variety of intergroup settings and types of contact: it was observed in prospective face-to-face ethnic contact (Anglo- ethnic Australians; the study described earlier), in retrospective accounts of face-to-face cross-national and intergenerational contact (Japanese-British nationals; Greenland & Brown, 1999, Study 2; young and older Americans; Paolini et al., 2010, Study 2). We detected it in television-mediated or parasocial contact (Latino and non-Latino Americans; Paolini et al., 2014, Study 2), and in people's responses to imagined contact across the ethnic divide (Latino-non-Latino Americans, Paolini et al., 2014, Study 3; Turkish-Greek Cypriots, Paolini et al., 2014, Study 4), and as far as across minimal laboratory-based groups (Paolini et al., 2010).

The ubiquity of negative valence asymmetries in social categorization does not however equate to the invariance of these effects. According to functional and motivational analyzes (Oakes et al., 1994), category salience should reflect a dynamic interaction between the qualities of the contact experiences *in the present* and the qualities of preexisting, chronic individual expectations about the groups involved and contact with these groups *in the past*. We found evidence for the moderating effects of individuals' histories of past contact in four samples and across three conflict-ridden societies (Paolini et al., 2014). In a first test with Catholic and Protestant university students in Northern Ireland, for instance, having fewer face-to-face visits of cross-group student friends—i.e. lack of positive contact—during participants' present time at the university typically predicted higher category salience. This basic pattern of negative contact's prominence, however, was significantly reduced among those with more pre-university contact opportunities and completely nullified among those with a larger quantity of pre-university contact.

Altogether the moderating findings of Paolini et al. (2014) indicate that positive and extensive histories of intergroup contact act as protective factors against (and significantly limit the size of) negative valence asymmetries; thus, the disproportionate influence of negative contact appears only, or primarily, among those who had a history of limited *past* contact with the out-group or low quality of contact. Having found these moderating findings and having found them in settings characterized by entrenched histories of intergroup conflict or recent flares of acute animosity (cf. Northern Ireland and Cyprus vs. Arizona's Southern border at times of immigration policy changes) is encouraging. These findings suggest that more extensive and intimate prior contact *early in life* has a protective function against negative contact *later in life* even in these virulent societies. Longitudinal and developmental studies are now needed to establish this with confidence.

Our research has more recently progressed testing valence asymmetries in the distal outcome of *out-group evaluations*—including prejudice and stereotyping. Significant evidence of greater effects of negative (vs. positive) contact was first gathered by Barlow and colleagues (2012). Across eight independent samples from Australia and the US and multiple indices of prejudice, quantity of negative contact emerged as a stronger and more consistent predictor of increased prejudice against Black Australians, Muslim Australians, asylum seekers and Black Americans, than quantity of positive contact did for decreased prejudice against these groups. In so doing, this research provides insight into the complex interactions between the effects of quantity and valence (or quality) of intergroup contact.

Other studies comparing the effects of positive and negative intergroup contact on out-group attitudes have corroborated the findings of Barlow et al. (2012), as well as started identifying meaningful moderations. Dhont and Van Hiel (2009), for example, also reported that the prejudice exacerbating effects of majority members' negative contact with immigrants by far outweighed the prejudice attenuating effects of positive contact. However, in their research it was evident that, at least within their Flemish convenience samples from the general community, negative contact's prominence was apparent among ideologically intolerant individuals (i.e. high in right-wing authoritarianism [RWA] and social dominance orientation [SDO]), but not among ideologically tolerant individuals (i.e. low in RWA and SDO). Our research in the border regions of five Central European countries has also returned evidence of negative contact's prominence in out-group evaluations (in Austria, the Czech Republic, Germany, Poland and Slovakia; Graf et al., 2014). There, we found that negative contact's prominence held only when contact valence appraisals were framed around the characteristics and behaviors of the contact partners (e.g. "she was unfriendly"), but not when contact valence was framed around the contact situation (e.g. "I did not enjoy the meeting").

These moderating patterns speak against a general prominence of negativity (cf. Baumeister et al., 2001). They suggest that variations in contact valence are most pernicious for intergroup relations when individuals see the world through ideologically tainted lenses or focus on the qualities of their contact counterpart; contact valence would be relatively inconsequential when people's views do not essentialize status differences in society (e.g. when they are low in RWA and SDO) and their focus is on contextual factors of the contact experience. Hence, it is a specific type of negativity—that experienced as inherently associated with the out-group and its members—that would be most dangerous and detrimental for intergroup relations.

Other recent research directly comparing the effects of positive and negative contact has returned a less uniform picture. Contrary to Barlow et al. (2012), Dhont and Van Hiel (2009), and Graf et al. (2014), Stark, Flache and Veenstra (2013) found no evidence of valence asymmetry: in Dutch classrooms, positive and negative attitudes towards classmates of different ethnicity generalized (cross-sectionally, as well as longitudinally) onto attitudes towards these ethnic groups *to the same degree*. We explain these comparable effects of positive and negative contact with the specifics of institutionalized settings, like schools, where contact is carefully structured and monitored by authorities so that negative exchanges with out-group members never reach the strength of negative contact as it can be experienced in unstructured and uncontrolled settings (cf. Barlow et al., 2012; Graf et al., 2014). An independent study of youngsters' contact with minorities in the Netherlands (Bekhuis, Ruiter, & Coenders, 2013) supports this interpretation. These scholars compared positive and negative contact in social settings that varied in degree of structuring, monitoring and sanctioning by authorities (e.g. classroom vs. neighborhood). As in Stark et al. (2013), Bekhuis et al. (2013) found that positive and negative contact had equal effects on ethnic attitudes in highly structured, monitored and sanctioned contexts; negative contact was instead more influential than positive contact in unstructured and unregulated settings. Yet another study with a representative German community sample documented a full reversal of the effect, with positive contact predicting attitudes towards foreigners more than negative contact did (Pettigrew, 2008; Pettigrew & Tropp, 2011; however see Barlow et al., 2012, and Graf et al., 2014, for some critical appraisals of their methodology).

All in all, to date there is relatively more evidence of negative contact's prominence on out-group evaluations. There is some meaningful evidence of null effects of contact valence and some isolated and to-date-unexplained evidence for positive contact's prominence (however see Paolini & McIntyre, 2016). The main problem with the bulk of these tests is that by being correlational and from the field, their findings are most likely subjected to self-selection biases and reverse causation.

To put negative valence asymmetries under more stringent test, away from these important confounds, we recently performed a meta-analysis of 35 years of experimental research on individual-to-group generalization within the stereotype change tradition (Paolini & McIntyre, 2016). Generalization of liking (or disliking) of out-group members to the liking (or disliking) of the out-group as a whole lies at the heart of intergroup contact effects (for a similar point, see Brown & Hewstone, 2005; Pettigrew & Tropp, 2011). The similar focus on generalization effects allows us to use studies on individual-to-group generalization to assess viable explanations and mechanisms for valence asymmetries in intergroup contact. Also, since most tests in the stereotype change tradition are experimental, these individual-to-group generalization experiments offer the welcomed source of data—free from selection biases and reverse causation—that is still missing in most of the intergroup contact research. Eligible studies for our meta-analysis were those that had randomly allocated participants to contrasting conditions asking to form first impressions of *either* positive *or* negative members of a negatively stereotyped out-group and subsequently asked them to judge the out-group as a whole (first impression paradigm studies; Garcia-Marquez & Mackie, 1999). Critical to the selection was the inclusion of a control condition in these studies' design against which to assess the size of individual-to-group generalizations.

Within a data pool of fourtyeight tests and 2,299 participants from varied settings, we found convincing meta-analytical, experimental evidence of negative valence asymmetries in out-group evaluations: generalized changes in out-group evaluations, relative to control, were significantly larger among those who had been randomly assigned to forming an impression of negative members of a negatively stereotyped out-group than among those who had been assigned to form an impression of positive members of that negatively stereotyped out-group (Paolini & McIntyre, 2016). This means that, consistent with predictions for negative intergroup valence asymmetries in stigmatizing contexts, negative generalizations after negative out-group experiences are larger than positive generalizations after positive experiences. Hence, where positive changes are most urgently needed, there seems to be a readiness for negative intergroup dynamics to progressively deteriorate at a faster rate than they can possibly improve under positive contact.

In the next section, we turn our attention to data on the greater prevalence of positive (vs. negative) contact and discuss how this quality of contact ecologies might be the first and most accessible antidote against the supremacy of negativity in unstructured settings.

Attenuating negativity's prominence with positivity's prevalence

In our research in five Central European countries (Graf et al., 2014), we aimed to reconcile the opposing outlooks on the positive effects of intergroup contact in past contact research, as summarized in Pettigrew and Tropp's (2006) meta-analysis, and the more recent research on negative valence asymmetry. We approached this using a design that afforded the assessment of both frequency and impact of positive and negative contact. Simultaneous considerations of positive and negative contact's prevalence and prominence revealed that, at least in naturalistic, non-conflict-laden contexts, the greater prevalence of positive contact may compensate for the greater prominence of negative contact, thus leading to modest net improvements in out-group attitudes after intergroup contact, despite the greater impact of negative contact.

Evidence of greater prevalence of positive (vs. negative) intergroup contact has been documented in various settings and is in line with a more basic finding, established in general psychology, that positive events outnumber negative events in people's everyday experiences (Peeters, 1971). Pettigrew (2008) reported a ratio of positive to negative contact frequencies of 9:4 in a probability community sample from Germany. Dhont and Van Hiel (2009, Study 2) returned an approximate positive–negative ratio of 4:2 in a convenience sample of adults from Belgium. Barlow et al. (2012, Study 2) published a ratio of 5:3 drawing from White Americans surveyed for their direct contact with Black Americans. While interesting and encouraging, this prevalence data relies on *explicit* measures of contact valence, and as such require participants' retrospective awareness of the frequency of positive and negative events. This awareness might be either unavailable or inaccurate (for an extensive discussion, Schwarz, 2007).

In our Central European study (Graf et al., 2014), we remedied to these methodological problems with unobtrusive measures of contact valence. We asked our participants from five different countries to freely describe their experiences of cross-border contact without any valence probes. Later we had multiple independent judges code these contact descriptions with respect to contact valence. Critically, the contact descriptions were coded for positivity and negativity only when participants had spontaneously included valence appraisals in their descriptions. When spontaneous valence appraisals were missing, contact positivity and negativity were coded as absent (this approach resulted in contact descriptions being coded as exclusively positive, exclusively negative, both positive and negative, or not evaluative at all).

These unobtrusive measures are more valid assessments of contact valence because they are less susceptible to the biases that afflict explicit and deliberate measures.

Yet, they returned a similar pattern of contact prevalence; the exact positive-negative ratios depended on the specific analytical approach employed. When contrasting only positive against negative contact experiences, we found a positive-negative ratio of 4:1 for both person- and situation-framed valences. When we included non-evaluative contact descriptions, positive contact experiences still exceeded negative ones by 2:1, again independently of contact valence framing.

Ecological analyzes of people's ordinary contact experiences need to include a careful consideration of the specific intergroup context, and an appreciation of key differences between different types of contact. For instance, we expect key features of contact—e.g. whether contact is structured-unstructured, intimate-casual, supervised-unsupervised—to impact on positive-negative contact's relative prevalence (and as a result, on the net impact of outcomes). Relatedly, things might look quite differently depending on whether one studies contact that is first-hand and face-to-face, like in the research summarized above, or instead socially mediated, through in-group friends, gossips, storytelling or the media. Socially mediated contact may be more often negative than positive because of its susceptibility to propaganda and the shaping influence of ideology (Fiedler & Walther, 2004).

Similarly, we are far from arguing that positive contact's prevalence, as detected in non-segregated societies without overt conflict and with low perceived threat, will necessarily extend to conflict-ridden settings (however, see Husnu & Paolini, 2016, for initial evidence of positive contact prevalence in Cyprus). In conflict-ridden societies, the damaging effects of negative contact, instead of being attenuated by the greater prevalence of positive contact, might rather be further compounded by the higher prevalence of negative contact. Consistent with this reasoning, greater prevalence *and* greater prominence of negative contact were reported in police officers' experiences of interracial contact with immigrants in Belgium by Dhont, Cornelis and Van Hiel (2010), and in soldiers' reports during peacekeeping operations in conflict areas abroad by Boniecki and Britt (2003). This suggests that, in order to fully appreciate the interplay between contact prevalence and prominence, the complex social reality of real intergroup relations around the globe needs to be considered, and to be integrated with a close analysis of the ecology of different types and conditions of contact, as they naturally manifest in a variety of settings.

Research comparing positive and negative contact is at its infancy and we see already many promising venues for future investigation opening in front of us. In the final pages of this chapter, we prioritize a discussion of those that we consider having greatest potential to revolutionize our discipline by disputing traditional notions of what constitute positive and negative effects of intergroup contact and what contact positivity and negativity really mean.

Future research: deconstructing contact positivity and negativity further

Several prominent scholars have in recent years emphasized the necessity to enlarge the pool of outcomes assessed in intergroup contact research beyond out-group attitudes/prejudice (Dixon, Levine, Reicher, & Durrheim, 2012; Hodson, Costello, & MacInnis, 2013; Pettigrew & Tropp, 2011; Wright & Lubensky, 2009), so to improve our pulse for individuals' readiness to engage in diverse actions that can challenge social injustice (e.g. support for minorities' rights and collective action on minorities' behalf). We share these views and welcome the early signs of this methodological diversification also in research on intergroup valence asymmetries (e.g. Aberson, 2015; Paolini & McIntyre, 2016). Fortunately, over the years, this debate has become more than a methodological discussion (e.g. Tausch, Saguy, & Bryson, 2015; Wright & Lubensky, 2009): it is contributing to bring positive *and negative* intergroup contact in sharp focus and is offering a prime opportunity to revisit and possibly reconsider what we regard as the "ultimate good" for intergroup relations and the very ideological and political foundation of our discipline.

What is good or bad for intergroup relations is not a given; it reflects what we *regard* as final, ideal destination and *desirable* end point for intergroup dynamics. And it is important to appreciate that alternative end points are not necessarily complementary or mutually compatible: as Tausch et al. (2015) eloquently put it, the standard effects of positive intergroup contact are potentially at odds with the very preconditions for collective action (cf., higher perceived group similarities, Tam et al., 2007; improved out-group attitudes, Pettigrew & Tropp, 2006; vs. awareness of inequalities, Van Zomeren, Spears, Fischer, & Leach, 2004; negative views of the advantaged group, Simon & Klandermans, 2001). Hence, since the early days of research on the "sedative effects" of positive intergroup contact (see below), we have learnt that striving to achieve harmonious intergroup relations and peace between opposing groups—*one* desirable end point—can at times detract from our ability to build an equitable and fairer society—*another* desirable end point.

By disputing the very existence of a single positive intergroup outcome for contact, as a discipline we also become more sensitive to appreciating different viewpoints and agendas. Collective action, for instance, can be approached from the eyes of the stigmatized, disadvantaged group, as well as from the perspective of the privileged, high-status group. In this specific area, we expect comparisons between positive and negative contact to likely thrive and return some interesting valence, as well as minority-majority asymmetries.

A number of studies have demonstrated that positive intergroup contact with majority members can lower disadvantaged groups' motivation to challenge social injustice by dampening minority members' ability to recognize the injustice that their group suffers (Dixon, Durrheim, Tredoux, Tropp, Clack, & Eaton, 2010; Saguy & Chernyak-Hai, 2012; Saguy, Tausch, Dovidio, & Pratto, 2009; Tausch et al., 2015; Tropp, Hawi, Van Laar, & Levin, 2012). This "sedative effect" of positive contact has been documented in several contexts: among Black respondents in post-apartheid South Africa, among Arabs and Ethiopian-Jews in Israel, among African and Latino Americans. Curiously, this fast growing literature is so far also characterized by a positivity bias (e.g. a focus on intergroup friendships; Cakal, Hewstone, Schwaer, & Heath, 2011; Tausch et al., 2015; Tropp et al., 2012).

As a consequence, we do not know yet what happens to minorities' collective action intentions when they have negative contact with majority members. As long as perceptions of inequalities are critical to fuelling people's motivation to engage in actions aimed at restoring social injustice, we would expect sharp dissociations of effects of positive and negative contact for members of disadvantaged groups: negative contact might boost rather than sedate minority members' collective efforts at improving the in-group's standing, at least when negativity is appraised and framed as reflecting historical and unfair intergroup disadvantage (vs. inherent and unchangeable deficiencies of the in-group or the self).

Positive and negative contact should impact on privileged majorities' collective action intentions also—but in very different ways. Investigating these effects is important because, as Pettigrew and Tropp (2011) rightly noted, as far as high status groups hold power and access to resources in society, as minorities step forward, majorities need to be prepared to progressively step back and away from their privileges. Hence, investigations of majority's willingness (or lack of willingness) to stand up *for* (or *against*) minorities' rights are also critical if any sizeable and sustained social change and a more equitable redistribution of resources are to take place.

Positive contact with members of minority groups may boost majority members' willingness to support minority's causes, whereas negative contact might do the exact opposite. We recently tested this possibility looking at majority members' *actual* collective *actions* (vs. intentions) in the context of Slovakia's 2015 referendum (Zingora & Graf, 2016). This referendum was initiated by the group Alliance for Family and backed by the conference of Catholic Slovak Bishops to block gay couples' rights in areas of registered partnership and children adoption. As such, it offered a prime opportunity to assess heterosexuals' actual referendum voting, as a measure of political support (vs. opposition) to homosexual minority rights. In this context, we found a marked dissociation of effects between heterosexuals' positive and negative past contact with gay people: as anticipated, positive contact predicted heterosexuals' boycott of the anti-gay referendum and more positive out-group attitudes, whereas negative contact predicted heterosexuals' voting to restrict homosexuals' rights and more negative attitudes. The effects on collective action were mediated by lower (vs. higher) perceived threat from gay people but not by attitudes towards gay people (Zingora & Graf, 2016).

Hence, while we expect negative contact to encourage social mobilization among minorities, our results demonstrate that negative contact may diminish majority members' actual support for disadvantaged minorities. Also, the findings show that, among majority members, we do not necessarily observe the same dissociation of effects for positive contact on out-group attitudes *versus* collective action that has been found for minority members. Among high status groups, positive contact can improve attitudes towards disadvantaged out-groups *and also* enhance their willingness to support minorities' struggle for social justice (Zingora & Graf, 2016). This is exactly what Dixon, Durrheim, Tredoux, Tropp, Clack, Eaton et al. (2010)

and Cakal et al. (2011) found in the South-African context when measuring both White Africans' attitudes towards Blacks and their support for (pro-Black) race-compensatory and race-preferential policies; this is what Pettigrew and Tropp (2011) detected among White Americans with close ties with Black Americans in their reanalysis of Jackman and Crane's (1986) classic study.

Ultimately, whether positive (vs. negative) contact brings about positive (vs. negative) intergroup gains depends on whose perspective one is taking— e.g. majority/minority—and what kind of change one is pursuing—e.g. lessened prejudices and a peaceful society *versus* social justice and an equitable society.

Here, we wish to push this deconstruction of contact positivity and negativity a step further. Although experimentation using *objective* operationalizations of contact valence still has its place (Paolini & McIntyre, 2016) and was important in instigating an interest in positive-negative contact comparisons (e.g. Paolini et al., 2010), we have grown into believing that when it comes to defining what is positive and what is negative contact, "beauty is in the eye of the beholder" and "there are many shades of grey": contact valence is a fundamentally *subjective* experience, which is exposed to a host of modulating influences impacting on its downstream consequences.

In our investigation of cross-national contact in Central Europe (Graf et al., 2014), we proved that the psychological framing and attributional processes individuals initiate when engaging in spontaneous contact valence appraisals ultimately moderate the relationship between contact valence and intergroup perceptions: negative intergroup experiences shaped out-group attitudes more heavily than positive intergroup experiences when contact valence was attributed to the characteristics of the contact partners; whereas the magnitude of these effects was comparable (and small) when contact valence was attributed to the contact situation. Hence, it is *not* contact positivity and negativity *per se* that counts; rather how that experience is psychologically constructed by those directly (and potentially indirectly) involved that seems to matter.

The same intergroup interaction should therefore result in very different outcomes for the individual and the groups depending on whether contact negativity or positivity are interpreted and constructed as reflecting the contact partners' own/group (vs. others') responsibilities, their inherent and stable (vs. unstable) qualities, or rather unavoidable and uncontrollable circumstances (e.g. long-term and structural injustices vs. avoidable and controllable factors). The exact emotions that infuse and underpin these valenced intergroup experiences should also matter. While all negative, we know that anger, sadness, disgust and pity have very distinct cognitive antecedents and behavioral consequences (e.g. Fiske, Cuddy, Glick, & Xu, 2002; Mackie, Devos, & Smith, 2000). In our laboratory, we have recently started unpacking contact positivity and negativity in terms of their experienced source (e.g. what the out-group vs. in-group contact partner did or said), as well as in terms of distinct emotions (e.g. happiness vs. sadness/anger). Preliminary findings point to the complexity and relational nature of the attributional processes behind people's appraisals of valence in intergroup contexts. So, for instance, the sadness associated to an in-group member can be readily reframed as anger for an out-group member's actions.

We call for research that looks boldly at the subjective and reconstructive nature of people's appraisals of valence and emotional dimensions of intergroup contact (see also Pettigrew & Tropp, 2011, p. 168). This can take the shape of in-depth qualitative analyzes of people's ordinary daily experiences (e.g. Hammack, Pilecki, & Merrilees, 2014; Petrjánošová & Graf, 2012), as well as a revival of attribution research within contact research (Graf et al., 2014). A particularly fertile ground for variations in valence framing and attributions is, for instance, offered by *ambivalent* contact experiences. Ambivalence in appraisals refers to the coexistence of positive and negative features attributed to a single intergroup interaction. In close-up analysis of free reports of ambivalent contact (Graf, Paolini, Rubin, Harwood, & Hewstone, 2016), we found that, when valence was subjectively constructed around the interaction partners, the out-group attitudes of those with ambivalent contact fell predictably between those with purely negative and purely positive contact. However, when valence was framed around *aspects of the contact situation*, the attitudes of participants with ambivalent contact did not differ from those with purely positive contact—suggesting that in this instance, the positive features of the contact situation (within the ambivalent experience) buffered against the detrimental effects of the negative features. On the other hand, the positive features attributed to the contact partners were *not sufficiently* potent to neutralize the harmful effects of the coexisting negative features.

It is important to recognize that ambivalence does not only apply to single intergroup interactions; it can also characterize the overall pool of individuals' past contact experiences. With a growing number of intergroup exchanges in today's multicultural societies, people's histories of contact are likely to include a mixture of positivity and negativity, as well as vary in intensity (e.g. experiencing misunderstanding vs. verbal assault). Future studies may want to assess (e.g. with diary method) not only the valence of participants' past intergroup experiences but also enquire about their *perceived* intensity or *weight* to shed light on how valence *and* intensity interact to impact on important intergroup processes.

Closing remarks

In the opening of this chapter, we acknowledged the legacy of Allport (1954) that inspired the rich tradition of intergroup contact research, steadily growing over the following decades (Pettigrew & Tropp, 2011). It is thrilling to see how the topics of interest within this highly socially relevant theory have vigorously evolved to address the challenges of complex and ever changing intergroup relations. In concluding our recount of the recent research efforts around contact positivity and negativity, we hope it is evident that the time is now ripe for a new generation of intergroup contact research. We call for more nuanced analyzes of the subjective meaning of intergroup contact for the individual and groups (including subjective valences, emotions and their experienced sources). One promising avenue to enrich current intergroup contact theory is the one that considers contact valence through complex processes of attribution and reconstruction, embedded in motivational and affective states. Another is that of studies that focus on the complex effects of positive, negative and ambivalent contact (experienced with different intensity and in different contexts) and thus mapping more closely onto the complexities of the dynamic relationships between contact, attitudes and intergroup actions.

For this to be possible, we need to understand what individuals and groups in contact expect, experience and try to achieve through their intergroup exchanges and invite studies that, looking beyond out-group attitudes as an outcome, make us reflect further on alternative ultimate states for intergroup relations—including intergroup harmony and more just societies.

Notes

The compilation of this chapter was supported by a grant from the Czech Science Foundation (13–25656S) and from the Institute of Psychology, Academy of Sciences of the Czech Republic (RVO: 68081740) awarded to Sylvie Graf, and an Australian Research Council grant (DP0770704) awarded to Stefania Paolini.

References

Aberson, C.L. (2015). Positive intergroup contact, negative intergroup contact, and threat as predictors of cognitive and affective dimensions of prejudice. *Group Processes and Intergroup Relations, 18*, 743–60. doi: 10.1177/1368430214556699

Aberson, C.L., & Gaffney, A.M. (2009). An integrated threat model of explicit and implicit attitudes. *European Journal of Social Psychology, 39*, 808–30. doi: 10.1002/ejsp.582

Allport, G.W. (1954). *The nature of prejudice.* New York, NY: Addison-Wesley.

Amir, Y. (1976). The role of intergroup contact in change of prejudice and ethnic relations. In P.A. Katz (Ed.), *Towards the elimination of racism* (pp. 245–308). New York, NY: Pergamon Press.

Baker, P.E. (1934). *Negro–White adjustment.* New York, NY: Association Press.

Barlow, F.K., Paolini, S., Pedersen, A., Hornsey, M.J., Radke, H.R.M., Harwood, J., . . . & Sibley, C.G. (2012). The contact caveat: Negative contact predicts increased prejudice more than positive contact predicts reduced prejudice. *Personality and Social Psychology Bulletin, 38*, 1629–43. doi: 10.1177/0146167212457953

Baumeister, R.F., Bratslavsky, E., Finkenauer, C., & Vohs, K.D. (2001). Bad is stronger than good. *Review of General Psychology, 5*, 323–70. doi: 10.1037/1089-2680.5.4.323

Bekhuis, H., Ruiter, S., & Coenders, M. (2013). Xenophobia among youngsters: The effect of interethnic contact. *European Sociological Review, 29*, 229–42. doi: 10.1093/esr/jcr057

Boniecki, K.A., & Britt, T.W. (2003). Prejudice and the peacekeeper. In T.W. Britt & A.B. Adler (Eds.), *The psychology of the peacekeeper: Lessons from the field* (pp. 53–70). Westport, CT: Praeger Press.

Brophy, I.N. (1946). The luxury of anti-Negro prejudice. *Public Opinion Quarterly, 9*, 456–66. doi: 10.1086/265762

Brown, R., & Hewstone, M. (2005). An integrative theory of intergroup contact. *Advances in Experimental Social Psychology, 37*, 255–343. doi: 10.1016/S0065-2601(05)37005-5

Cakal, H., Hewstone, M., Schwaer, G., & Heath, A. (2011). An investigation of the social identity model of collective action and the "sedative" effect of intergroup contact amongst Black and White students in South Africa. *British Journal of Social Psychology, 50*, 606–27. doi: 10.1111/j.2044-8309.2011.02075.x

Crisp, R.J., & Turner, R.N. (2012). The imagined contact hypothesis. *Advances in experimental social psychology, 46*, 125–82. doi: 10.1016/B978-0-12-394281-4.00003-9

Dhont, K., Cornelis, I., & Van Hiel, A. (2010). Interracial public-police contact: Relationships with police officers' racial and work-related attitudes and behaviour. *International Journal of Intercultural Relations, 34*, 551–60. doi: 10.1016/j.ijintrel.2010.07.004

Dhont, K., & Van Hiel, A. (2009). We must not be enemies: Interracial contact and the reduction of prejudice among authoritarians. *Personality and Individual Differences, 46*, 172–7. doi: 10.1016/j.paid.2008.09.022

Dixon, J., Durrheim, K., Tredoux, C., Tropp, L., Clack, B., & Eaton, L. (2010). A paradox of integration? Interracial contact, prejudice reduction, and perceptions of racial discrimination. *Journal of Social Issues, 66*, 401–16. doi: 10.1111/j.1540-4560.2010.01652.x

Dixon, J., Durrheim, K., Tredoux, C., Tropp, L., Clack, B., Eaton, L., & Quayle, M. (2010). Challenging the stubborn core of opposition to equality: Racial contact and policy attitudes. *Political Psychology, 31*, 831–55. doi: 10.1111/j.1467-9221.2010.00792.x

Dixon, J., Levine, M., Reicher, S., & Durrheim, K. (2012). Beyond prejudice: Are negative evaluations the problem? Is getting us to like one another more the solution? *Behavioral and Brain Sciences, 35*, 1-15. doi: 10.1017/S0140525X11002214.

Fiedler, K., & Walther, E. (2004). *Stereotyping as inductive hypothesis testing*. New York, NY: Psychology Press.

Fiske, S.T. (1980). Attention and weight in person perception: The impact of negative and extreme behavior. *Journal of Experimental Research in Personality, 22*, 889–906.

Fiske, S.T., Cuddy, A.J., Glick, P., & Xu, J. (2002). A model of (often mixed) stereotype content: Competence and warmth respectively follow from perceived status and competition. *Journal of Personality and Social Psychology, 82*, 878–902. doi: 10.1037//0022-3514.82.6.878

Garcia-Marques, L., & Mackie, D.M. (1999). The impact of stereotype incongruent information on perceived group variability and stereotype change. *Journal of Personality and Social Psychology, 77*, 979–90. doi: 10.1037/0022-3514.77.5.979

Graf, S., Paolini, S., & Rubin, M. (2014). Negative intergroup contact is more influential, but positive intergroup contact is more common: Assessing contact prominence and contact prevalence in five Central European countries. *European Journal of Social Psychology, 44*, 536–47. doi: 10.1002/ejsp.2052

Graf, S., Paolini, S., Rubin, M., Harwood, J., & Hewstone, M. (2016). The effect of positive, negative and ambivalent intergroup contact experiences on outgroup attitudes. *Manuscript in preparation.*

Greenland, K., & Brown, R. (1999). Categorization and intergroup anxiety in contact between British and Japanese nationals. *European Journal of Social Psychology, 29*, 503–21. doi: 10.1002/(SICI)1099-0992(199906)29:4<503::AID-EJSP941>3.0.CO;2-Y

Hammack, P.L., Pilecki, A., & Merrilees, C. (2014). Interrogating the process and meaning of intergroup contact: Contrasting theoretical approaches. *Journal of Community and Applied Social Psychology, 24*, 296–324. doi: 10.1002/casp.2167

Harwood, J., Paolini, S., Joyce, N., Rubin, M., & Arroyo, A. (2011). Secondary transfer effects from imagined contact: Group similarity affects the generalization gradient. *British Journal of Social Psychology, 50*, 180–9. doi: 10.1348/014466610X524263

Hewstone, M., & Swart, H. (2011). Fifty-odd years of intergroup contact: From hypothesis to integrated theory. *British Journal of Social Psychology*, *50*, 374–86. doi: 10.1111/j.2044–8309.2011.02047.x

Hodson, G., Costello, K., & MacInnis, C.C. (2013). Is intergroup contact beneficial among intolerant people? Exploring individual differences in the benefits of contact on attitudes. In G. Hodson & M. Hewstone (Eds.), *Advances in intergroup contact* (pp. 49–80). London, UK: Psychology Press.

Husnu, S., & Paolini, S. (2016). Freely-chosen positive (vs. negative) imagined contact: Exploring mechanisms and consequences in a conflict-ridden setting. *Manuscript in preparation*.

Huston, T.L., Caughlin, J.P., Houts, R.M., Smith, S.E., & George, L.J. (2001). The connubial crucible: Newlywed years as predictors of marital delight, distress, and divorce. *Journal of Personality and Social Psychology*, *80*, 237–525. doi: 10.1037/0022–3514.80.2.237

Jackman, M.R., & Crane, M. (1986). "Some of my best friends are black . . .": Interracial friendship and white racial attitudes. *Public Opinion Quarterly*, *50*, 459–86. doi: 10.1086/268998

Jackson, J.W. (1993). Contact theory of intergroup hostility: A review and evaluation of the theoretical and empirical literature. *International Journal of Group Tensions*, *23*, 43–65.

Kuhn, M.H., & McPartland, T.S. (1954). An empirical investigation of self-attitudes. *American Sociological Review*, *19*, 68–76. doi: 10.2307/2088175

Lewicka, M., Czapinski, J., & Peeters, G. (1992). Positive–negative asymmetry or "When the heart needs a reason". *European Journal of Social Psychology*, *22*, 425–34. doi: s10.1002/ejsp.2420220502

Mackie, D.M., Devos, T., & Smith, E.R. (2000). Intergroup emotions: Explaining offensive action tendencies in an intergroup context. *Journal of Personality and Social Psychology*, *79*, 602–16. doi: 10.1037/0022–3514.79.4.602.

Matlin, M.W., & Stang, D.J. (1978). *The Pollyanna principle*. Cambridge, MA: Schenkman.

Mazziotta, A., Mummendey, A., & Wright, S.C. (2011). Vicarious intergroup contact effects: Applying social-cognitive theory to intergroup contact research. *Group Processes and Intergroup Relations*, *14*, 255–74. doi: 10.1177/1368430210390533

Oakes, P.J., Haslam, S.A., & Turner, J.C. (1994). *Stereotypes and social reality*. Oxford, UK: Blackwell.

Paolini, S., Harwood, J., & Rubin, M. (2010). Negative intergroup contact makes group memberships salient: Explaining why intergroup conflict endures. *Personality and Social Psychology Bulletin*, *36*, 1723–38. doi: 10.1177/0146167210388667

Paolini, S., Harwood, J., Rubin, M., Husnu, S., Joyce, N., & Hewstone, M. (2014). Positive and extensive intergroup contact in the past buffers against the disproportionate impact of negative contact in the present. *European Journal of Social Psychology*, *44*, 548–62. doi: 10.1002/ejsp.2029

Paolini, S., & McIntyre, K. (2016). Several reasons why evil is stronger than good in intergroup relations: Taking tests of negative valence asymmetry from the field back to the laboratory. *Under review*.

Peeters, G. (1971). The positive-negative asymmetry: On cognitive consistency and positivity bias. *European Journal of Social Psychology*, *1*, 455–74. doi: 10.1002/ejsp.2420010405

Petrjánošová, M., & Graf, S. (2012). "The Austrians were surprised that I didn"t speak German': The role of language in Czech-Austrian relations. *Human Affairs*, *22*, 539–57. doi: 10.2478/s13374–012–0043-y

Pettigrew, T.F. (2008). Future direction for intergroup contact theory and research. *International Journal of Intercultural Relations*, *32*, 187–99. doi: 10.1016/j.ijintrel.2007.12.002

Pettigrew, T.F., & Tropp, L.R. (2006). A meta-analytical test of the intergroup contact theory. *Journal of Personality and Social Psychology*, *90*, 751–83. doi: 10.1037/0022–3514.90.5.751

Pettigrew, T.F., & Tropp, L.R. (2011). *When groups meet: The dynamics of intergroup contact.* New York, NY: Psychology Press.

Reynolds, K.J., Turner, J.C., & Haslam, S. (2000). When are we better than them and they worse than us? A closer look at social discrimination in positive and negative domains. *Journal of Personality and Social Psychology, 78,* 64–80. doi: 10.1037/0022–3514.78.1.64

Rook, K.S. (1984). The negative side of social interaction: Impact on psychological well-being. *Journal of Personality and Social Psychology, 46,* 1097–08. doi: 10.1037/0022–3514.46.5.1097

Rothbart, M., & John, O.P. (1985). Social categorization and behavioral episodes: A cognitive analysis of the effect of intergroup contact. *Journal of Social Issues, 41,* 81–104. doi: 10.1111/j.1540–4560.1985.tb01130.x

Rothbart, M., & Park, B. (1986). On the confirmability and disconfirmability of trait concepts. *Journal of Personality and Social Psychology, 50,* 131–42. doi: 10.1037/0022–3514.50.1.131

Rozin, P., & Royzman, E.B. (2001). Negativity bias, negativity dominance, and contagion. *Personality and Social Psychology Review, 5,* 296–320. doi: 10.1207/S15327957PSPR0504–2

Saguy, T., & Chernyak-Hai, L. (2012). Intergroup contact can undermine disadvantaged group members' attributions to discrimination. *Journal of Experimental Social Psychology, 48,* 714–20. doi: 10.1016/j.jesp.2012.01.003

Saguy, T., Tausch, N., Dovidio, J.F., & Pratto, F. (2009). The irony of harmony: Positive intergroup contact produces false expectations for equality. *Psychological Science, 20,* 114–21. doi: 10.1111/j.1467–9280.2008.02261.x

Schiappa, E., Gregg, P.B., & Hewes, D.E. (2005). The parasocial contact hypothesis. *Communication Monographs, 72,* 92–115. doi: 10.1080/0363775052000342544

Schwarz, N. (2007). Retrospective and concurrent self-reports: The rationale for real-time data capture. In A.A. Stone, S. Shiffman, A.A. Atienza, & L. Nebeling (Eds.), *The science of real-time data capture: Self-reports in health research* (pp. 11–26). New York, NY: Oxford University Press.

Simon, B., & Klandermans, B. (2001). Towards a social psychological analysis of politicized collective identity: Conceptualization, antecedents, and consequences. *American Psychologist, 56,* 319–31. doi: 10.1037/0003–066X.56.4.319

Singer, H.A. (1948). The veteran and race relations. *Journal of Educational Sociology, 21,* 397–408. doi: 10.2307/2263899

Stark, T.H., Flache, A., & Veenstra, R. (2013). Generalization of positive and negative attitudes toward individuals to outgroup attitudes. *Personality and Social Psychology Bulletin, 39,* 608–22. doi: 10.1177/0146167213480890

Tam, T., Hewstone, M., Cairns, E., Tausch, N., Maio, G., & Kenworthy, J.B. (2007). The impact of intergroup emotions on forgiveness in Northern Ireland. *Group Processes and Intergroup Relations, 10,* 119–35. doi: 10.1177/1368430207071345

Tausch, N., Saguy, T., & Bryson, J. (2015). The implications of intergroup contact for social change: Its impact on individual mobility and collective action intentions among members of a disadvantaged group. *Journal of Social Issues, 71,* 536–53. doi: 10.1111/josi.12127

Taylor, S.E. (1991). Asymmetrical effects of positive and negative events: The mobilization-minimization hypothesis. *Psychological Bulletin, 110,* 67–85. doi: 10.1037//0033–2909.110.1.67

Tropp, L.R., Hawi, D., Van Laar, C., & Levin, S. (2012). Cross-ethnic friendships, perceived discrimination, and their effects on ethnic activism over time: A longitudinal investigation of three ethnic minority groups. *British Journal of Social Psychology, 51,* 257–72. doi: 10.1111/j.2044–8309.2011.02050.x

Turner, J.C., Hogg, M.A., Oakes, P.J., Reicher, S.D., & Wetherell, M.S. (1987). *Rediscovering the social group: A self-categorization theory.* Oxford, UK: Blackwell.

Van Zomeren, M., Spears, R., Fischer, A., & Leach, C.W. (2004). Put your money where your mouth is! Explaining collective action tendencies through group-based anger and group efficacy. *Journal of Personality and Social Psychology, 87,* 649–64. doi: 10.1037/0022–3514.87.5.649

Vezzali, L., Hewstone, M., Capozza, D., Giovannini, D., & Wölfer, R. (2014). Improving intergroup relations with extended and vicarious forms of indirect contact. *European Review of Social Psychology, 25,* 314–89. doi: 10.1080/10463283.2014.982948

Wright, S.C., Aron, A., McLaughlin-Volpe, T., & Ropp, S.A. (1997). The extended contact effect: Knowledge of cross-group friendships and prejudice. *Journal of Personality and Social psychology, 73,* 73–90. doi: 10.1037/0022–3514.73.1.73

Wright, S.C., & Lubensky, M. (2009). The struggle for social equality: Collective action vs. prejudice reduction. In S. Demoulin, J.P. Leyens, & J.F. Dovidio (Eds.), *Intergroup misunderstandings: Impact of divergent social realities* (pp. 291–310). New York, NY: Psychology Press.

Zingora, T., & Graf, S. (2016). *From intergroup contact with gay people and Roma to voting on restriction of gay rights: The role of intergroup threat and attitudes.* Manuscript under review.

7

THE EXTENDED INTERGROUP CONTACT HYPOTHESIS

State of the art and future developments

Loris Vezzali and Sofia Stathi

Key words: extended contact, vicarious contact, indirect contact, intergroup relations, prejudice reduction

More than 60 years of research have revealed that direct, face-to-face contact between members of different groups, especially when characterized by Allport's (1954) optimal conditions (i.e. equal status, cooperation, common goals, institutional support), reduces prejudice (Hodson & Hewstone, 2013). However, strategies that seek to utilize direct contact are often difficult to put into practice. For instance, people may lack contact opportunities, especially in segregated, conflictual or post-conflictual contexts (e.g. Psaltis, Pachoulides, Lytras, Philipou, & Beyli, 2011). Moreover, people may resist positive interactions with out-group members due to high levels of initial prejudice or intergroup anxiety (Stathi, Crisp, Turner, West, & Birtel, 2012). In addition, when considering the implementation of direct contact interventions, organizational difficulties can deem them impractical. The review by Paluck and Green (2009) indirectly supports the contention that interventions based on direct contact may be difficult to implement, showing that only 10% of reviewed experimental field studies on prejudice reduction were based on direct contact.

Research conducted in the last two decades revealed that also indirect intergroup contact, a term referring to forms of contact without face-to-face interaction, can improve intergroup relations. In particular, research has focused primarily on two indirect contact forms: (a) extended contact, that is knowing or observing in-group members interacting positively with out-group members (Wright, Aron, McLaughlin-Volpe, & Ropp, 1997); (b) imagined contact, that is mentally simulating a positive interaction with out-group members (Crisp & Turner, 2012).

In this chapter, we will focus on extended contact. After providing an overview of theoretical perspectives and research on extended contact, we will describe the most recent developments of the extended contact hypothesis. Finally, we will indicate some further avenues for future research.

The extended intergroup contact hypothesis

According to Wright et al. (1997), people do not need to personally know out-group members in order to reduce prejudice. Rather, the mere knowledge that in-group members have a close relation with individuals belonging to the out-group, or in fact observing intergroup interactions, is sufficient for improving out-group attitudes. Wright et al. (1997) identified the rationale to support extended contact in three advancements of the contact hypothesis (Allport, 1954): first, the importance attributed to cross-group friendships as a form of highly qualitative contact (Davies, Tropp, Aron, Pettigrew, & Wright, 2011); second, the key role that anxiety reduction has in mediating contact effects (Pettigrew & Tropp, 2008); and third, the importance of membership salience in the generalization of the positive attitudes developed during contact (Brown & Hewstone, 2005). Although these advancements pertain to direct contact research, Wright et al. (1997) propose that they may also underlie the new concept of extended contact. In other words, the authors suggest that extended contact may exert its effects based on the above advancements in direct contact research.

Specifically, Wright et al. (1997) argued that extended contact should be effective because it capitalizes on the knowledge of friendships between in-group and out-group members, and it is characterized by low levels of anxiety and high membership salience. Knowing of or observing a cross-group interaction should be less anxiety-provoking than actually taking part in it. Moreover, it should increase the salience of group membership to a greater extent than being actually involved in the contact situation. According to Wright et al. (1997), in fact, group salience should be higher in extended than in direct contact, because knowing of or observing cross-group interactions should make the distinct categories of the interacting partners perceptually noticeable (for empirical evidence, see Vezzali, Saguy, Andrighetto, Giovannini, & Capozza, 2016). According to Brown and Hewstone (2005), the effects of contact generalize only when group membership between individuals is salient during contact, because category salience enhances the representative-ness of the interaction partners (and thus, favors generalization of attitudes to the whole out-group category). Based on this argument, enhanced category salience during extended contact should favor the generalization of positive effects outside the immediate context.

Wright et al. (1997) further point out that extended contact should benefit from the role of social norms, based on the idea that when group membership is salient, individuals are more likely to adhere to group norms (Tajfel & Turner, 1979). Knowing of or observing cross-group interactions should in fact point to inclusive and favorable norms regarding contact (see also section on Underlying processes and effects of extended contact).

Theoretical accounts explaining the effects of extended contact

Wright et al. (1997) suggested that the extended contact hypothesis is consistent with the theoretical perspective provided by balance theory (Heider, 1958), which states that individuals should try to avoid unbalanced states that are cognitively uncomfortable. In an extended contact relationship, three targets are considered: the perceiver, an in-group member and an out-group member. The relations are between the perceiver and the in-group member, between the in-group member and the out-group member, between the perceiver and the out-group member. If the perceiver has a positive relation with the in-group member, the in-group member has a positive relation with the out-group member, but the perceiver has a negative relation with the out-group member, this creates an unbalanced state for the perceiver that can be resolved by improving the attitude towards the out-group member.

Turner, Hewstone, Voci, Paolini and Christ (2007; see also Dovidio, Eller, & Hewstone, 2011) suggested that the premises of extended contact are also consistent with social cognitive theory (Bandura, 1986). Observing others provides information on social norms (see Hodson, Harry, & Mitchell, 2009; Wright et al., 1997) and patterns of behavior that individuals can adopt (observational learning). In the case of extended contact, individuals may learn positive responses towards the out-group by observing in-group peers interacting with out-group members.

Vezzali, Hewstone, Capozza, Giovannini and Wölfer (2014) proposed two additional theoretical accounts that may serve to explain the extended contact effects. The first is vicarious dissonance theory (Cooper & Hogg, 2007), deriving from cognitive dissonance theory (Festinger, 1957). According to this theory, the observation of a close person engaging in behaviors inconsistent with personal attitudes can create vicarious dissonance. In the case of extended contact, knowing of or observing an in-group member behaving positively towards an out-group member would be in contrast to one's own negative attitudes towards the out-group; to resolve this inconsistency, the individual may also improve personal attitudes towards the out-group.

Finally, the vicarious self-perception model (Goldstein & Cialdini, 2007) could also account for the extended contact effects. This model is based on the self-perception theory (Bem, 1972), which states that the observation of one's own behavior may provide insights into personal attitudes. According to the vicarious self-perception model, such processes may also operate vicariously, when observing the behavior of a close other. Applied to extended contact, observing an in-group member, a close person who shares group membership with the individual, interacting positively with the out-group would indicate that this person, and consequently the self (given the closeness between the self and the in-group), has positive out-group attitudes.

Underlying processes and effects of extended contact

Originally, Wright et al. (1997) proposed four processes that may explain the effects of extended contact. The first is represented by inclusion of the other in the self (IOS; Aron, Aron, & Smollan, 1992). To the extent that individuals who share a group membership are spontaneously included in the self (Smith & Henry, 1996), and that people engaging in a close relationship are perceived as a single cognitive unit (Sedikides, Olsen, & Reis, 1993), observing an in-group member engaging in a positive relationship with out-group members should increase psychological closeness towards the out-group.

The second mediator is intergroup anxiety, which is also one of the most important mediators of the relationship between direct contact and prejudice (Brown & Hewstone, 2005; Pettigrew & Tropp, 2008). Wright et al. (1997) noted that the anxiety triggered by knowing of or observing a cross-group relationship is likely to be lower than the anxiety that is experienced during an actual intergroup encounter. Therefore, the authors hypothesized that reduced anxiety could work as an additional mechanism of extended contact.

In-group and out-group norms represent the third and fourth mediators respectively, as proposed by Wright et al. (1997). The rationale is that, since group membership should be more salient when knowing of or observing a cross-group interaction than when being immersed in it, extended contact should increase the likelihood of individuals self-categorizing as group members and accepting in-group norms (Tajfel & Turner, 1979). Thus, when the observed interaction between in-group and out-group is positive, observers are likely to assume that the in-group is positively oriented towards the out-group. Similarly, knowing of or observing a positive intergroup interaction can also provide indications regarding out-group norms, suggesting that the out-group is positively inclined towards the observers' in-group. These positive in-group and out-group norms should in turn mediate the effects of extended contact on out-group attitudes (Vezzali, Stathi, Giovannini, Capozza, & Visintin, 2015).

Turner, Hewstone, Voci and Vonofakou (2008; see also Gómez, Tropp, & Fernandez, 2011) provided the initial evidence for the simultaneous mediation by the four mechanisms proposed by Wright et al. (1997). The authors conducted two cross-sectional studies examining the relationship between Whites and Asians in the UK from the perspective of White British university students (Study 1) and high-school students (Study 2). Results revealed that extended contact was associated with increased IOS (a measure of closeness between the self and the out-group), reduced intergroup anxiety, increased perceptions that in-group and out-group are positively oriented towards contact (in-group and out-group norms). In turn, these variables simultaneously mediated the effects of extended contact on improved out-group attitudes.

In addition to these four mechanisms, research has identified several further mediators of extended contact, both cognitive (e.g. self-disclosure; Turner, Hewstone, & Voci, 2007) and affective (e.g. out-group trust; Tam, Hewstone, Kenworty, & Cairns, 2009, Study 2; for a review see Vezzali et al., 2014).

The extended contact hypothesis started to attract stronger interest among scholars since 2004, when Paolini, Hewstone, Cairns and Voci (2004) demonstrated in two cross-sectional studies focusing on Catholics and Protestants in Northern Ireland that both direct and extended contact were simultaneously associated with improved out-group attitudes and greater perceptions of out-group variability. This work provided evidence that extended contact has effects that go beyond those of direct contact and that the two strategies are complementary to each other. Moreover, the authors provided the first empirical evidence that intergroup anxiety mediated the extended contact effects.

There is now strong evidence that extended contact is an effective strategy for improving intergroup relations. Vezzali et al. (2014) conducted an extensive review of a total of niney one studies, revealing widespread effects of extended contact across several target groups, age groups and situations. Overall, the studies employed experi-mental, correlational and longitudinal designs. Effects of extended contact span across several outcome variables in addition to out-group attitudes (Turner et al., 2008), including improved behavioral intentions (Paolini, Hewstone, & Cairns, 2007) and actual intergroup behavior (Vezzali et al., 2015), less stereotyping (Munniksma, Stark, Verkuyten, Flache, & Veenstra, 2013), reduced out-group infrahumanization (Capozza, Falvo, Trifiletti, & Pagani, 2014) and more positive intergroup expectations (Gómez et al., 2011). Importantly, research, although still limited, demonstrates that extended contact is equally effective in improving attitudes among both majority and minority groups (e.g. Gómez et al., 2011; Turner, Hewstone, & Voci, 2007). This represents a considerable advantage over direct contact strategies, which instead are more effective among majority members (Tropp & Pettigrew, 2005).

In the above sections, we outlined the extended contact hypothesis, the theoretical perspectives that underlie it, relevant mediating processes and research supporting its effectiveness. We will now focus on the most recent advancements of the extended contact literature, before concluding with important directions for future research. The first advancement is the theoretical and methodo-logical distinction between extended and vicarious contact. The second is the use of social networks analysis as a method with ample potential for the extended contact literature.

Extended contact vs. vicarious contact

One of the most relevant recent advancements in the extended contact literature is the distinction between extended and vicarious contact. Originally, Wright et al. (1997) labelled both the knowledge of in-group members having out-group friends, and the observation of these interactions, as extended contact. Research conducted since the formulation of the extended contact hypothesis, however, has suggested that knowing of versus observing cross-group interactions represent two distinct indirect contact forms. We argue that it is important to disentangle the two forms of indirect contact in terms of theoretical underpinnings, methods and processes involved so that prejudice reduction interventions based on their principles are better tailored and more effective.

Dovidio et al. (2011) defined *extended contact* as the knowledge that an in-group member has out-group friends. Vezzali et al. (2014) in their review defined extended contact as the knowledge that in-group and out-group members have contact. This definition allows for extended contact to occur even outside the boundaries of cross-group friendships, is consistent with empirical research (e.g. Andrighetto, Mari, Volpato, & Behluli, 2012) and makes extended contact more comparable to vicarious contact (see below). For extended contact to occur, in-group members provide individuals with information concerning their cross-group contacts. A typical measure of extended contact consists in simply asking participants about the number of in-group members they know who have out-group friends. For instance, Turner, Hewstone and Voci (2007, Study 2) asked White and Asian high-school students, respectively, to report the number of in-group friends and family members who had out-group friends. Results revealed an indirect association between extended contact and more positive out-group attitudes via increased self-disclosure towards out-group members and reduced intergroup anxiety.

In contrast, *vicarious contact* was defined by Dovidio et al. (2011; see also Vezzali et al., 2014) as the observation of an interaction between in-group and out-group members (and one that is not necessarily between friends). Studies on vicarious contact are usually experimental, and contact is typically manipulated by asking participants to watch video clips displaying cross-group interactions. For instance, Mazziotta, Mummendey and Wright (2011, Study 1) asked German participants to watch videos where German individuals had positive contact with Chinese people. Results revealed that, compared to control conditions showing intra-group interactions, watching intergroup interactions resulted in improved attitudes towards Chinese people, as well as a greater desire to have contact with them.

Vezzali et al. (2014) further specified a specific form of vicarious contact, where cross-group interactions are observed via the media. For instance, Vittrup and Holden (2011) selected short video clips from popular TV shows characterized by a racially diverse cast that depicted positive interactions between members of different ethnic groups (e.g. *Sesame Street*). After watching these video clips, compared to a control condition where no video was shown, White children displayed more positive attitudes towards Black people.

Importantly, however, cross-group interactions depicted in the media may provide individuals with examples of negative relations between in-group and out-group members. In other words, they may expose viewers to *negative* vicarious contact. An example is provided by Weisbuch, Pauker and Ambady (2009), who found in a series of correlational and experimental studies that White people in television displayed negative nonverbal behavior towards Black people. Watching these subtly negative interactions led to an increase in implicit prejudice among White viewers, which also related to more negative explicit out-group attitudes.

In their extensive review, Vezzali et al. (2014) considered ad-hoc stories, books, newspapers and radio programs, in which perceivers read or hear about intergroup contact, as forms of vicarious contact via the media. For example, in a series of studies by Cameron and colleagues (e.g. Cameron, Rutland, Brown, & Douch, 2006), children were asked to read ad-hoc short stories of friendships between in-group and out-group characters, and to discuss the stories with the experimenters over the course of multiple sessions. Results of these experimental interventions revealed positive effects on stereotyping and willingness to engage in contact with the out-group.

Theoretical perspectives underlying the effects of extended and vicarious contact

Regarding the theoretical underpinning of vicarious contact, we point again to social cognitive theory (Bandura, 1986), which in this case is even more relevant than when explaining extended contact. The core of social cognitive theory is based on the idea that the observation of others provides important information on how to behave and on social norms. Although knowing about a cross-group interaction can change perceptions of both in-group and out-group norms (Turner et al., 2008), models of behavior are perceptually more likely to be learned from direct observation (i.e. vicarious contact), where the actual behavior is likely to be the main focus of the scene, than when individuals are told a story about an intergroup encounter (i.e. extended contact), which may include several details unrelated to actual behaviors.

Also the model of vicarious self-perception (Goldstein & Cialdini, 2007) may be better used to explain the effects of vicarious rather than of extended contact. Since self-perception theory (Bem, 1972), on which the vicarious self-perception model is based, states that it is the *observation* of behavior that allows to infer personal attitudes, it follows that it is the observation of a cross-group interaction (i.e. vicarious contact) that can be especially informative of personal attitudes. This speculation is reinforced by the fact that self-perception processes are often automatic and mostly based on a superficial elaboration of information (Goldstein & Cialdini, 2007). Although observing a cross-group interaction (vicarious contact) does not necessarily require a high degree of awareness, being attentive to an in-group member's account of his/her cross-group contact (extended contact) implies the use of attentional resources and, consequently, the individual's awareness. Note that self-perception processes generally affect attitudes that are less relevant or central for the individual (Bem, 1972). It is thus possible that vicarious self-perception processes have greater effects on intergroup attitudes that are less relevant to the individual, or directed at groups for which previous attitudes do not exist. On the other hand, vicarious self-perception processes may be less suited to change intergroup attitudes that are more central to individuals, that is, established intergroup attitudes. Future research may delve into the two theories and test the specific predictions for both extended and vicarious contact, contributing this way to a potential theoretical differentiation between the two strategies.

In contrast, we argue that balance theory (Heider, 1958) may be equally suited for both extended and vicarious contact, because both knowing of or observing a positive cross-group relationship may heighten the salience of the imbalance between the different unit relations (individual-in-group member; in-group member-out-group member; individual-out-group member), creating the need to restore a balanced state. Similarly, vicarious dissonance theory (Cooper & Hogg, 2007) can be applied to both extended and vicarious contact. In fact, individuals may note that an in-group member has a certain attitude towards the out-group (i.e. positive attitude) which is inconsistent with the personal attitude (i.e. negative attitude) in both indirect contact forms. However, the extent to which balance theory (Heider, 1958) and vicarious dissonance theory (Cooper & Hogg, 2007) explain the effects of extended and vicarious contact may vary, suggesting another avenue that future research can explore.

A new theoretical model of extended and vicarious contact

Based on available evidence, Vezzali et al. (2014) proposed a theoretical model (Figure 7.1) identifying antecedents, consequences, mediating and moderating processes of both extended and vicarious contact forms, which we will summarize below. Importantly, the model does not clearly distinguish between extended and vicarious contact, since research has yet to provide direct comparisons of the two indirect contact forms; it allows, however, for predictions that may help disentangle them.

Environmental conditions are the antecedents of extended and vicarious contact (Figure 7.1). Social and family network diversity, as well as heterogeneous societal settings, are prerequisite conditions for the two forms of contact. In fact, in these contexts where the likelihood of direct intergroup contact is higher, individuals are more likely to be told by in-group members about their cross-group friendships, and to observe cross-group interactions. However, in these contexts where the likelihood of cross-group contact is high, the possibility of negative intergroup contact is also evident, thus potentially exposing individuals to both positive and negative extended contact. In contrast, media that depict intergroup interactions represent a prerequisite for vicarious contact only.

Although extended contact has been identified as a primarily cognitive experience (Paolini et al., 2007), research has demonstrated that extended and vicarious contact exert their effects through both a cognitive and an affective route (Figure 7.1). The two routes are not necessarily independent; rather, they can affect each other. For instance, cognitive factors may precede affective factors (Capozza et al., 2014). To the extent that both extended and vicarious contact effects are mediated by both cognitive and affective processes, it is difficult at present to identify processes unique to one of the two indirect contact forms.

Moderators identified by previous research are grouped into three categories (Figure 7.1). The first refers to *contextual conditions*, such as segregation; for instance, effects of extended contact are stronger when individuals have low levels of direct contact (Christ et al., 2010). The second refers to *situational perceptions*, like group categorization. For example, Cameron et al. (2006) demonstrated that generalization of vicarious contact effects is higher when dual identities rather than a common in-group identity or individual characteristics are salient. The third category of moderators refers to individual differences. There is evidence, for

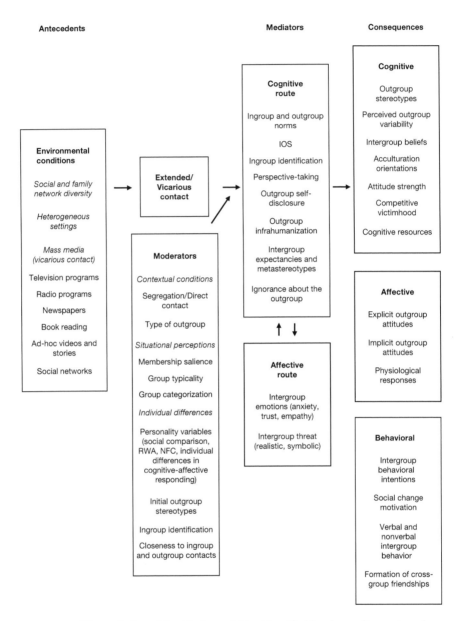

FIGURE 7.1 Theoretical model with the variables identified by the studies reviewed by Vezzali et al. (2014). RWA = right-wing authoritarianism. NFC = need for closure. Source: Vezzali et al. (2014). copyright © European Association of Social Psychology, reprinted by permission of Taylor & Francis Ltd, www.tandfonline.com on behalf of European Association of Social Psychology.

instance, that the effects of extended contact are moderated by personality variables such as right-wing authoritarianism (Hodson et al., 2009).

Existing research does not differentiate which factors are more likely to moderate extended or vicarious contact. However, different predictions can be made. For instance, one could reasonably predict that, all things being equal, membership salience is higher when observing than when knowing of a cross-group interaction (posited that in-group-out-group distinctions are perceptually visible). If this prediction is correct, then individual differences (which should play little role when membership is salient; Tajfel & Turner, 1979) are more likely a moderator of extended than of vicarious contact effects.

The effects of vicarious and extended contact span from cognitive to affective to behavioral (Figure 7.1). Again, existing research does not allow us to disentangle the two indirect contact forms, although it is possible to make different predictions. For example, nonverbal behavior is a more likely outcome of vicarious contact, where it can be directly observed from role models, rather than of extended contact (Weisbuch et al., 2009).

In addition, observing a cross-group interaction does not necessarily require strong attentional resources; therefore, vicarious contact may sometimes elicit low-elaboration processes. In contrast, attentional resources should be generally higher when individuals are told about a cross-group encounter (extended contact), with the consequence of a greater likelihood to elicit high-elaboration processes. Since attitudes should be stronger and more resistant to change when formed after high- rather than low-elaboration processes (Petty & Cacioppo, 1986), we argue that, at least in some circumstances, reduced prejudice stemming from extended contact will be more resistant to change than reduced prejudice stemming from vicarious contact. However, this is a hypothesis that remains to be tested.

It should be noted that extended and vicarious contact have generally been investigated with different paradigms: whereas research on extended contact is mostly correlational or longitudinal, vicarious contact studies are mostly experimental. In fact, in the review by Vezzali et al. (2014), 92% of the reviewed extended contact studies were correlational or longitudinal, whereas 90% of the vicarious contact studies were experimental. Encompassing these methodological differences in the effort to understand the unique features and psychological processes relevant to extended and vicarious contact poses an interesting challenge for scholars.

The social network perspective

Recent research has taken into consideration the possibility of applying social network analysis (SNA) to the study of extended contact. SNA represents a scientific approach to the investigation of ties between members of a network. This approach goes beyond individual characteristics of network members to explain their behavior, by assuming that interdependencies between members contribute to defining behavioral patterns within a network (Borgatti & Halgin, 2011).

Wölfer, Faber and Hewstone (2015) advocate the use of SNA for the examination of both intragroup and intergroup relations, and highlight some strengths of this approach: (a) it allows considering more objective information than self-reports, based on actual patterns of relationships between network members; (b) it permits the examination of complex interaction patterns, including indirect connections between network members; (c) it can shed light on influence processes within the network; (d) it provides information on latent psychological entities within the network, such as small groups, and (e) it allows examining social structures across different levels of analysis - individual, group and network level. Importantly, SNA may have both cross-sectional as well as longitudinal applications, which can be especially useful when seeking to capture how social structures change and evolve over time.

SNA may be especially useful in the examination of extended and vicarious contact. This is because, as noted above, it allows the examination of indirect connections between members of a network. Furthermore, when using self-reported data, individuals may provide biased information on the number of their in-group friends, and on the number of their in-group friends' out-group friends. In fact, individuals may not be aware of in-group members' social networks (cf. Vezzali et al., 2015).

The first research to adopt a social network perspective in the study of extended contact is by Munniksma et al. (2013), who tested initial out-group stereotypes as a moderator of the longitudinal effects of extended contact among Dutch high-school students (the out-group was Turks). The authors, by focusing their analysis on small social settings, used an extended intergroup friendship measure that excluded direct friendships. They asked participants to nominate their five best friends within the class. This way, they obtained information on both direct friendships as well as on indirect connections between class members. When computing the extended contact measure, they considered as extended contact only the extended contact with out-group peers who were not also nominated as participants' own friends. In other words, if a participant's in-group friend had an out-group friend who was also a friend of the participant, this was not considered as extended contact. This way, they considered the "pure" effect of extended contact, which would be difficult to capture with an analysis solely based on self-reports. Results revealed that extended contact, assessed 3 months after entering high-school, related to more positive out-group stereotypes 6 months later, but only among participants with initially unfavorable out-group stereotypes.

Vezzali et al. (2014) however caution against the exclusive reliance on social network data. In fact, at least in small social networks such as small classrooms, individuals indirectly connected to an out-group member through an in-group member are likely to also be direct friends with the out-group member. In other words, individuals are likely to have both direct and extended contact with the out-group member (this may partly explain the common moderate to strong correlation between direct and extended contact indices). Considering only "pure" extended contact (i.e. excluding participants who have at the same time both direct and extended contact with an out-group member) would cause the exclusion of a large number of data, which would undermine, at least partly, the understanding of social network processes, and possibly reduce the replication of findings from the extended contact literature.

Wölfer and Hewstone (2014) used a two-step procedure to combine SNA with self-reports. They first asked seventh-grade students from Germany, Netherlands and Sweden to indicate their five best classroom friends. Second, they considered these nominated in-group friends' self-reports, by averaging their self-reported intergroup contact. This way, they took advantage of both social network data and self-reports, which allowed them to have more objective data (provided by nominations) and information on the social network beyond the classroom level (provided by self-reports, where nominated friends indicated their out-group friends in general, beyond the strict boundaries of the classroom). The results of multilevel analyzes revealed that extended contact obtained by combining direct nominations and self-reports predicted out-group attitudes among both majority and minority members, also when controlling for a number of key variables such as direct contact and number of in-group friends.

Stark (2015), by taking advantage of social network data, provided an insight into the role of social networks in understanding the patterns of cross-group friendships based on the initial level of prejudice displayed by individuals. Stark reasoned that the finding that more prejudiced individuals avoid intergroup contact (Binder et al., 2009) may not depend on active avoidance of out-group members, but could be explained by the in-group members' social network. Participants were Dutch adolescents; the out-group was represented by Turkish and Moroccan classmates. Results revealed that more prejudiced participants had fewer cross-group friendships than those less prejudiced, an effect that was due to the tendency to avoid being friends with in-group members who had out-group friends (an index based on friendship nominations at the level of the classroom). Interestingly, indirect evidence for this effect was provided by Jacoby-Senghor, Sinclair and Smith (2015), who found that Whites with higher implicit bias towards Blacks avoided Whites with Black friends, because of expecting to feel less comfortable with Black targets.

Results by Stark (2015) are key because they provide a basic insight into the role of social network in guiding behavior. In Stark's research (2015), knowing about in-group members with out-group friends led to the avoidance of these in-group members. This finding offers new perspectives in extended contact research, by showing that the knowledge that in-group members have out-group friends is not sufficient to reduce negative intergroup behavior, and that friendship choices, even within the in-group, rely at least in part on the wider social network structure.

This preliminary set of studies provides initial support that SNA is useful in the examination of extended and vicarious contact. We encourage future research to take advantage of this methodological perspective in combination with classic self-report measures in order to gain a deeper understanding of the dynamics involved in extended and vicarious contact processes.

Future directions

In the previous sections, we suggested that the distinction between extended and vicarious contact and the adoption of a social network perspective in the examination of extended and vicarious contact represent important theoretical advancements. We also noted that in both cases research is still in its infancy, and we suggest that these advancements represent important avenues for future studies.

A further area of development is the examination of when direct and indirect contact strategies should be implemented; moreover, it will be important to examine how they may be combined to maximize their effects in the effort to reduce prejudice. Direct contact, which requires that each individual has face-to-face contact with an out-group member, may be particularly useful in highly diverse settings. However, even in these contexts prejudiced individuals may find a way to avoid contact, by directly avoiding out-group members or by selecting their in-group friendships among in-group members with fewer out-group friends, thus reducing the chances of establishing out-group friendships themselves (Stark, 2015). Instead, strategies such as extended contact, vicarious contact and imagined contact may be useful in segregated settings, like post-conflict contexts, when contact opportunities are low, or the implementation of a direct contact intervention is not cost-effective. We note, however, that extended or vicarious forms of contact also require that in-group and out-group members have some degree of contact in the wider social network. Instead, imagined contact can be applied in completely segregated or homogeneous contexts. Future research may provide empirical support to these speculations.

Various authors suggested that direct and indirect contact strategies are complementary and can be used in combination. For instance, extended or vicarious contact, and imagined contact, can be used as preparatory strategies for direct intergroup contact (Crisp & Turner, 2012; Turner, Hewstone, Voci, et al., 2007). Crisp and Turner (2012) proposed a continuum of contact strategies, arguing that imagined contact can be used as the first stage of an intervention, since, especially in contexts with low contact opportunities, it can be the only way to foster the willingness to engage with the out-group. In the second stage, where hopefully the social network has become more diverse, extended contact may be highly effective in spreading the effects of still isolated cross-group contacts. Finally, at later stages, when social norms about integration have become more popular and behavioral intentions are more positive, actual contact can have maximal effects.

However, other combinations of strategies are possible. For instance, since a direct contact intervention may be costly and difficult to implement, applying direct contact interventions only among some in-group and out-group members, and then using extended contact principles to spread its effects among a larger group could be beneficial. Research on how to combine contact strategies in order to significantly improve intergroup attitudes is surprisingly scarce. Future research can test which are the most effective combinations of strategies in given contexts.

A further area that we consider interesting for future exploration concerns negative extended and vicarious contact. Research on direct contact has recently highlighted some important characteristics of negative direct contact, indicating that its effects are stronger than those of positive contact (Barlow et al., 2012). There is also initial evidence that negative extended (Mazziotta, Rohmann, Wright, De Tezanos-Pinto, & Lutterbach, 2015) and vicarious contact (Weisbuch et al., 2009) lead to negative out-group attitudes. Research should explore the unique features of negative extended or vicarious contact, its underlying processes and its cognitive and affective consequences. These studies may also consider how extended and vicarious contact evolve over time. Generally, in extended contact studies, participants are asked to report the number of in-group friends who have out-group friends at a given time. However, it would be interesting to explore what happens when a cross-group friendship ends, and how this information affects people's attitudes.

Closing remarks

In this chapter, we reviewed the extended contact hypothesis, its theoretical underpinnings (Wright et al., 1997) and evidence of its effectiveness as a prejudice reduction technique. We then discussed two recent developments in the literature, the distinction between extended and vicarious contact, and the benefits of incorporating SNA in the study of extended contact, both of which in our opinion are likely to drive future research in the field. Moreover, we highlighted two further relevant domains that have potential to grow in the next years. The first concerns the identification of where and when contact strategies can be more effective and how they can be combined to be maximally beneficial. The second relates to the examination of negative extended and vicarious contact.

It should be noted that research on extended contact is rapidly growing, with the majority of studies having been conducted after 2007. This research has identified several other topics that deserve further examination, such as the role of closeness to in-group and out-group contacts, the operationalization of extended and vicarious contact interventions in the field and beyond educational settings, the reciprocal interplay between cognitive and affective processes in mediating extended and vicarious contact effects, the role played by different mass media in producing vicarious contact effects, the use of novel behavioral and implicit measures. Within the length restrictions of this chapter, we only focused on some of the developments that can further expand the extended contact hypothesis both in terms of theory and methodology. However, despite the growing interest, we believe that research on extended and vicarious contact is still in its infancy, and future work may provide important insights regarding the reduction of prejudice in the society at large.

Note

We would like to thank Gordon Hodson for his feedback on an earlier version of this chapter.

References

Allport, G.W. (1954). *The nature of prejudice*. New York, NY: Addison-Wesley.

Andrighetto, L., Mari, S., Volpato, C., & Behluli, B. (2012). Reducing competitive victimhood in Kosovo: The role of extended contact and common ingroup identity. *Political Psychology, 33,* 513–29. doi: 10.1111/j.1467-9221.2012.00887.x

Aron, A., Aron, E.N., & Smollan, D. (1992). Inclusion of other in the self scale and the structure of interpersonal closeness. *Journal of Personality and Social Psychology, 63,* 596–612. doi: 10.1037/0022-3514.63.4.596

Bandura, A. (1986). *Social foundations of thought and action: A social cognitive theory*. Englewood Cliffs, NJ: Prentice- Hall, Inc.

Barlow, F.K., Paolini, S., Pedersen, A., Hornsey, M.J., Radke, H.R.M., Harwood, J., . . . & Sibley, C.G. (2012). The contact caveat: Negative contact predicts increased prejudice more than positive contact predicts reduced prejudice. *Personality and Social Psychology Bulletin, 38,* 1629–43. doi: 10.1177/0146167212457953

Bem, D.J. (1972). Self-perception theory. In L. Berkowitz (Ed.), *Advances in experimental social psychology* (Vol. 6, pp. 1–99). New York, NY: Academic Press.

Binder, J., Zagefka, H., Brown, R., Funke, F., Kessler, T., & Mummendey, A. (2009). Does contact reduce prejudice or does prejudice reduce contact? A longitudinal test of the contact hypothesis among majority and minority groups in three European countries. *Journal of Personality and Social Psychology, 96,* 843–56. doi: 10.1037/a0013470

Borgatti, S., & Halgin, D.S. (2011). On network theory. *Organization Science, 22,* 1168–81. doi: 10.1287/orsc.1100.0641

Brown, R., & Hewstone, M. (2005). An integrative theory of intergroup contact. *Advances in Experimental Social Psychology, 37,* 255–343. doi: 10.1016/S0065-2601(05)37005-5

Cameron, L., Rutland, A., Brown, R., & Douch, R. (2006). Changing children's intergroup attitudes toward refugees: Testing different models of extended contact. *Child Development, 77,* 1208–19. doi: 10.1111/j.1467-8624.2006.00929.x

Capozza, D., Falvo, R., Trifiletti, E., & Pagani, A. (2014). Cross-group friendships, extended contact, and humanity attributions to homosexuals. *Procedia – Social and Behavioral Sciences, 114,* 276–82. doi: 10.1016/j.sbspro.2013.12.698

Christ, O., Hewstone, M., Tausch, N., Wagner, U., Voci, A., Hughes, J., & Cairns, E. (2010). Direct contact as a moderator of extended contact effects: Cross-sectional and longitudinal impact on outgroup attitudes, behavioral intentions, and attitude certainty. *Personality and Social Psychology Bulletin, 36,* 1662–74. doi: 10.1177/0146167210386969

Cooper, J., & Hogg, M.A. (2007). Feeling the anguish of others: A theory of vicarious dissonance. *Advances in experimental social psychology, 39,* 359–403. doi: 10.1016/S0065-2601(06)39007-7

Crisp, R.J., & Turner, R.N. (2012). The imagined contact hypothesis. *Advances in experimental social psychology, 46,* 125–82. doi: 10.1016/B978-0-12-394281-4.00003-9

Davies, K., Tropp, L.R., Aron, A., Pettigrew, T.F., & Wright, S.C. (2011). Cross-group friendships and intergroup attitudes: A meta-analytic review. *Personality and Social Psychology Review, 15,* 332–51. doi: 10.1177/1088868311411103

Dovidio, J.F., Eller, A., & Hewstone, M. (2011). Improving intergroup relations through direct, extended and other forms of in direct contact. *Group Processes and Intergroup Relations, 14,* 147–60. doi: 10.1177/1368430210390555

Festinger, L. (1957). *A theory of cognitive dissonance*. Stanford, CA: Stanford University Press.

Goldstein, N.J., & Cialdini, R.B. (2007). The spyglass self: A model of vicarious self-perception. *Journal of Personality and Social Psychology, 92,* 402–17. doi: 10.1037/0022-3514.92.3.402

Gómez, A., Tropp, L.R., & Fernandez, S. (2011). When extended contact opens the door to future contact: Testing the effects of extended contact on attitudes and intergroup expectancies in majority and minority groups. *Group Processes and Intergroup Relations, 14,* 161–73. doi: 10.1177/1368430210391119

Heider, F. (1958). *The psychology of interpersonal relations.* New York, NY: Wiley.

Hodson, G., Harry, H., & Mitchell, A. (2009). Independent benefits of contact and friendship on attitudes toward homosexuals among authoritarians and highly identified heterosexuals. *European Journal of Social Psychology, 39,* 509–25. doi: 10.1002/ejsp.558

Hodson, G., & Hewstone, M. (Eds.) (2013). *Advances in intergroup contact.* New York, NY: Psychology Press.

Jacoby-Senghor, D.S., Sinclair, S., & Smith, C.T. (2015). When bias binds: Effect of implicit outgroup bias on implicit affiliation. *Journal of Personality and Social Psychology, 109,* 415–33. doi: 10.1037/a0039513

Mazziotta, A., Mummendey, A., & Wright, S.C. (2011). Vicarious intergroup contact effects: Applying social-cognitive theory to intergroup contact research. *Group Processes and Intergroup Relations, 14,* 255–74. doi: 10.1177/1368430210390533

Mazziotta, A., Rohmann, A., Wright, S.C., De Tezanos-Pinto, P., & Lutterbach, S. (2015). (How) does positive and negative extended cross-group contact predict direct cross-group contact and intergroup attitudes? *European Journal of Social Psychology, 45,* 653–67. doi: 10.1002/ejsp.2110

Munniksma, A., Stark, T.H., Verkuyten, M., Flache, A., & Veenstra, R. (2013). Extended intergroup friendships within social settings: The moderating role of initial outgroup attitudes. *Group Processes and Intergroup Relations, 16,* 752–70. doi: 10.1177/13684302137 86207

Paluck, E.L., & Green, D.P. (2009). Prejudice reduction: What works? A critical look at evidence from the field and the laboratory. *Annual Review of Psychology, 60,* 339–67. doi: 10.1146/annurev.psych.60.110707.163607

Paolini, S., Hewstone, M., & Cairns, E. (2007). Direct and indirect intergroup friendship effects: Testing the moderating role of the affective-cognitive bases of prejudice. *Personality and Social Psychology Bulletin, 33,* 1406–20. doi: 10.1177/0146167207304788

Paolini, S., Hewstone, M., Cairns, E., & Voci, A. (2004). Effects of direct and indirect cross group friendship on judgements of Catholics and Protestants in Northern Ireland: The mediating role of anxiety-reduction mechanism. *Personality and Social Psychology Bulletin, 30,* 770–86. doi: 10.1177/0146167203262848

Pettigrew, T.F., & Tropp, L.R. (2008). How does intergroup contact reduce prejudice? Meta-analytic tests of three mediators. *European Journal of Social Psychology, 38,* 922–34. doi: 10.1002/ejsp.504

Petty, R.E., & Cacioppo, J.T. (1986). *Communication and persuasion: Central and peripheral routes to attitude change.* New York, NY: Springer.

Psaltis, C., Pachoulides, C., Lytras, E., Philipou, G., and Beyli, Z. (2011). Representations of history and intergroup relations in Cyprus. *Final report of Cyprus civil society in action,* CRIS 2008/168–265.

Sedikides, C., Olsen, N., & Reis, H.T. (1993). Relationships as natural categories. *Journal of Personality and Social Psychology, 64,* 71–82. doi: 10.1037/0022-3514.64.1.71

Smith, E.R., & Henry, S. (1996). An in-group becomes part of the self: Response time evaluation. *Personality and Social Psychology Bulletin, 22,* 635–42. doi: 10.1177/014616 7296226008

Stark, T.H. (2015). Understanding the selection bias: Social network processes and the effect of prejudice on the avoidance of outgroup friends. *Social Psychology Quarterly, 78,* 127–50. doi: 10.1177/0190272514565252

Stathi, S., Crisp, R.J., Turner, R.N., West, K., & Birtel, M. (2012). Using mental imagery to promote positive intergroup relations. In D.W. Russel & C.A. Russel (Eds.), *The psychology of prejudice: Interdisciplinary perspectives on contemporary issues* (pp. 235–50). Hauppauge, NY: Nova.

Tajfel, H., & Turner, J.C. (1979). An integrative theory of intergroup conflict. In W.G. Austin & S. Worchel (Eds.), *The social psychology of intergroup relations* (pp. 33–47). Monterey, CA: Brooks/Cole.

Tam, T., Hewstone, M., Kenworthy, J.B., & Cairns, E. (2009). Intergroup trust in Northern Ireland. *Personality and Social Psychology Bulletin, 35*, 45–59. doi: 10.1177/014616 7208325004

Tropp, L.R., & Pettigrew, T.F. (2005). Relationships between intergroup contact and prejudice among minority and majority status groups. *Psychological Science, 16*, 951–7. doi: 10.1111/j.1467-9280.2005.01643.x

Turner, R.N., Hewstone, M., & Voci, A. (2007). Reducing explicit and implicit outgroup prejudice via direct and extended contact: The mediating role of self-disclosure and intergroup anxiety. *Journal of Personality and Social Psychology, 93*, 369–88. doi: 10.1037/0022-3514.93.3.369

Turner, R.N., Hewstone, M., Voci, A., Paolini, S., & Christ, O. (2007). Reducing prejudice via direct and extended cross-group friendship. *European Review of Social Psychology, 18*, 212–55. doi: 10.1080/10463280701680297

Turner, R.N., Hewstone, M., Voci, A., & Vonofakou, C. (2008). A test of the extended contact hypothesis: The mediating role of intergroup anxiety, perceived ingroup and outgroup norms, and inclusion of the outgroup in the self. *Journal of Personality and Social Psychology, 95*, 843–60. doi: 10.1037/a0011434

Vezzali, L., Hewstone, M., Capozza, D., Giovannini, D., & Wölfer, R. (2014). Improving intergroup relations with extended and vicarious forms of indirect contact. *European Review of Social Psychology, 25*, 314–89. doi: 10.1080/10463283.2014.982948

Vezzali, L., Saguy, T., Andrighetto, L., & Giovannini, D., & Capozza, D. (2016). *When intergroup contact can backfire. The content of intergroup encounters and desire for equality.* Under review.

Vezzali, L., Stathi, S., Giovannini, D., Capozza, D., & Visintin, E.P. (2015). "And the best essay is . . .": Extended contact and cross-group friendships at school. *British Journal of Social Psychology, 54*, 601–15. doi: 10.1111/bjso.12110

Vittrup, B., & Holden, G.W. (2011). Exploring the impact of educational television and parent-child discussions on children's racial attitudes. *Analyses of Social Issues and Public Policy (ASAP), 11*, 82–104. doi: 10.1111/j.1530-2415.2010.01223.x

Weisbuch, M., Pauker, K., & Ambady, N. (2009). The subtle transmission of race bias via televised nonverbal behavior. *Science, 326*, 1711–14. doi: 10.1126/science.1178358

Wölfer, R., Faber, N., & Hewstone, M. (2015). Social network analysis in the science of groups: Cross-sectional and longitudinal applications for studying intra- and intergroup behavior. *Group Dynamics: Theory, Research, and Practice, 19*, 45–61. doi: 10.1037/gdn0000021

Wölfer, R., & Hewstone, M. (2014, July). Effects of intergroup contact: Network analytic enrichment of traditional measures. In K. Phalet (Ed.), (Chair), School diversity: Bridging minority and majority group perspectives. *Symposium conducted at the meeting of the European Association of Social Psychology.* Amsterdam, Netherlands.

Wright, S.C., Aron, A., McLaughlin-Volpe, T., & Ropp, S.A. (1997). The extended contact effect: Knowledge of cross-group friendships and prejudice. *Journal of Personality and Social Psychology, 73*, 73–90. doi: 10.1037/0022–3514.73.1.73

8

A FUTURE FOCUS FOR IMAGINED CONTACT

Advances in and beyond intergroup relations

Rose Meleady and Richard J. Crisp

Key words: imagined contact, indirect contact, intergroup relations, mental imagery, prejudice reduction

Intergroup contact, or interaction with a member(s) of a different group, represents one of the most widely used social-psychological interventions for reducing prejudice (Allport, 1954). Pettigrew and Tropp's (2006) meta-analysis of over 500 studies confirms that there is a fundamental, robust and positive impact of contact on intergroup attitudes (Pettigrew & Tropp, 2006). In this chapter, we focus on a complementary implementation of intergroup contact known as *imagined contact*. Imagined contact involves the mental simulation of a social interaction with a member or members of an out-group (Crisp & Turner, 2009, 2012). Despite being a relatively new technique, there have been rapid developments in the imagined contact field. More than seventy studies have now provided evidence of the efficacy of imagined contact as a simple and versatile prejudice reduction intervention (Miles & Crisp, 2014). In this chapter, we take stock of the progress made in the imagined contact field to date and offer an agenda for continued investigation.

In Part I, we provide a brief review of the current state of the art on imagined contact. We illustrate how imagined contact has been shown to impact a range of phenomena related to promotion of positive intergroup relations. In Part II, we consider future directions for imagined contact research. We identify several remaining questions that we believe will be important to address relating to the use of imagined contact as a tool to reduce prejudice and break down barriers between groups. Finally, in Part III we go on to review recent research that advances new techniques arising from the imagined contact literature that illustrate its wider applicability to a range of domains. In particular, we focus on new applications of imagined contact theory to the areas of economic decision-making, virtual cooperation and innovation training.

Imagined intergroup contact

Intergroup contact occurs when members of different cultural groups interact and come to know each other in ways that cut across group fault lines. This integration of different social groups has been shown to powerfully reduce prejudice between them (Allport, 1954; Pettigrew & Tropp, 2006). While it is now beyond any doubt that positive intergroup contact can reduce prejudice, its implementation is more problematic. Getting groups to interact across group lines is not always straightforward. For example, many societies remain highly segregated, and even in multicultural communities, interracial communication is often fleeting or superficial (e.g. Dixon & Durrheim, 2003; Graham & Cohen, 1997). Recently, a solution has presented itself in the form of a new technique called imagined contact. The imagined contact hypothesis is the idea that simply imagining intergroup contact with an out-group member may promote more positive intergroup attitudes and prepare individuals for future contact (Crisp & Turner, 2009, 2012).

At first glance, one may expect strategies of mental simulation to be relatively insubstantial, especially set against the visceral realities of intergroup conflict and deep-rooted prejudices. However, a brief examination of its use in other domains reveals mental simulation to be a powerful tool to elicit behavior change (for review see Crisp, Birtel, & Meleady, 2011). For instance, health psychologists have used mental imagery to foster the achievement of health-related goals (e.g. Greitemeyer & Würz, 2006; Sherman & Anderson, 1987). Clinicians have incorporated mental simulation into relapse prevention techniques (Marlatt & Gordon, 1985) and to improve motor learning in rehabilitation settings (Page, Levine, Sisto, & Johnston, 2001). Consumer researchers have capitalized on peoples' capacity for mental simulation to facilitate purchase intentions (e.g. Escalas & Luce, 2003, 2004). Furthermore, it has been used in education to improve students' academic achievement (e.g. Pham & Taylor, 1999; Ratcliff et al., 1999). The beneficial use of mental simulation to improve performance and motivation in sports settings has also been documented by a number of athletes and is supported by a large body of research (e.g. Feltz & Landers, 1983). In social psychology, research shows that simply imagining a particular social context can have the same effect on attitudes and behavior as the real experience (Blair, Ma, & Lenton, 2001; Garcia, Weaver, Moskowitz, & Darley, 2002).

The theoretical significance and applied utility of mental simulation therefore provides a sound basis for its application to the area of intergroup relations. If imagining a particular social context can activate the same processes as the direct experience, it follows that when people imagine intergroup contact they should engage in processes that parallel the processes involved in actual intergroup contact. For example, they may think about how they would feel during the interaction, and how this would influence their perceptions of that out-group member. In turn, this should lead to more positive evaluations of the out-group, similar to the effects of face-to-face contact (Turner, Crisp, & Lambert, 2007). This contention has now received a great deal of empirical support (for meta-analysis of over seventy studies, see Miles & Crisp, 2014). In what follows, we provide an overview of research that demonstrates the impact of imagined contact on a range of phenomena related to the reduction of prejudice and intergroup bias.

Intergroup Attitudes and Stereotypes. Turner et al. (2007) provided the first demonstration of the ability of imagined contact to improve intergroup attitudes. In three experiments, the authors demonstrated that participants asked to imagine a positive interaction with an out-group member subsequently expressed more positive attitudes towards those groups, compared to participants who did not. Two studies showed that young participants who imagined themselves engaging in a positive interaction with an elderly person subsequently showed less in-group favoring bias in attitudinal evaluations. The third study replicated this bias-reduction effect with a different stigmatized group. Heterosexual male participants who imagined talking to a homosexual man subsequently evaluated homosexual men, in general, more positively.

Even from the earliest enquiry, then, it is clear that simply imagining positive contact experiences with social groups that differ from our own can make us feel warmer towards that group. Subsequent research has replicated the positive attitudinal effects of imagined contact across a range of target groups successfully reducing stigma on the basis of nationality (e.g. Stathi & Crisp, 2008; Vezzali, Crisp, Stathi, & Giovannini, 2015), ethnicity (e.g. Husnu & Crisp, 2010; Stathi, Cameron, Hartley, & Bradford, 2014), religion (e.g. Birtel & Crisp, 2012b; Turner & Crisp, 2010), as well as mental health (e.g. West & Bruckmüller, 2013; West, Holmes, & Hewstone, 2011) and weight (e.g. Turner & West, 2012). These attitudinal effects of imagined contact have been observed at both the explicit and implicit level (Turner & Crisp, 2010; Vezzali, Capozza, Giovannini, & Stathi, 2012).

Beyond affective intergroup attitudes, research has also shown that imagined contact successfully reduces negative intergroup cognitions. Stathi, Tsantila and Crisp (2012), for instance, found that participants who imagined a positive encounter with a schizophrenic person reported weakened stereotypic perceptions of schizophrenic people in general. Similarly, Brambilla, Ravenna and Hewstone (2012) found that imagined contact enhanced perceptions of warmth and competence of envied and paternalized groups, respectively (see also Cameron, Rutland, Turner, Holman-Nicolas, & Powell, 2011; Giacobbe, Stukas, & Farhall, 2013). Imagined contact has even been shown to reduce susceptibility to stereotype threat, where the awareness of a negative stereotype held towards one's own group inadvertently produces stereotype confirmatory decrements in behavior (Abrams et al., 2008; Crisp & Abrams, 2009).

Emotions. Intergroup interactions have the potential for creating intense social anxiety because people do not want to appear prejudiced or be perceived as incompetent communicators. This negative affect evoked by the prospect of having to engage in an intergroup encounter is known as intergroup anxiety (Stephan & Stephan, 1985). Intergroup anxiety can lead to the expectation that intergroup interactions will be difficult (Britt, Boniecki, Vescio, Biernat, & Brown, 1996) and to the avoidance of intergroup interactions altogether (Plant & Devine,

2003). If contact does occur, feelings of intergroup anxiety can poison the interaction (Shelton & Richeson, 2005). Importantly, imagined contact has been shown to successfully reduce these fears and negative expectations. Turner et al. (2007) established that reductions in intergroup anxiety statistically explained the effect of imagined contact on out-group attitudes. This mediating role of intergroup anxiety has subsequently been replicated across task variants and target out-groups (e.g. Birtel & Crisp, 2012a; Husnu & Crisp, 2010; Stathi, Crisp, Turner, West, & Birtel, 2012; Turner et al., 2007; West et al., 2011).

Beyond anxiety, other friendship related emotions also seem to play a role in the imagined contact effect. Imagined contact has been shown to increase out-group trust, broadly defined as a positive expectation about the intentions and behavior of an out-group towards the in-group (Lewicki, McAllister, & Bies, 1998). Turner, West and Christie (2013) found that, compared to participants in a control condition, participants who imagined contact with an asylum seeker (Study 1), or a gay man (Study 2), reported more positive attitudes towards, and trust in members of the out-group (see also Pagotto, Visintin, De Iorio, & Voci, 2013). Imagined contact can also increase empathy with the out-group. Kuchenbrandt, Eyssel and Seidel (2013) found that German students who imagined a positive, cooperative encounter with a stranger from the Roma community expressed significantly more empathy towards this group than participants who completed a no-contact control condition. Husnu and Crisp (2015) have also demonstrated that imagined contact enhanced perspective taking—the cognitive component of empathy. Participants who imagined contact reported less out-group prejudice as a result of taking the perspective of the out-group or "putting themselves in their shoes".

Behavior. Research suggests that imagined contact techniques may prove important not just because they serve to combat stereotypes and encourage more positive attitudes and emotions, but because they also foster an interest in engaging in future interactions with out-group members. Husnu and colleagues first demonstrated this effect in the context of prolonged conflicts in Cyprus (Crisp, Husnu, Meleady, Stathi, & Turner, 2010; Husnu & Crisp, 2010). Turkish Cypriot and Greek Cypriot participants who imagined having contact with members of the opposite group subsequently expressed greater intentions to positively engage with the previously stigmatized groups in the future (see also Asbrock, Gutenbrunner, & Wagner, 2013; Birtel & Crisp, 2012b; Stathi, Crisp, & Hogg, 2011). This effect has been shown to last at least one week following the experimental session (Vezzali, Capozza, Stathi, & Giovannini, 2012; Vezzali, Stathi, Crisp, & Capozza, 2015) and can be enhanced by instructions to form an elaborated imagined contact scenario that specifies when and where the interaction took place (Husnu & Crisp, 2010).

In a similar vein, imagined contact has also been shown to increase contact self-efficacy. Perceptions of self-efficacy represent another important variable known to precede and predict behavior (Bandura, 1986). Across three studies, Stathi and colleagues (2011) demonstrate that after imagining positive contact with a single out-group member, participants felt more confident in their ability to interact effectively with the out-group in general. These results are complemented by evidence that imagined contact can also change approach and avoidance behavioral tendencies. Turner and colleagues (2013) observed that after imagined contact, participants reported an increased desire to get to know and spend time with members of the out-group, and a weaker desire to keep their distance from them (see also Vezzali, Crisp, et al., 2015, Study 2).

While the previous findings rely on self-reported measures of approach behavior, Turner and West (2012) have provided corroborating evidence with an unobtrusive behavioral measure of approach. Participants were informed that they would shortly be taking part in a discussion with an out-group member, either an obese individual (Study 1) or a Muslim person (Study 2). Participants were asked to set out two chairs in preparation for this discussion. The distance placed between the chairs by the participant constituted the dependent variable. In both studies, participants who had engaged in an imagined contact manipulation subsequently placed the chairs significantly closer than those in the control condition. Taken together, these findings suggest that imagined contact can be used as a pre-contact tool to help prepare people for direct contact. Mentally rehearsing a positive encounter with a member of a target out-group removes contact inhibitions that go hand in hand with existing prejudices and leads to a more positive approach towards the out-group.

Other research has demonstrated that when individuals do come into some form of contact with out-group members, imagined contact can help oil the wheels of social interaction. Birtel and Crisp (2012a) examined whether imagined contact may counteract the detrimental effect of intergroup anxiety on the quality of intergroup communication. Participants were asked to record a video message to introduce themselves to an out-group member. Independent coders rated the quality of nonverbal communicative behavior within the videos, including how relaxed or strained, open or guarded the participant appeared. The authors reported that while higher anxiety predicted lower quality of communication, this relationship was eliminated following imagined contact. West and colleagues have recently supported these findings within the context of a face-to-face interaction (West, Turner, & Levita, 2015). The target out-group in this case was people with schizophrenia. After completing either the imagined contact or control simulation, participants were asked to have a two-minute conversation with a person with schizophrenia (actually, a confederate). Imagined contact was found to buffer against physiological stress in anticipation of the interaction, and improve the perceived quality of the interaction. These findings are important because they suggest that imagined contact may not only encourage individuals to seek out direct contact, but help ensure that these experiences are maximally effective when they do occur.

Advances in intergroup relations

The application of mental simulation techniques to the area of intergroup relations has provided an intervention capable of reducing prejudice when actual contact is impossible or unlikely. As we have seen, there is now consistent evidence that imagined contact can have a beneficial effect on a range of phenomena related to the reduction of intergroup bias. Of course, there are questions that are still outstanding. In this section of the chapter, we offer an agenda for future investigations concerning the ability for imagined contact to reduce prejudice and break down barriers between different social groups. Specifically, we focus on three key questions that we believe represent important next steps for the field.

1. *How Far-Reaching is the Behavioral Impact of Imagined Contact?* Intergroup contact research has been criticized for an excessive focus on self-reported attitudes (as has indeed the field of social psychology more generally, Baumeister, Vohs, & Funder, 2007). Notwithstanding the considerable evidence that imagined contact can improve intergroup attitudes, the ultimate goal of contact interventions is an improvement in intergroup relations. It is positive behavior towards members of other groups that is most likely to result in a harmonious society (Turner et al., 2013). It is therefore important for research to investigate the effects of imagined contact on indicators of positive intergroup behavior, as well as attitudes. As we have seen, some progress has recently been made towards this aim. We now have a growing collection of studies demonstrating that imagined contact can reduce interpersonal distance (Turner & West, 2012) and improve intergroup communication (Birtel & Crisp, 2012a; West et al., 2015). Going forward, we believe one of the most important goals for imagined contact research is to extend this evidence base on the behavioral consequences of imagined contact.

It will be important to understand, for instance, whether imagined contact reduces discriminatory behavior. So far, the few studies that have employed behavioral measures following imagined contact have measured only behavior towards the out-group. As yet, we have no data on how behavior towards out-group members following imagined contact compares to that towards in-group members (but see Stathi et al., 2014, for an investigation focusing on intergroup attitudes that showed bias was reduced by increases in out-group evaluations). Without this comparison, we cannot conclude that imagined contact necessarily reduces intergroup behavioral bias (it may, for instance, simply increase positive behaviors to both in-group and out-group members to the same extent, maintaining the intergroup differentiation). Future research should go on to measure behavior towards in-group members to provide a point of comparison. This will allow us to confirm whether any in-group favoring bias present in baseline conditions are reduced or eliminated following imagined contact.

It will also be important to examine behavior within the context of an actual intergroup encounter. So far, research has measured behavior within anticipated, or virtual encounters, with the exception of West and colleagues (2015) who asked participants to interact with a confederate who was alleged to have schizophrenia. After imagining a positive encounter with someone with schizophrenia, participants were asked to have a 2-minute conversation with the confederate. The confederate reported that interactions with participants in the imagined contact conditions were generally more positive in nature than participants in the control condition. It will now be important for research to replicate the results of this single study. Replications that extend these findings to other intergroup contexts when cues to the out-group status of the interaction partner are more salient (e.g. skin color, accent), and where behavior is monitored over a longer period of time will also be important. Further, if the encounter occurs with a real out-group member (rather than a confederate), it will also be possible to investigate whether, by changing the way the participant behaves towards them, imagined contact may have knock-on effects for the out-group member's intergroup attitudes.

Studying behavior within the context of intergroup encounters will also provide the opportunity to study other behaviors beyond interaction quality. For example, if imagined contact oils the wheels to social interaction, we may expect that imagining contact prior to the completion of a problem-solving task with an out-group member will improve performance and productivity by reducing losses from poor coordination (Diehl & Stroebe, 1987). Such findings would be informative for organizations and attempts to increase performance in diverse workgroups.

2. *Does Imagined Contact Increase the Likelihood of Engaging in Actual, Direct Contact in the "Real World"?* One of the primary functions of imagined contact may be as a pre-contact tool to increase individuals' readiness to pursue and sustain future, direct intergroup contact (Crisp et al., 2010). While two comparative investigations have provided encouraging results regarding the relative strength of imagined and direct contact interventions on intergroup attitudes (Giacobbe et al., 2013; Vezzali, Stathi, et al., 2015), imagined contact techniques will have the widest benefits if they not only encourage more tolerant attitudes and positive behavior, but also help break down barriers to future, direct contact between groups. In this way, imagined contact may lead to a cascade of contact, with further benefits for intergroup relations (Crisp & Turner, 2009).

It has been robustly established that imagined contact increases individuals' intentions to engage in future cross-group interactions (Asbrock et al., 2013; Birtel & Crisp, 2012b, Husnu & Crisp, 2010; Stathi et al., 2014; Vezzali, Capozza, Stathi, et al., 2012; Vezzali, Crisp, et al., 2015). In fact, meta-analytic tests reveal that the effects of imagined contact on intentions are stronger than its effect on attitudes (Miles & Crisp, 2014). It is less well established, however, whether such intentions translate into actual contact experience. Some evidence has recently been provided by Vezzali, Crisp and colleagues (2015, Study 2). The authors asked a cohort of Italian students who were about to embark on a college exchange program to imagine a positive encounter with a native from the host country. A questionnaire administered on their return revealed that, compared to those who did not complete the intervention, students reported less anxiety towards natives; reduced anxiety was in turn associated with spending more time with natives during a subsequent foreign exchange trip.

While these findings from Vezzali, Stathi and colleagues (2015) are encouraging regarding the potential for imagined contact to increase the likelihood that direct contact will be instigated, the only evidence we have so far still relies on self-reported measures. There are, of course, limitations to using questionnaires that ask people to report what they will do, or what they have done. People often fail to translate their intentions into action, and accordingly behavioral intentions do not always correlate highly with actual behavior ("intention-behavior gap"; Sheeran, 2002). Moreover, self-reported subjective measures of past behavior (as well as hypothetical future behaviors) may be biased by social desirability concerns (Ganster, Hennessey, & Luthans, 1983) and motivations to appear unprejudiced (Plant & Devine, 1998). Put simply, people will not always do what they say they will do, and have not always done what they say they have done. For this reason, it is important that these results are supplemented with other methodological approaches, beyond self-reports.

Although they are more resource-intensive, observational methods may be of value here. For instance, if participants are incidentally placed in a holding area with several other individuals, some in-group members and some out-group members, where do they sit, who do they talk to? Does imagined contact increase the chance that individuals will initiate a conversation with an out-group member? Might contact-seeking behavior even generalize to other out-groups, beyond the target for imagined contact? (For discussion of such secondary transfer effects of imagined contact, see Harwood, Paolini, Joyce, Rubin, & Arroyo, 2011). Concepts from social network analysis may also have utility. For instance, researchers could examine the degree of intergroup connectedness in children's social networks following school-based imagined contact interventions. How might imagined contact experiences perpetuate through children's social networks over time? We know that imagined contact increases intentions to engage in future contact, as well as approach tendencies towards out-groups. It will now be important to go one step further and demonstrate that these effects are translated into actual direct contact experience. Greater methodological diversification may help answer this remaining question.

3. *Can Imagined Contact Buffer Against the Detrimental Effects of Negative Direct Contact Experiences?* We also identify the possible use of imagined contact to protect against the harmful effects of negative contact experience as another important line for future research. Little attention has been paid to the possible effects of negative contact experiences. This is potentially problematic—increasing social diversity will provide opportunities for both positive and negative contact (Barlow et al., 2012). Some recent findings have shown that while positive contact is reliably associated with decreases in prejudice and social distance, negative contact is associated with increased prejudice (Aberson, 2015; Barlow et al., 2012, Dhont & Van Hiel, 2009; Graf, Paolini, & Rubin, 2014; Pettigrew & Tropp, 2011). Indeed findings suggest that although negative contact experiences generally occur less frequently than positive experiences (Graf et al., 2014), they may be more strongly linked to increased prejudice than positive contact is to its reduction (Barlow et al., 2012; Dhont & Van Hiel, 2009; Paolini, Harwood, & Rubin, 2010). These recent findings highlight a need for more research to understand how we can limit the potential of negative contact to poison intergroup relations. Here, we call for research to consider the contribution of imagined contact to this aim.

Paolini and colleagues (2014) provided some initial evidence that past experience of positive intergroup contact may buffer against the impact of subsequent negative experiences. They had previously demonstrated that negative contact causes higher category salience than positive contact (Paolini et al., 2010). Given that category salience facilitates the generalization process by which attitudes towards the contacted out-group member generalize to the out-group as a whole (Brown & Hewstone, 2005), this may explain why negative contact has a greater capacity to increase prejudice than positive contact has to decrease it. Importantly, in a second investigation, Paolini and colleagues (2014) demonstrated that this effect was eliminated when individuals had a prior history of high quality intergroup contact.

If past experiences of positive contact can protect against the detrimental effects of negative encounters, it would be interesting to examine whether imagined contact could work in a similar way. We know that there is power in the very concept of contact. Could imagined contact therefore represent a means of building or strengthening this catalog of positive contact experience that protects against the harmful effects of discrete negative contact experiences? Might individuals be less inclined to generalize negative feelings towards the contacted individual to the out-group as a whole after imagined contact exposure? We believe that investigating the possibility of implementing imagined contact as a tool to buffer against negative contact experiences represents an important, and timely, direction for future research.

It will also be interesting to examine whether imagined contact can buffer against negative contact experiences by reducing the propensity to interpret them as such in the first place. Imagined contact has been shown to increase individuals' expectations that future contact will be positively toned (Husnu & Crisp, 2010). It is also well-established that we have a general tendency to search for and attend to information consistent with our expectations more readily than information that disconfirms our expectations (Trope & Thompson, 1997). Might it therefore be the case that, when imagined contact is used as a precursor to contact, behaviors exhibited by out-group members, particularly more ambiguous behaviors, may be more be likely to be construed positively rather than negatively? In other words, after imagined contact individuals may be more willing to give out-group members the "benefit of doubt", and see the positives in their actions. It will be interesting for future research to examine whether imagined contact may help to avoid potential misinterpretations that can blight encounters and worsen intergroup relations.

Advances beyond intergroup relations

While the focus of current imagined contact applications has been to improve intergroup relations, we argue that they may have broader utility even beyond this domain. In this final section, we introduce some recent research programs that have begun to implement imagined contact techniques to tackle a broad range of issues, some of which are quite distal to the domain in which it was first developed.

We examine three new applications: to economic decision-making, virtual cooperation and innovation training.

Economic Decision-Making. We have recently adopted methods from behavioral economics to consider how imagined contact may influence decisions when individuals encounter so-called "social dilemmas". A social dilemma describes a situation in which individuals must decide between behavior that benefits the self, or behavior that benefits the collective (Dawes, 1980). The dilemma arises because individuals are always individually better off when they choose the personally rewarding, non-cooperative choice. However, if all individuals do this, everyone will end up worse off than if they all chose to cooperate and work together. The earliest paradigm developed to study social dilemmas is the prisoner's dilemma (Axelrod, 1980; Rapoport & Chammah, 1965). The prisoner's dilemma is based upon a hypothetical prison-sentencing scenario in which two individuals are suspected of a crime. The police have insufficient evidence to arrest either suspect so they are both taken into questioning and offered the same deal. If one suspect testifies against his accomplice, and the accomplice remains silent, the betrayer will walk free and the accomplice will receive a long prison sentence. If both suspects testify against each other, they will both receive an intermediate prison sentence. If both remain silent, they will both receive a short prison sentence. Each suspect must make their decision individually, without knowing that of the other. So, in this situation, each prisoner is better off testifying than remaining silent. However, the outcome obtained when both testify is worse than if they had both remained silent.

These social dynamics can be modelled in the laboratory using experimental economic games (Axelrod, 1980; Rapoport & Chammah, 1965). The prisoner's dilemma game usually involves two decision makers. Each decision maker is asked to make a private, binary choice between either a cooperative or non-cooperative option. Participants receive monetary payoffs as a function of their choice, and the choice of the other participant. The non-cooperative choice represents the dominant choice as it provides a higher payoff than the cooperative choice. However, if both players select the non-cooperative choice, they both receive lower payment than if both had cooperated. Joint welfare is maximized when both participants choose to cooperate.

In a recent study, we examined the effect of imagined contact on cooperation towards an out-group member within the prisoner's dilemma game (Meleady & Seger, 2016). The study was conducted with an online community sample via Amazon's Mechanical Turk (MTurk). An analysis of the demographics of MTurk workers shows that the majority of users are located in either America or India (Ross, Irani, Silberman, Zaldivar, & Tomlinson, 2010). We utilized this dichotomy within our experimental procedure. Participants were recruited from America, and the target out-group was Indians. Participants were randomly assigned to either an imagined contact or control condition. They were then told that they were going to be asked to complete a two-player financial decision-making task with another participant recruited for this study from either America or India. In fact, participants were always told they had been assigned to a partner from the national out-group. Participants choose whether to cooperate with this individual in pursuit of joint welfare, or compete in pursuit of their own selfish interests. The results demonstrated that participants were more likely to make the prosocial, cooperative choice when they had previously imagined a positive encounter with a member of the out-group (vs. control). This effect held when accounting for the role of previous contact with the out-group, as well as participant's tendency to respond in socially desirable ways.

In a second study, we sought to replicate these findings and confirm that they held in the reverse intergroup context. This time, Indians were the participant group, and Americans became the target out-group. The results confirmed that Indian participants were more likely to exhibit cooperative (vs. competitive) behavior towards Americans when they had first imagined positive contact with a member of the out-group. In a third study, we then turned to consider mediating processes. Reverting back to the American sample with Indians as the target out-group, we found that the effect of imagined contact on economic behavior was mediated by increased trust towards the out-group partner. After imagined contact, participants were more trusting of their out-group partner, and thus more inclined to make the cooperative choice that carries the risk of exploitation.

These initial findings suggest that imagined contact may help to resolve the tension between individual gain and social efficiency. The prisoner's dilemma used within these investigations has important applications to economics and business. Imagine two competing firms, say UltraTech and TechStar. Each firm must individually decide on a pricing strategy. They best exploit their shared market when they both charge a similarly high price. A company could choose however to set a competitive low price and win customers away from the rival. In this situation, the low pricing strategy is comparative to testifying and the high price is comparative to remaining silent. While the low price represents each firm's dominant strategy, the outcome when both companies employ this strategy is worse for each than that of both cooperating (Wiley, 1988). It remains for future research to consider whether the simulated social interaction techniques developed within the imagined contact domain could be implemented into training techniques to promote optimal outcomes in business settings.

Virtual Cooperation. Recently, we have conducted a program of research that used an adapted imagined contact technique to improve group decision-making across "virtual networks" (i.e. where actual or direct interaction between group or team members is not possible; Meleady, Hopthrow, & Crisp, 2013). Social dilemmas occur not just between individuals (or groups), but also within groups. A group of friends faces a social dilemma, for instance when dining out at a restaurant and agreeing to split the bill evenly. If individuals act out of self-interest, they could enjoy a steak at a bargain price as the extra cost of this meal is split among the group. However, if everyone reasons accordingly, the group will end up with an extremely large bill and everyone will be worse off than if they had all ordered modestly. In these situations, the pursuit of self-interest leads to less optimal collective outcomes.

One of the most consistent findings in experimental social dilemmas research is the positive effect group discussion has on cooperative decision-making (Sally, 1995). The most widely accepted explanation of the group discussion effect suggests that discussion provides group members with the opportunity to develop, and become committed to, a perceived group consensus to cooperate. This coordination of behavior serves to reduce the fear of exploitation and risk associated with the cooperative choice (Bouas & Komorita, 1996; Kerr & Kaufman-Gilliland, 1994). However, while this group discussion effect is robust among laboratory groups, many real-world dilemmas are not faced by small face-to-face groups, but by large and often faceless groups (e.g. residents deciding whether to honor a hose pipe ban, or contribute their time towards a neighbourhood watch scheme). Direct communications among all decision makers is therefore often not a feasible solution to the problem (Messick & Brewer, 1983).

Our investigation examined whether the benefits of group discussion could be capitalized upon indirectly through an adapted imagined contact technique (Meleady et al., 2013). The imagery instructions used were based on those developed in the imagined contact literature, requiring participants to imagine themselves engaging in a social interaction for several minutes, and to write a few lines to describe what they had imagined. However, rather than asking participants to imagine an interaction with a single person from an out-group, they instead imagined an interaction with multiple members of their fellow, decision-making group. Participants were told that they had been assigned to a group of six to take part in a virtual group decision-making task (an N-player prisoner's dilemma, or public good dilemma). Participants assigned to the experimental condition were asked to imagine engaging in a group discussion with the other group members in which they reached a consensus to cooperate. Those in the control condition instead listed reasons in favor of the cooperative choice. We found reliable evidence across five studies that cooperation decisions were successfully elevated in the imagined group discussion condition compared to the control. Imagined discussion successfully encouraged cooperation among group members with both cooperative and competitive prior motives (McClintock, 1978), and persisted even when participants imagined they were part of a larger decision-making group (twelve or twenty four persons).

Consistent with research on imagined intergroup contact, we found that imagined group discussion activated concepts consonant with those underlying the direct experience. The effect of imagined group discussion was statistically explained by expectations of a cooperative group consensus, the same process underlying the direct group discussion effect (Bouas & Komorita, 1996; Kerr & Kaufman-Gilliland, 1994). We can conclude that, in the absence of the opportunity for direct negotiation among decision makers, imagined contact and adapted imagined contact techniques may provide an effective way of encouraging collectively rational decision-making. Much like we observe in the imagined intergroup contact domain, imagined group discussion activates processes paralleling those underlying the effects of direct group discussion and thereby encourages cooperative group decision-making.

It remains now for future research to test these techniques within more applied contexts. These techniques may also be valuable in the workplace for instance. In organizations, it is often crucial that members devote extra time, energy and effort to interdependent tasks and actions that benefit the group or organization (De Cremer & van Knippenberg, 2002). Imagined contact techniques may provide a versatile and inexpensive tool to help convert employees' motivation from self-interest to collective interest. These techniques may be implemented when face-to-face negotiations between team members prove expensive or unfeasible (e.g. within multi-national organizations). Indeed, even when sizes are small enough to allow direct communication among all decision makers, direct discussion can be logistically difficult, especially given the recent rise of the remote employee during the Internet era. Imagined contact techniques could provide a simple and versatile approach to maximizing virtual work. We argue that future research should productively consider how imagined contact techniques may present unique implications for development of effective and efficient teamwork, both between and within groups.

Innovation Training. Another interesting extension of imagined contact techniques has asked participants to imagine themselves in a stereotypical or counter-stereotypical role. That is, instead of being asked to imagine interacting with a given target, participants are asked to imagine *being* that person. This work is grounded in research that suggests that exposure to experiences that challenge individuals' existing expectations and perspectives can facilitate improvements in cognitive flexibility—a key component of innovation in problem solving (Crisp & Meleady, 2012; Crisp & Turner, 2011).

When individuals are exposed to experiences that challenge their stereotypes, it requires them to inhibit easily accessible information and engage in more elaborate, systematic processing (Fiske & Neuberg, 1990; Hutter & Crisp, 2006). Importantly, research shows that just as with physical exercise, repeatedly "working out" the brain literally improves its processing power (Jaeggi, Buschkuehl, Jonides, & Shah, 2011; Muraven, Baumeister, & Tice, 1999). The idea then, is that exposure to counter-stereotypes can train a more active and complex cognitive style.

Di Bella and Crisp (2016) employed an adapted imagined contact technique as a tool to provide exposure to a counter-stereotypical experience. The participant group of interest here was female undergraduate students who were studying STEM subjects (science, technology, engineering and math). This is a group who is persistently confronted with gender stereotypes, which can actually impair performance (known as the "stereotype threat" effect; Steele & Aronson, 1995). Importantly, Di Bella and Crisp found that imagined contact can provide a tool to overcome these challenges. Participants were asked to imagine themselves in either a stereotypical career role (nursing) or counter-stereotypical career role (computing). Results demonstrated that women who completed the counter-stereotypical imagination task subsequently displayed superior performance on a quantitative judgment test. It seems then that using imagined contact as a tool to actively confront the stereotypes may help inoculate these individuals from the negative impact of stereotype "threats" and even help boost the brain's "innovation muscle".

In terms of applications, one could envision how imagined contact techniques could be integrated into campaigns to improve recruitment and retention of people in to unconventional career routes. It is well documented, for instance, that there is a "leaky pipeline" problem in education relating to gender. At the undergraduate level, approximately half of students in STEM programs are women, yet only 27 percent of the people working in STEM-related occupations end up being female (Di Bella & Crisp, 2015). Behavioral science can contribute to efforts to increase the number of women in these occupations. For instance, the application of counter-stereotypic imagery techniques in education may be one of the ways we can counter the negative impact of stereotypes on aspiration and ambition. The extended benefits of countering stereotypic bias in this way are potentially wide-ranging. For instance, research illustrates that diversity at work, as in other domains, can stimulate greater levels of creativity and innovative thinking across the board (Crisp & Turner, 2011, Galinsky et al., 2015).

Closing remarks

Imagined contact offers a way of accessing the benefits of intergroup contact where actual contact is unlikely or impossible. With all the attention now devoted to this topic, imagined contact research is advancing rapidly in many directions. There is now consistent evidence that imagined contact can impact a range of outcomes related to the promotion of positive intergroup relations. In this chapter, we outlined the research conducted to date, and identified a number of further lines of enquiry that we believe will be important to firmly establish imagined contact as a powerful strategy to generate behavioral change within the realm of intergroup relations. We also reviewed several emerging research programs that suggest the benefits of imagined contact techniques may extend even beyond prejudice reduction. We hope that research will continue to thrive by investigating how imagined contact may be of value not only as a means for improving intergroup relations, but also as a way of fostering individual and collective capabilities in domains key to our future potential, prosperity, progress and growth.

References

Aberson, C.L. (2015). Positive intergroup contact, negative intergroup contact, and threat as predictors of cognitive and affective dimensions of prejudice. *Group Processes and Intergroup Relations, 18*, 743–60. doi: 10.1177/1368430214556699.

Abrams, D., Crisp, R.J., Marques, S., Fagg, E., Bedford, L., & Provias, D. (2008). Threat inoculation: Experienced and imagined intergenerational contact prevents stereotype threat effects on older people's math performance. *Psychology and Aging, 25*, 934–9. doi: 10.1037/a0014293

Allport, G.W. (1954). *The nature of prejudice*. New York, NY: Addison-Wesley.

Asbrock, F., Gutenbrunner, L., & Wagner, U. (2013). Unwilling, but not unaffected–Imagined contact effects for authoritarians and social dominators. *European Journal of Social Psychology*, *43*, 404–12. doi: 10.1002/ejsp.1956

Axelrod, R. (1980). More effective choice in the Prisoner's Dilemma. *Journal of Conflict Resolution*, *24*, 379–403. doi: 10.1177/002200278002400301

Bandura, A. (1986). *Social foundations of thought and action: A social cognitive theory*. Englewood Cliffs, NJ: Prentice-Hall, Inc.

Barlow, F.K., Paolini, S., Pederson, A., Hornsey, M.J., Radke, H.R., Harwood, J., ... & Sibley, C.G. (2012). The contact caveat: Negative contact predicts increased prejudice more than positive contact predicts reduced prejudice. *Personality and Social Psychology Bulletin*, *38*, 1629–43. doi: 10.1177/0146167212457953

Baumeister, R.F., Vohs, K.D., & Funder, D.C. (2007). Psychology as the science of self-reports and finger movements: Whatever happened to actual behaviour. *Perspectives on Psychological Science*, *2*, 396–403. doi: 10.1111/j.1745-6916.2007.00051.x

Birtel, M.D., & Crisp, R.J. (2012a). Imagining intergroup contact is more cognitively difficult for people higher in intergroup anxiety but this does not detract from its effectiveness. *Group Processes and Intergroup Relations*, *15*, 744–61. doi: 10.1177/1368430212443867

Birtel, M.D., & Crisp, R.J. (2012b). "Treating" prejudice: An exposure-therapy approach to reducing negative reaching towards stigmatized groups. *Psychological Science*, *23*, 1379–86. doi: 10.1177/0956797612443838

Blair, I.V., Ma, J.E., & Lenton, A.P. (2001). Imagining stereotypes away: The moderation of implicit stereotypes through mental imagery. *Journal of Personality and Social Psychology*, *81*, 828–41. doi: 10.1037//0022-3514.81.5.828

Bouas, K.S., & Komorita, S.S. (1996). Group discussion and cooperation in social dilemmas. *Personality and Social Psychology Bulletin*, *22*, 1144–50. doi: 10.1177/01461672962211005

Brambilla, M., Ravenna, M., & Hewstone, M. (2012). Changing stereotype content through mental imagery: Imagining intergroup contact promotes stereotype change. *Group Processes and Intergroup Relations*, *15*, 305–15. doi: 10.1177/1368430211427574

Britt, T.W., Boniecki, K.A., Vescio, T.K., Biernat, M., & Brown, L.M. (1996). Intergroup anxiety: A person x situation approach. *Personality and Social Psychology Bulletin*, *22*, 1177–88. doi: 10.1177/01461672962211008

Brown, R., & Hewstone, M. (2005). An integrative theory of intergroup contact. *Advances in Experimental Social Psychology*, *37*, 255–343. doi: 10.1016/S0065-2601(05)37005-5

Cameron, L., Rutland, A., Turner, R., Holman-Nicolas, R., & Powell, C. (2011). "Changing attitudes with a little imagination": Imagined contact effects on young children's intergroup bias. *Anales de Psicología*, *27*, 708–17.

Crisp, R.J., & Abrams, D. (2009). Improving intergroup attitudes and reducing stereotype threat: An integrated contact model. *European Review of Social Psychology*, *19*, 242–84. doi: 10.1080/10463280802547171

Crisp, R.J., Birtel, M., & Meleady, R. (2011). Mental simulations of social thought and action: Trivial tasks or tools for transforming social policy. *Current Directions in Psychological Science*, *20*, 261–4. doi: 10.1177/0963721411413762

Crisp, R.J., Husnu, S., Meleady, R., Stathi, S., & Turner, R.N. (2010). From imagery to intention: A dual route model of imagined contact effects. *European Review of Social Psychology*, *21*, 188–236. doi: 10.1080/10463283.2010.543312

Crisp, R.J., & Meleady, R. (2012). Adapting to a multicultural future. *Science*, *336*, 853–5. doi: 10.1126/science.1219009

Crisp, R.J., & Turner, R.N. (2009). Can imagined interactions produce positive perceptions? Reducing prejudice through simulated social contact. *American Psychologist*, *64*, 231–40. doi: 10.1037/a0014718

Crisp, R.J., & Turner, R.N. (2011). Cognitive adaptation to the experience of social and cultural diversity. *Psychological Bulletin, 137*, 242–66. doi: 10.1037/a0021840

Crisp, R.J., & Turner, R.N. (2012). The imagined contact hypothesis. *Advances in experimental social psychology, 46*, 125–82. doi: 10.1016/B978-0-12-394281-4.00003-9

Dawes, R.M. (1980). Social dilemmas. *Annual Review of Psychology, 31*, 169–93. doi: 10.1146/annurev.ps.31.020180.001125

De Cremer, D., & van Knippenberg, D. (2002). How do leaders promote cooperation? The effects of charisma and procedural fairness. *Journal of Applied Psychology, 87*, 858–66. doi: 10.1037/0021-9010.87.5.858

Dhont, K., & Van Hiel, A. (2009). We must not be enemies: Interracial contact and the reduction of prejudice among authoritarians. *Personality and Individual Differences, 46*, 172–7. doi: 10.1016/j.paid.2008.09.022

Di Bella, L., & Crisp, R.J. (2015). The perls of being a female scientist *Scientific American Mind*.

Di Bella, L., & Crisp, R.J. (2016). Women's adaptation to STEM domains promotes resilience and lesser reliance on heuristic thinking. *Group Processes and Intergroup Relations, 19*, 184–201. doi: 10.1177/1368430215596074

Diehl, M., & Stroebe, W. (1987). Productivity loss in brainstorming groups: Toward the solution of a riddle. *Journal of Personality and Social Psychology, 53*, 497–509. doi: 10.1037/0022-3514.53.3.497

Dixon, J.A., & Durrheim, K. (2003). Contact and the ecology of racial division: Some varieties of informal segregation. *British Journal of Social Psychology, 42*, 1–23. doi: 10.1348/014466603763276090

Escalas, J.E., & Luce, M.F. (2003). Process versus outcome thought focus and advertising. *Journal of Consumer Psychology, 13*, 246–54. doi: 10.1207/S15327663JCP1303–06

Escalas, J.E., & Luce, M.F. (2004). Understanding the effects of process-focused versus outcome-focused thought in response to advertising. *Journal of Consumer Research, 31*, 274–85. doi: 10.1086/422107

Feltz, D.L., & Landers, D.M. (1983). The effects of mental practice on motor skill learning and performance: A meta-analysis. *Journal of Sport Psychology, 5*, 271–351.

Fiske, S.T., & Neuberg, S.L. (1990). A continuum model of impression formation, from category-based to individuating processes: Influence of information and motivation on attention and interpretation. *Advances in experimental social psychology, 23*, 1–74. doi: 10.1016/S.065–2601(08)603017–2

Galinsky, A.D., Todd, A.R., Homan, A.C., Phillips, K.W., Apfelbaum, E.P., Sasaki, S.J., . . . & Maddux, W.W. (2015). Maximizing the gains and minimizing the pains of diversity: A policy perspective. *Perspectives on Psychological Science, 10*, 742–8. doi: 10.1177/1745691615598513

Ganster, D.C., Hennessey, H.W., & Luthans, F. (1983). Social desirability response effects: Three alternative models. *Academy of Management Journal, 26*, 321–31. doi: 10.2307/255979

Garcia, S.M., Weaver, K., Moskowitz, G.B., & Darley, J.M. (2002). Crowded minds: The implicit bystander effect. *Journal of Personality and Social Psychology, 83*, 843–53. doi: 10.1037/0022-3514.83.4.843

Giacobbe, M.R., Stukas, A.A., & Farhall, J. (2013). The effect of imagined versus actual contact with a person with a diagnosis of schizophrenia. *Basic and Applied Social Psychology, 35*, 265–71. doi: 10.1080/01973533.2013.785403

Graf, S., Paolini, S., & Rubin, M. (2014). Negative intergroup contact is more influential, but positive intergroup contact is more common: Assessing contact prominence and contact prevalence in five Central European countries. *European Journal of Social Psychology*, *44*, 536–47. doi: 10.1002/ejsp.2052

Graham, J.A., & Cohen, R. (1997). Race and sex as factors in children's sociometric ratings and friendship choices. *Social Development*, *6*, 355–72. doi: 10.1111/j.1467-9507.1997. tb00111.x

Greitemeyer, T., & Würz, D. (2006). Mental simulation and the achievement of health goals: The effect of goal difficulty. *Cognition, Imagination, and Personality*, *25*, 239–51. doi: 10.2190/d4ua-rqfq-0h5t-w9yy

Harwood, J., Paolini, S., Joyce, N., Rubin, M., & Arroyo, A. (2011). Secondary transfer effects from imagined contact: Group similarity affects the generalization gradient. *British Journal of Social Psychology*, *50*, 180–9. doi: 10.1348/014466610X524263

Husnu, S., & Crisp, R.J. (2010). Imagined intergroup contact: A new technique for encouraging greater inter-ethnic contact in Cyprus. *Peace and Conflict: Journal of Peace Psychology*, *16*, 97–108. doi: 10.1080/10781910903484776

Husnu, S., & Crisp, R.J. (2015). Perspective-taking mediates the imagined contact effect. *International Journal of Intercultural Relations*, *44*, 29–34. doi: 10.1016/j.ijintrel.2014.11.005

Hutter, R.R.C., & Crisp, R.J. (2006). Implications of cognitive busyness for the perception of category conjunctions. *Journal of Social Psychology*, *146*, 253–6. doi: 10.3200/SOCP. 146.2.

Jaeggi, S.M., Buschkuehl, M., Jonides, J., & Shah, P. (2011). Short- and long-term benefits of cognitive training. *Proceedings of the National Academy of Sciences of the United States of America*, *108*, 10081–6. doi: 10.1073/pnas.1103228108

Kerr, N.L., & Kaufman-Gilliland, C.M. (1994). Communication, commitment, and co-operation in social dilemmas. *Journal of Personality and Social Psychology*, *66*, 513–29. doi: 10.1037/0022–3514.66.3.513

Kuchenbrandt, D., Eyssel, F., & Seidel, S.K. (2013). Cooperation makes it happen: Imagined intergroup cooperation enhances the positive effects of imagined contact. *Group Processes and Intergroup Relations*, *16*, 635–47. doi: 10.1177/1368430212470172

Lewicki, R.J., McAllister, D.J., & Bies, R.J. (1998). Trust and distrust: New relationships and realities. *The Academy of Management Review*, *23*, 438–58. doi: 10.5465/AMR.1998. 926620

Marlatt, G.A., & Gordon, J.R. (1985). *Relapse prevention: Maintenance strategies in addictive behaviour change*. New York, NY: Guilford.

McClintock, C.G. (1978). Social values: Their definition, measurement and development. *Journal of Research & Development in Education*, *12*, 121–37.

Meleady, R., Hopthrow, T., & Crisp, R.J. (2013). Simulating social dilemmas: Promoting cooperative behaviour through imagined group discussion. *Journal of Personality and Social Psychology*, *104*, 839–53. doi: 10.1037/a0031233

Meleady, R., & Seger, C. (2016). Imagined contact encourages prosocial behaviour towards outgroup members. *Group Processes and Intergroup Relations*. doi: 10.1177/13684302 15612225

Messick, D.M., & Brewer, M.B. (1983). Solving social dilemmas: A review. In L. Wheeler & P. Shaver (Eds.), *Review of personality and social psychology* (pp. 11–44). Beverly Hills, CA: Sage.

Miles, E., & Crisp, R.J. (2014). A meta-analytic test of the imagined contact hypothesis. Group Processes and Intergroup Relations, 17, 3–26. doi: 10.1177/1368430213510573

Muraven, M., Baumeister, R., & Tice, D.M. (1999). Longitudinal improvement of self-regulation through practice: Building self-control strength through repeated exercise. *Journal of Social Psychology*, *139*, 446–57. doi: 10.1080/00224549909598404

Page, S.J., Levine, P., Sisto, S., & Johnston, M. (2001). A randomized, efficacy and feasibility study of imagery in acute stroke. *Clinical Rehabilitation, 15*, 233–402. doi: 10.1191/026921501672063235

Pagotto, L., Visintin, E.P., De Iorio, G., & Voci, A. (2013). Imagined intergroup contact promotes cooperation through outgroup trust. *Group Processes and Intergroup Relations, 16*, 209–16. doi: 10.1177/1368430212450057

Paolini, S., Harwood, J., & Rubin, M. (2010). Negative intergroup contact makes group memberships salient: Explaining why intergroup conflict endures. *Personality and Social Psychology Bulletin, 36*, 1723–38. doi: 10.1177/0146167210388667

Paolini, S., Harwood, J., Rubin, M., Husnu, S., Joyce, N., & Hewstone, M. (2014). Positive and extensive intergroup contact in the past buffers against the disproportionate impact of negative contact in the present. *European Journal of Social Psychology, 44*, 548–62. doi: 10.1002/ejsp.2029

Pettigrew, T.F., & Tropp, L.R. (2006). A meta-analytic test of intergroup contact theory. *Journal of Personality and Social Psychology, 90*, 751–83. doi: 10.1037/0022-3514.90.5.751

Pettigrew, T.F., & Tropp, L.R. (2011). *When groups meet: The dynamics of intergroup contact.* New York, NY: Psychology Press.

Pham, L.B., & Taylor, S.E. (1999). From thought to action; effects of process- versus outcome-based mental simulations on performance. *Personality and Social Psychology Bulletin, 25*, 250–60. doi: 10.1177/0146167299025002010

Plant, E.A., & Devine, P.G. (1998). Internal and external motivation to response without prejudice. *Journal of Personality and Social Psychology, 75*, 811–32. doi: 10.1037/0022-3514.75.3.811

Plant, E.A., & Devine, P.G. (2003). The antecedents and implications of interracial anxiety. *Personality and Social Psychology Bulletin, 29*, 790–801. doi: 10.1177/0146167203029006011

Rapoport, A., & Chammah, A.M. (1965). *Prisoner's dilemma.* Ann Arbor, MI: University of Michigan Press.

Ratcliff, C.D., Czuchry, M., Scarberry, N.C., Thomas, J.C., Dansereau, D.F., & Lord, C.G. (1999). Effects of directed thinking on intentions to engage in beneficial activities: Actions versus reasons. *Journal of Applied Social Psychology, 29*, 994–1009. doi: 10.1111/j.1559-1816.1999.tb00136.x

Ross, J., Irani, L., Silberman, M.S., Zaldivar, A., & Tomlinson, B. (2010). Who are the crowdworkers? Shifting demographics in mechanical turk. In E. Mynatt & D. Schoner (Eds.), *CHI EA '10: Proceedings of the 28th of the international conference extended abstracts on human factors in computing systems* (pp. 2863–72). New York, NY: ACM.

Sally, D. (1995). Conversation and cooperation in social dilemmas: A meta-analysis. *Rationality and Society, 7*, 58–92. doi: 10.1177/1043463195007001004

Sheeran, P. (2002). Intention-behaviour relations: A conceptual and empirical review. *European Review of Social Psychology, 12*, 1–36. doi: 10.1080/14792772143000003

Shelton, J.N., & Richeson, J.A. (2005). Intergroup contact and pluralistic ignorance. *Journal of Personality and Social Psychology, 88*, 91–107. doi: 10.1037/0022-3514.88.1.91

Sherman, S.J., & Anderson, C.A. (1987). Decreasing premature termination from psychotherapy. *Journal of Social and Clinical Psychology, 5*, 298–312.

Stathi, S., Cameron, L., Hartley, B., & Bradford, S. (2014). Imagined contact as a prejudice-reduction intervention in schools: The underlying role of similarity and attitudes. *Journal of Applied Social Psychology, 44*, 536–46. doi: 10.1111/jasp.12245

Stathi, S., & Crisp, R.J. (2008). Imagining intergroup contact promotes projection to outgroups. *Journal of Experimental Social Psychology, 44*, 943–57. doi: 10.1016/j.jesp.2008.02.003

Stathi, S., Crisp, R.J., & Hogg, M.A. (2011). Imagined intergroup contact enables member-to-group generalization. *Group Dynamics: Theory, Research and Practice, 15*, 275–84. doi: 10.1037/a0023752

Stathi, S., Crisp, R.J., Turner, R.N., West, K., & Birtel, M. (2012). Using mental imagery to promote positive intergroup relations. In D.W. Russel & C.A. Russel (Eds.), *The psychology of prejudice: Interdisciplinary perspectives on contemporary issues* (pp. 235–50). Hauppauge, NY: Nova Science Publishers.

Stathi, S., Tsantila, K., & Crisp, R.J. (2012). Imagining intergroup contact can combat mental health stigma by reducing anxiety, avoidance and negative stereotyping. *Journal of Social Psychology, 152*, 746–57. doi: 10.1080/00224545.2012.697080

Steele, C.M. & Aronson, J. (1995). Stereotype threat and the intellectual test performance of African Americans. *Journal of Personality and Social Psychology, 69*, 797–811. doi: 10.1037/0022-3514.69.5.797

Stephan, W.G., & Stephan, C.W. (1985). Intergroup anxiety. *Journal of Social Issues, 41*, 157–75. doi: 10.1111/j.1540-4560.1985.tb01134.x

Trope, Y., & Thompson, E.P. (1997). Looking for truth in all the wrong places? Asymmetric search of individuating information about stereotyped group members. *Journal of Personality and Social Psychology, 73*, 229–41. doi: 10.1037/0022-3514.73.2.229

Turner, R.N., & Crisp, R.J. (2010). Imagining intergroup contact reduces implicit prejudice. *British Journal of Social Psychology, 49*, 129–42. doi: 10.1348/014466609X419901

Turner, R.N., Crisp, R.J., & Lambert, E. (2007). Imagining intergroup contact can improve intergroup attitudes. *Group Processes and Intergroup Relations, 10*, 427–41. doi: 10.1177/1368430207081533

Turner, R.N., & West, K. (2012). Behavioural consequences of imagining intergroup contact with stigmatized outgroups. *Group Processes and Intergroup Relations, 15*, 193–202. doi: 10.1177/1368430211418699

Turner, R.N., West, K., & Christie, Z. (2013). Out-group trust, intergroup anxiety, and out-group attitude as mediators of the effect of imagined intergroup contact on intergroup behavioural tendencies. *Journal of Applied Social Psychology, 43*, 196–205. doi: 10.1111/jasp.12019

Vezzali, L., Capozza, D., Giovannini, D., & Stathi, S. (2012). Improving implicit and explicit intergroup attitudes using imagined contact: An experimental intervention with elementary school children. *Group Processes and Intergroup Relations, 15*, 203–12. doi: 10.1177/1368430211424920

Vezzali, L., Capozza, D., Stathi, S., & Giovannini, D. (2012). Increasing outgroup trust, reducing infrahumanization, and enhancing future contact intentions via imagined intergroup contact. *Journal of Experimental Social Psychology, 48*, 437–40. doi: 10.1016/j.jesp.2011.09.008

Vezzali, L., Crisp, R.J., Stathi, S., & Giovannini, D. (2015). Imagined intergroup contact facilitates intercultural communication for college students on academic exchange programmes. *Group Processes and Intergroup Relations, 18*, 66–75. doi: 10.1177/1368430214527853

Vezzali, L., Stathi, S., Crisp, R.J., & Capozza, D. (2015). Comparing direct and imagined intergroup contact among children: Effects on outgroup stereotypes and helping intentions. *International Journal of Intercultural Relations, 49*, 46–53. doi: 10.1016/j.ijintrel.2015.06.009

West, K., & Bruckmüller, S. (2013). Nice and easy does it: How perceptual fluency moderates the effectiveness of imagined contact. *Journal of Experimental Social Psychology, 49*, 254–62. doi: 10.1016/j.jesp.2012.11.007

West, K., Holmes, E., & Hewstone, M. (2011). Enhancing imagined contact to reduce prejudice against people with schizophrenia. *Group Processes and Intergroup Relations, 14*, 407–28. doi: 10.1177/1368430210387805

West, K., Turner, R.N., & Levita, L. (2015). Applying imagined contact to improve physiological responses in anticipation of intergroup interactions and the perceived quality of these interactions. *Journal of Applied Social Psychology, 45*, 425–36. doi: 10.1111/jasp.12309

Wiley, J.S. (1988). Reciprocal altruism as a felony: Antitrust and the Prisoner's Dilemma. *Michigan Law Review, 86*, 1906–28. doi: 10.2307/1289073

9

INTERGROUP CONTACT AMONG CHILDREN

Lindsey Cameron and Rhiannon N. Turner

Key words: intergroup contact, cross-group friendship, children, prejudice

Intergroup contact theory and research have benefitted from a long tradition of academics focused on understanding *children's* experience of intergroup contact. This is a particularly important area of research because children typically spend a large proportion of their lives in educational contexts, where—provided there is sufficient diversity—high-quality contact between members of different social groups is relatively easy to introduce. Furthermore, as structured learning environments, schools are an ideal context in which to implement contact-based *interventions*. Moreover, when one considers that intergroup attitudes and experiences garnered in childhood provide the building blocks of adult social attitudes and intergroup behaviors (Abrams & Killen, 2014), the value of understanding the experience and impact of contact and childhood is palpable.

In the past 10 years, research on contact in schools has gained momentum as leading psychologists have drawn together social and developmental perspectives to understand the impact of intergroup contact in childhood (e.g. Bigler & Liben, 2007; Rutland & Killen, 2015; Rutland, Killen, & Abrams, 2010). In this chapter, we will highlight recent research that demonstrates the unique theoretical, methodological and applied insights *developmental* social psychology can provide regarding the power of intergroup contact, the underlying processes of the intergroup contact effect and the design and implementation of contact-based interventions. We will identify a number of current and future lines of enquiry that are critical for the advancement of our understanding of intergroup contact in childhood, and among adults.

Intergroup contact in schools: contemporary developmental social psychological research

Seventy years of developmental social psychology research has demonstrated the positive impact of intergroup contact on children's intergroup attitudes and behaviors, across a range of intergroup contexts, including nondisabled–disabled, German–Turkish, African American-European American, to name a few (Aboud et al., 2012; Beelmann & Heinemann, 2014; Lemmer & Wagner, 2015). A key strength of this developmental research is the breadth of positive outcomes of intergroup contact that have been uncovered. Intergroup contact among children has been linked with more positive intergroup attitudes (Davies, Tropp, Aron, Pettigrew, & Wright, 2011; Turner, Tam, Hewstone, Kenworthy, & Cairns, 2013), more prosocial behavioral intentions (Abbott & Cameron, 2014) and inclusive, diverse friendships (Bagci, Kumashiro, Smith, Blumberg, & Rutland, 2014; Feddes, Noack, & Rutland, 2009; Jugert, Noack, & Rutland, 2011).

Žeželj, Jakšic and Jošic (2015), for example, examined the impact of supervised contact between Serbian and Roma children in schools. They found that Serbian children with more contact subsequently held more positive attitudes towards Roma in general. Meanwhile, Vezzali and Giovannini (2012) found that secondary school pupils in Italy who had experienced more high quality contact with immigrants (i.e. the interaction was viewed as being more pleasant) held more positive attitudes towards members of that group, but were also more positive towards two groups unrelated to the initial contact, the disabled and gay people.

Research has also identified outcomes unique to the developmental literature including how children manage diverse friendship groups (Ruck, Park, Killen, & Crystal, 2011), the impact of contact on children's developing socio-cognitive capacities such as perspective-taking (Vezzali & Giovannini, 2012), moral reasoning (Crystal, Killen, & Ruck, 2008), cultural openness (Abbott & Cameron, 2014) and wider cultural perspectives (Gieling, Thijs, & Verkuyten, 2014; Verkuyten, Thijs, & Bekhuis, 2010).

Cross-group friendship

One form of contact that has dominated the field is the study of *cross-group friendship* (e.g. Davies et al., 2011; Pettigrew & Tropp, 2008; Turner, Hewstone, Voci, Paolini, & Christ, 2007). Research has consistently identified cross-group friendship as a particularly effective form of contact, among adults and children, and in multiple social contexts (e.g. Davies et al., 2011; Pettigrew & Tropp, 2008; Turner, Hewstone, & Voci, 2007). Among many positive outcomes, children with cross-group friendships are more positive towards the out-group (e.g. Feddes et al., 2009; Titzmann, Brenick, & Silbereisen, 2015), report reduced anxiety about interacting with out-group members and trust the out-group more (Davies et al., 2011; Turner & Feddes, 2011; Turner, Hewstone, & Voci, 2007).

Turner, Hewstone and Voci (2007) examined the impact of cross-group friendship in the context of White–South Asian relations in the UK. They found that White school children aged 8–11 years and White and South Asian students aged 11–15 years with cross-group friends held more positive out-group attitudes. More recently, Turner, Tam et al. (2013) examined cross-group friendship in high schools in Northern Ireland, where intergroup relations are marred by a history of conflict, and segregation between the Catholic and Protestant communities persists. Children attending integrated (mixed Catholic and Protestant) schools reported more cross-group friendships than children attending segregated (either Catholic or Protestant) schools. Moreover, across both types of schools, children with more cross-group friendships also expressed greater empathy, more self-disclosure, and a more positive general attitude towards the other community.

As with intergroup contact in general, research on cross-group friendships among children has also identified a range of benefits that extend beyond intergroup relations, such as increased social competence (e.g. Lease & Blake, 2005) and increased self-esteem, well-being and resilience (Bagci et al., 2014; Fletcher, Rollins, & Nickerson, 2004). Children with cross-group friends also show greater leadership potential and appear to be more popular (Kawabata & Crick, 2008; Lease & Blake, 2005).

Cross-group friendship appears to be a pivotal form of intergroup contact in achieving outcomes that are essential for good intergroup relations. One reason for this is that these friendships are typically prolonged and intimate and involve shared activities across different social contexts and over different situations. Such contact is more likely to lead to positive intergroup attitudes (e.g. Davies et al., 2011; Wagner, van Dick, Pettigrew, & Christ, 2003). Other drivers of the cross-group friendship effect include opportunity for mutual self-disclosure (Davies et al., 2011; Turner, Hewstone, & Voci, 2007), and reduced intergroup anxiety (Paolini, Hewstone, Cairns, & Voci, 2004; Stephan & Stephan, 1985; Turner & Feddes, 2011). For instance, Turner, Hewstone and Voci (2007) found that the positive relationship between cross-group friendship and out-group attitude among White British and South Asian primary school children (aged 7–11 years) was mediated by reduced intergroup anxiety (De Tezanos-Pinto, Bratt, & Brown, 2010; Jasinskaja-Lahti, Mahonen, & Liebkind, 2011; Swart, Hewstone, Christ, & Voci, 2011; Žeželj et al., 2015).

Although children in diverse settings have the *opportunity* to form cross-group friendships, a recent debate has emerged regarding whether children take up these opportunities. The evidence to date from social developmental psychology research is mixed (see Thijs & Verkuyten, 2014, for a review). Some research has shown that children's friendship groups often do not reflect the ethnic make-up of the school: cross-race friendships are relatively uncommon (Aboud & Sankar, 2007; McDonald et al., 2013; Wilson, Rodkin, & Ryan, 2014), particularly among minority group members (Verkuyten & Kinket, 2000), are less durable and decline with age (Aboud et al., 2012).

On the other hand, recent studies paint a more optimistic picture. Children attending more diverse schools report holding more inclusive, diverse friend-ships (Bagci et al., 2014; Feddes et al., 2009; Jugert et al., 2011; Schachner, Brenick, Noack, van de Vijver, & Heizmann, 2015). For instance, in the context of Northern Ireland, Turner, Tam et al. (2013) found that children in more diverse schools (i.e. attended by Catholic and Protestant pupils) reported more cross-group friends. Meanwhile Bagci et al. (2014) also found evidence that cross-group friendships were thriving in the "super-diverse" schools of Greater London. In other words, children in mixed schools do appear to be taking up the opportunities available to them to hold cross-group friendships.

Intergroup contact interventions

Developmental social psychologists have also turned their attention to the development of contact-based interventions for use in schools. Educational programs that bring together children from different backgrounds (i.e. contact interventions) are used widely in schools (e.g. school twinning), but their design and implementation is often based on practitioners' intuition and experience, and the programs are rarely evaluated (Cameron & Rutland, 2016; Cameron & Turner, 2010). Moreover, educators rarely take into account the principles of intergroup contact when managing existing diversity in schools. This is in part due to academics' lack of engagement with practitioners, and a failure to translate research findings into practical tips on creating successful contact (see for exception Aboud et al., 2012; McKeown, 2015; Pfeifer, Brown, & Juvonen, 2007). This has led prominent social and developmental psychologists to make an urgent call for increased collaboration between practitioners and academics, which is crucial in order to maximize the impact of such education programs, and to effectively monitor their impact (e.g. Paluck & Green, 2009). Although there is much work to be done, developmental psychologists have been leading the way in terms of developing theory-based contact interventions and testing these in the field. Some key examples of such research will now be described.

Cooperative learning

One of the most established intergroup contact interventions used in schools is cooperative learning programs, such as the "jigsaw classroom" (e.g. Bratt, 2008). According to this approach, intergroup contact should be structured so as to require cooperation, in order to ensure a positive contact experience, the development of cross-group friendship and attitude change. Cummings, Williams and Ellis (2002) evaluated an intergenerational contact program, which was administered to 4th grade American children. Participants took part in a range of activities, scheduled over 8 weeks, which facilitated interaction, cooperation and collaboration between the child and a senior citizen. For example, in one task, children were asked to chart plants and their characteristics, for which they required the help of their senior partner. Results showed a significant strengthening of children's positive attitudes towards older adults following the intervention (see Bratt, 2008, for review).

Guerra and colleagues conducted a series of studies in which they not only evaluated the impact of a contact intervention, but also identified the type of contact that had maximal impact on intergroup attitudes (Guerra, Rebelo, Monteiro, & Gaertner, 2013; Guerra et al., 2010). In these studies, children experience intergroup contact over a series of weeks, while they work in diverse groups to complete a Survival Task. Guerra and colleagues also tested different forms of intergroup contact that varied in level of category salience to determine the most beneficial form of intergroup contact. In their 2013 paper, Guerra and colleagues found that children in the intervention conditions showed no significant bias (bias scores were not significantly different from zero), while children in the control group exhibited significant bias, suggesting that contact did have a significant impact on attitudes. Regarding the type of contact that was most powerful, intergroup bias was lower when the shared, Portuguese identity was emphasized (recategorization condition), but only among African Portuguese children.

Indirect contact

Another form of contact that has proven useful in the design of intergroup contact interventions for children is indirect contact. This is the experience of contact without face-to-face intergroup interaction (Crisp & Turner, 2009). An extensively investigated form of indirect contact is *extended contact*, where one is aware of or observes intergroup friendships among one's fellow in-group members (Wright, McLaughlin-Volpe, Aron, & Ropp, 1997). A number of studies have shown that young people who know in-group members with out-group friends hold more positive intergroup attitudes (e.g. De Tezanos-Pinto et al., 2010; Turner, Hewstone, & Voci, 2007; Turner, Tam, et al., 2013). For instance, in their study of Norwegian school students, De Tezanos-Pinto et al. (2010) demonstrated that those who knew in-group members with cross-group (ethnic minority) friends, held more positive attitudes towards ethnic minorities. Supporting evidence for this phenomenon has also been uncovered in the UK, among British White and South Asian teenagers in England, and Catholic and Protestant teenagers in Northern Ireland (Turner, Hewstone, & Voci, 2007; Turner, Tam, et al., 2013).

Researchers have tested a variety of interventions based on the principles of indirect contact, including extended contact and vicarious contact interventions, where children observe cross-group friendships in books and TV (e.g. Cameron, Rutland, Brown, & Douch, 2006; Vezzali, Stathi, & Giovannini, 2012). In a series of studies, Cameron and colleagues demonstrated the positive impact of story-based indirect contact interventions where children read and discussed a series of books featuring cross-group friendships (e.g. Cameron et al., 2006; Cameron, Rutland, Hossain, & Petley, 2011). Vezzali and colleagues (2012) examined the impact of books featuring positive intercultural contact on Italian teenagers' intergroup orientation. They found that Italian teenagers who read such books subsequently expressed more positive attitudes, reduced stereotyping, and a greater desire for future contact with immigrants. Importantly, the positive effect of indirect contact interventions appears to go beyond children's intergroup attitudes and intentions: recent research shows such interventions can also enhance cross-group friendship formation (Vezzali, Stathi, Giovannini, Capozza, & Visintin, 2015). There is also some evidence that learning about in-group peers' experience of contact through mass media can promote intergroup tolerance (Liebkind, Mahonen, Solares, Solheim, & Jasinskaja-Lahti, 2014; Liebkind & McAlister, 1999), as can watching

TV shows such as Sesame Street, which involve positive intergroup encounters (see Mares & Pan, 2013, for a review).

Another form of indirect contact that has been translated into prejudice-reduction intervention tools for use in schools is *imagined contact*. Imagined contact is the mental simulation of a social interaction with an out-group member (Crisp & Turner, 2009; see Miles & Crisp, 2014, for a meta-analysis). This technique typically asks participants to imagine interacting with a member of another group, hold a conversation with an out-group member on a bus for instance. Research has demonstrated its positive impact on intergroup attitudes, emotions, intentions and behavior (Miles & Crisp, 2014). For instance, Turner, West and Christie (2013) showed 16- to 17-year-old British high school students a picture of a same-gendered asylum seeker who had recently arrived from Zimbabwe. They were asked to imagine having a positive interaction with this individual, before writing a detailed outline of the interaction they imagined. Compared to control participants, students who imagined contact reported a greater desire to approach asylum seekers (e.g. get to know them, find out more about them), a relationship that was mediated by an increase in out-group trust.

An imagined contact intervention has also been developed for younger children. Stathi, Cameron, Hartley and Bradford (2014) used pictures and photos to create a child-friendly imagined contact intervention. Over three weekly sessions, White children used the pictures to create three stories about a day spent with an Asian child. Those who took part in the intervention subsequently held more positive intergroup attitudes, greater willingness to engage in future contact, and perceived themselves to be more similar to Asians, compared with a control group who did not undertake the intervention. Vezzali, Stathi, Crisp and Capozza (2015) have also developed an imagined contact intervention for use with young children, where the intervention is delivered in small cooperative groups. Importantly, the positive impact of this intervention increased intergroup helping intentions and reduced stereotypes 1 week after the intervention (see also Vezzali, Stathi, Crisp, Giovannini et al., 2015, Study 1).

The impact of indirect contact is underlined by a number of recent reviews that have highlighted the positive effect of indirect forms of contact among children and adults (Lemmer & Wagner, 2015; Miles & Crisp, 2014). In fact, recent research suggests that, with regards to short-term effects at least, there may be little difference between the impact of direct and indirect contact (Lemmer & Wagner, 2015; Vezzali, Stathi, Crisp, & Capozza, 2015). Furthermore, indirect contact interventions are appealing in a practical sense: they are relatively easy to implement, as they are cheaper, quicker and logistically easier to carry out than interventions involving direct contact. They are also thought to be particularly useful in contexts where opportunity for direct, face-to-face contact is limited (e.g. Cameron et al., 2011). However, it is important to acknowledge that indirect contact and simulated contact interventions have been met with some skepticism within developmental psychology, where the long-term impact of such interventions, and their ability to change negative attitudes, has been questioned (e.g. Bigler & Hughes, 2010).

The above research demonstrates the wide-ranging, positive impact of intergroup contact in childhood, affecting various aspects of children's intergroup attitudes, behavior and cognitive capacities, but also illustrates the ways in which developmental social psychology has advanced our understanding of intergroup contact. Furthermore, contact-based interventions provide a promising means of promoting positive intergroup attitudes in schools (Beelmann & Heinemann, 2014). However, findings around the relationship between opportunity for contact and the uptake of cross-group friendships are mixed, and much work remains to be done to integrate intergroup contact theory with practice. These questions form some of the main lines of current and future research for the field.

Future directions

In our review of contemporary research outlined above, we have illustrated the unique theoretical, methodological and applied insights *developmental* social psychology can provide regarding the study of intergroup contact. Here we outline directions for future research that are vital for our understanding of intergroup contact, and reflect these three areas of impact: theory, methods and practice.

Theoretical impact: bringing together social and developmental psychological approaches

Within developmental social psychology, there is currently a strong push for research, theories and prejudice-reduction interventions that take into account not only the impact of contact, but also the role of children's developing cognitive abilities in *shaping* how children perceive and experience contact and diversity. Leading academics argue that children's emerging socio-cognitive abilities provide a lens through which children experience diversity (e.g. Rutland & Killen, 2015). These abilities include socio-cognitive skills such as empathy and perspective-taking, reconciliation of attitudes and expectation of difference (Aboud, 1981; Aboud & Levy, 2000). In line with this argument, a number of theories have been developed that consider the role of social context (including contact, and perceived intergroup relations) and children's cognitive abilities in shaping intergroup attitudes and behaviors (e.g. Bigler & Liben, 2007; Rutland & Killen, 2015; Rutland et al., 2010). This emphasis on socio-cognitive development has implications for contact interventions: following their meta-analysis, Beelmann and Heinemann (2014) recommended that intergroup contact interventions to improve intergroup attitudes should be coupled with techniques to strengthen children's socio-cognitive abilities. Future research is needed to examine the complex interplay of children's emerging socio-cognitive abilities, and contact.

Identifying the predictors of cross-group friendship

Until recently, developmental (and adult) research has tended to focus on uncovering the impact of cross-group friendship on various attitudinal outcomes.

In other words, cross-group friendship is viewed as the "starting point" in the contact-attitude relationship. Relatively little attention has been paid to the individual and contextual conditions that *lead* to cross-group friendship. This limitation has been highlighted by numerous high-profile psychologists who call for more research to identify the predictors of cross-group friendship (e.g. Aboud & Sankar, 2007; Bagci et al., 2014; Thijs & Verkuyten, 2014; Turner & Cameron, 2016; Tropp, O'Brien, & Migacheva, 2014). According to Esses and Dovidio (2002), the bias in research to date means that "we know a great deal about what happens when different group members come into contact but we know little about the conditions likely to promote intergroup contact in the first place" (p. 1212; see also Davies et al., 2011).

A number of very recent studies have brought to light some potential barriers and promoters of cross-group friendship, including acculturation attitudes, identity and teachers' diversity attitudes (e.g. Grütter & Meyer, 2014; Schachner et al., 2015; Stefanek, Strohmeier, & van de Schoot, 2015). For instance, Stefanek et al. (2015) examined preference for same-cultural friendships in multicultural secondary schools in Austria, among non-immigrant, immigrant Turkish and immigrant former Yugoslavian adolescents aged between 13 and 17 years ($N = 256$). They found that both acculturation-related predictors (identity, cultural pride) and contextual variables (level of diversity in the classroom) predicted same-cultural friendships.

Other potential predictors of cross-group friendship are in-group and out-group norms for acceptance of cross-group friendship (e.g. De Tezanos-Pinto et al., 2010). In a rare qualitative study examining the predictors of cross-group friendship, Aboud and Sankar (2007) found that negative peer norms were often cited by children as a key barrier to cross-group friendship development. More recently, Tropp et al. (2014) found, among African and European American children aged 9 to 13 years, that holding inclusive peer norms (believing your friends want to include the out-group in their friendship group) predicted interest in cross-group friendship. Jugert et al. (2011) found that peer norms regarding the acceptability and likelihood of cross-group friendship shaped children's cross-group friendship choices: when more supportive peer norms were in place, subsequent cross-group friendships were more likely. Importantly, Jugert et al.'s findings were longitudinal and so the *direction* of causality, from norms and attitude to subsequent cross-group friendship, is clear. These findings held for majority and minority group children.

Schachner et al. (2015) examined the role of structural and normative conditions in predicting cross-group friendships among an ethnically diverse sample of adolescents ($N = 842$) in Germany, with an immigrant or non-immigrant background. Perceived contact norms of teachers and students were measured by asking children about perceived unequal treatment by teachers, support for contact by teachers, perceived unequal treatment by students, perceived support for contact by students and perceived support for cooperation by students. Perceived cultural difference was also measured. Analyzes revealed that immigrant children perceived more negative contact norms than non-immigrant children. Furthermore, the strongest predictor of cross-group friendships was the availability of out-group members to form friendships with. However, when controlling for opportunity for contact, reported cross-group friendship was significantly predicted by perceived norms for intergroup contact, and (negatively predicted by) perceived cultural differences. These findings were relatively consistent across the immigrant and non-immigrant children.

Meanwhile, a longitudinal study among children and adolescents showed that greater general self-efficacy, in addition to initial willingness to engage in contact and higher perceived societal norms supporting the friendship, predicted the development of cross-group friendship over time (Titzmann et al., 2015). To date, there has been very little research to examine the role of intergroup anxiety as a *predictor* of children's cross-group friendships, but multiple studies among adults point to its key role in determining frequency and success of future intergroup interactions. Adults who have lower intergroup anxiety are more likely to "approach" rather than avoid intergroup interactions, and these interactions are more successful (Page-Gould, Mendoza-Denton, & Tropp, 2008). Although we know little about the key drivers of young people's anxiety about cross-group friendship, it is likely that perceived difference and fear of breaking peer norms to "stick to their own" could be important factors.

Another critical requirement for cross-group friendships to emerge from the literature is the opportunity to maintain the friendship beyond the school gates, and meet friends across varied contexts in the wider community (Hughes, 2014; Stringer et al., 2009). Research has shown that active friendships, held across multiple settings, for instance doing homework together (Wagner et al., 2003), appear to have a particularly strong impact on intergroup attitudes. Indeed, Aboud and Sankar (2007) also identified lack of opportunity to play together in multiple settings outside of school as a major barrier to cross-group friendship.

In order to fully understand the changing face of cross-group friendship throughout children's development, it is essential that we identify the promoters and obstacles to such friendships, including socio-cognitive, contextual and societal barriers. In order to achieve this large-scale research, using mixed methods to study children's friendships over extended periods of time is essential. Findings from such research can be translated into successful contact interventions, and be used to advise diverse schools on how to create schools where diverse friendships can flourish.

Confidence in contact

A new perspective on intergroup contact that considers many of the predictors of cross-group friendship identified here provides a useful model by which to study cross-group friendships, and design interventions to promote such relationships. Uniquely, this empirically driven model has at its starting point the *predictors* of cross-group friendship, and has at its centerpiece what we believe is a major predictor of cross-group friendship: confidence in contact (Turner & Cameron, 2016). Confidence in contact can be defined as being "a state of readiness for positive contact, whereby children have the skills, beliefs, and experience for successful contact" (Turner & Cameron, 2016, p. 218). We argue that "confidence in contact" is driven by individual characteristics (e.g. socio-cognitive abilities such as empathy, intergroup anxiety, intergroup attitudes) and situational variables (e.g. peer norms, school climate). Children with high confidence in contact will feel comfortable during intergroup contact, and experience less intergroup anxiety prior to and during intergroup interactions, they will feel secure in the knowledge that they will be accepted by the out-group and they will have the skills necessary for successful intergroup interaction. They will be "contact-ready", open to form friendships with cross-group members should the opportunity arise, and benefit from the positive outcomes of successful cross-group friendship (Turner & Cameron, 2016). Future research is needed to test the specific pathways of this model. However, it is a promising line of enquiry, and reflects many of the themes identified in this chapter, bringing together a number of key potential predictors of cross-group friendship, including socio-cognitive skills, social norms, self-efficacy, anxiety and the social context.

Looking beyond intergroup attitudes

While the majority of research on intergroup contact has focused on its impact on intergroup attitudes, stereotypes and affect, there is a growing movement, particularly in social psychology, to examine the impact of contact on intergroup *behavior* and particularly involuntary behavioral responses (e.g. Page-Gould et al., 2008; West & Turner, 2014). One motivation behind this movement is that intergroup behavior shapes intergroup interactions. Therefore, in order to truly improve intergroup relations, contact should impact on these perhaps more resistant outcomes. Social psychologists working with adults are leading the way in this line of research, and have uncovered a positive effect of contact on participant seating preference, physiological anxiety responses and nonverbal behavior during intergroup interactions (Page-Gould et al., 2008; West & Turner, 2014).

Research examining the impact of contact on less explicit and more behavioral responses is also gathering pace in social developmental psychology. In the past 10 years, more implicit measures of children's attitudes and stereotypes have been developed (e.g. Dunham, Baron, & Banaji, 2008; Rutland, Cameron, Milne, & McGeorge, 2005). Researchers have also examined the impact of contact on more behavioral measures of intergroup orientation, such as prosocial intentions in intergroup bullying scenarios (Abbott & Cameron, 2014). The study of the impact of contact on actual behaviors is more limited, but research is gaining momentum. For instance, McKeown, Stringer and Cairns (2015) used behavioral mapping to examine the impact of contact on seating preferences of teenagers in Northern Ireland, and Al Ramiah, Schmid, Hewstone and Floe (2015) examined where children choose to sit in the cafeteria. Meanwhile, Leman and Lam (2008) observed conversation style used by children during intergroup interactions, and the impact on group membership of subsequent playmate choices. Determining the impact of contact (direct and indirect) on young people's interactions in intergroup situations, including nonverbal and verbal behaviors, anxiety during contact, and cooperation, is a critical line of future research for developmental psychologists researching contact with children.

Intercultural competence

Within the fields of diversity education and social developmental psychology, a shift in focus is beginning to emerge whereby researchers are moving away from the study of attitudes and stereotypes, but are instead focusing on more global world perspectives and abilities, both as predictors and outcomes of successful intergroup contact. One such perspective or concept is that of "intercultural competence" (Barrett, Byram, Lázár, Mompoint-Gaillard, & Philippou, 2014). This is a combination of attitudes, knowledge, understanding and skills, which enables one to understand and respect people who are different from oneself, interact effectively with those people who are different from oneself, establish positive cross-cultural relationships and have a firm grasp of one's own identity in culturally diverse settings (Barrett et al., 2014). According to the intercultural competence framework proposed by Barrett and colleagues, cultural openness includes attributes such as valuing diversity, cultural openness, tolerance of ambiguity, understanding diversity, knowledge of multiple groups' beliefs and values, perspective-taking, empathy and being able to adapt to new cultural environments (Barrett et al., 2014). Based on this framework, cross-group friendships are more likely should the individuals concerned have intercultural competence, but also high quality intergroup interaction should lead to the strengthening of these abilities, attitudes and skills. Psychological research examining the impact of contact on this phenomenon is limited, but growing. Abbott and Cameron (2014), for instance examined the impact of contact on cultural openness and prosocial behavioral intentions, and found that adolescents with more experience of diversity reported being more open to other cultures, which had a positive impact on their prosocial behavioral intentions.

Researchers have also identified the effect of contact on children and adolescents' wider perspectives on the social world, including assimilation, multiculturalism and in-group appraisal (Gieling et al., 2014; Verkuyten et al., 2010). Gieling et al. (2014) examined the impact of contact on native Dutch adolescents' political tolerance for dissenting beliefs and practices among Muslims, a salient out-group in this Dutch context. The researchers found that intergroup contact increased political tolerance, and this relationship was mediated by decreased assimilation ideology (i.e. the belief that immigrants should assimilate to the Dutch culture and give up their own culture as soon as possible). This is consistent with the idea that contact leads to deprovincialization: an enriched, and less egocentric, view of the world (see also Verkuyten et al., 2010).

This shift in perspective reflects a growing need to understand the wide-ranging impact contact and diversity can have on young people. Moreover, it reflects a shift in focus towards what we can learn from young people and how they adapt to and indeed thrive in diverse schools every day. This focus on the intercultural competence, attitudes, knowledge, understanding and skills required for successfully navigating diverse settings will, we believe, be a central focus of future research on intergroup contact.

The experience of contact among minority group members

The majority of intergroup contact research (among adults and children) focuses on the impact of contact among majority group members. However, in their meta-analysis, Tropp and Pettigrew (2005) report that the relationship between contact and prejudice is significantly weaker among minority, compared with majority group participants. To date, we know very little about what is driving this difference. Recent research such as that of Schachner and colleagues (2015) suggests that intergroup contact has a weaker effect on intergroup attitudes among minorities, because the contact conditions are less optimal for them and they perceive less supportive norms for contact. Likewise, the barriers to cross-group friendship may differ for majority and minority status children. When considering intergroup contact, minority children may be more concerned about being victimized or discriminated against, whereas majority children may be concerned about "saying the wrong thing" (Aboud & Sankar, 2007).

So far in this chapter, we have focused on the positive impact of contact on intergroup relations. However, researchers are becoming increasingly aware of the potential negative consequences of attending diverse schools, particularly among minority children and adolescents (e.g. Brown et al., 2013). For instance, Brown et al. (2013) examined the longitudinal relationship between British South Asian 5- to 11-year-olds' desire for intergroup contact, their developing ethnic and national identity, and their social adjustment. Analyzes revealed that children who were initially positive about and wanted more contact with the ethnic majority out-group and wanted to maintain their ethnic identity showed a subsequent increase in peer acceptance, but a decline in emotional well-being. The authors concluded that minority children with a high desire for contact may be opening themselves up to name-calling and peer rejection in diverse environments, as they attempt to form friendships with the ethnic majority group, with detrimental effects for their emotional well-being (see also Stefanek et al., 2015). Increasing our understanding of minorities' experience of contact (including the predictors and outcomes) is essential to the future of intergroup contact research, not least a key requirement of cross-group friendship is that it should be an enjoyable experience, requiring commitment, and being valued, by both parties.

Moving beyond the "two group" approach

The majority of research has focused on racial, ethnic and religious intergroup contact, usually between two distinct groups. However, researchers are increasingly pointing to the complexity and richness of diversity experienced by young people in their everyday lives, where they may attend school with children from a multitude of nationalities, ethnicities and religions (Stringer et al., 2009; Thijs & Verkuyten, 2014). In order to understand the cognitive and social consequences of growing up with this level of diversity, it is essential that intergroup contact research moves away from a two group model and considers more complex contact experiences.

Closing remarks

Contemporary research on intergroup contact in children has made a number of important theoretical, methodological and applied contributions to the field. Recent developmental social psychology theories have provided a unique perspective on contact, considering the way in which experience and impact of contact is shaped by children's developing cognitive abilities (Rutland & Killen, 2015), and also identifying the impact of contact on social, cognitive and behavioral outcomes. Moreover, developmental research provides an opportunity to study the impact of contact and diversity on a scale and quality not normally achievable among adult populations. Children (often) have a unique opportunity for cross-group friendships available to them in school, and identifying the conditions (individual, socio-cognitive and contextual) that predict such friendships is an important line of future research. The "confidence in contact" perspective may provide a useful framework through which to study the conditions for cross-group friendships, as it brings together situational and individual (including socio-cognitive) barriers to and predictors of cross-group friendship. Meanwhile, while there are examples of good practice provided in this chapter, more work needs to be done to translate research findings into practice. One of the most compelling recent developments in the study of intergroup contact and prejudice in children is the shift from considering the impact of contact on specific intergroup attitudes towards considering how the experience, skills and mind-sets of young people allow them to not only manage diversity, but thrive on it. To that end, the future of intergroup contact research in children, to our mind, involves the study of the experience of contact, diversity and friendship among diverse children, identifying the conditions for positive contact, examining the outcomes of such contact and understanding the processes underlying friendship development.

References

Abbott, N.J., & Cameron, L. (2014). What makes an assertive bystander? The effect of intergroup contact, empathy, cultural openness and in-group bias on assertive bystander intervention intentions. *Journal of Social Issues, 70,* 167–82. doi: 10.1111/josi.12053

Aboud, F.E. (1981). Egocentrism, conformity, and agreeing to disagree. *Developmental Psychology, 17,* 791–9. doi: 10.1037/0012–1649.17.6.791

Aboud, F.E., & Levy, S.R. (2000). Interventions to reduce prejudice and discrimination in children and adolescents. In S. Oskamp (Ed.), *Reducing prejudice and discrimination: The Claremont Symposium on Applied Social Psychology* (9th ed, pp. 269–93). Mahwah, NJ: Erlbaum.

Aboud, F.E., & Sankar, J. (2007). Friendship and identity in a language-integrated school. *International Journal of Behavioral Development, 31,* 445–53. doi: 10.1177/01650254070 81469

Aboud, F.E., Tredoux, C., Tropp, L.R., Brown, C.S., Niens, U., & Noor, N.M. (2012). Interventions to reduce prejudice and enhance inclusion and respect for ethnic differences in early childhood: A systematic review. *Developmental Review, 32,* 307–36. doi: 10.1016/j.dr.2012.05.001

Abrams, D., & Killen, M. (2014). Social exclusion of children: Developmental origins of prejudice. *Journal of Social Issues, 70,* 1–11. doi: 10.1111/josi.12043

Al Ramiah, A.A., Schmid, K., Hewstone, M., & Floe, C. (2015). Why are all the White (Asian) kids sitting together in the cafeteria? Resegregation and the role of intergroup attributions and norms. *British Journal of Social Psychology, 54,* 100–24. doi: 10.1111/bjso.12064

Bagci, S.C., Kumashiro, M., Smith, P.K., Blumberg, H., & Rutland, A. (2014). Cross-ethnic friendships: Are they really rare? Evidence from secondary schools around London. *International Journal of Intercultural Relations, 41,* 125–37. doi: 10.1016/j.ijintrel.2014.04.001

Barrett, M., Byram, M., Lázár, I., Mompoint-Gaillard, P., & Philippou, S. (2014). *Developing intercultural competence through education.* Strasbourg, France: Council of Europe Publishing.

Beelmann, A., & Heinemann, K.S. (2014). Preventing prejudice and improving intergroup attitudes: A meta-analysis of child and adolescent training programs. *Journal of Applied Developmental Psychology, 35,* 10–24. doi: 10.1016/j.appdev.2013.11.002

Bigler, R.S., & Hughes, J.M. (2010). Reasons for scepticism about the efficacy of simulated social contact interventions. *American Psychologist, 65,* 132–3. doi: 10.1037/a0018097

Bigler, R.S., & Liben, L.S. (2007). Developmental intergroup theory. Explaining and reducing children's social stereotyping and prejudice. *Current Directions in Psychological Science, 16,* 162–6. doi: 10.1111/j.1467-8721.2007.00496.x

Bratt, C. (2008). The jigsaw classroom under test: No effect on intergroup relations evident. *Journal of Community and Applied Social Psychology, 18,* 403–19. doi: 10.1002/casp.946

Brown, R., Baysu, G., Cameron, L., Nigbur, D., Rutland, A., Watters, C., . . . & Landau, A. (2013). Acculturation attitudes and social adjustment in British South Asian children: A longitudinal study. *Personality and Social Psychology Bulletin, 39,* 1656–67. doi: 10.1177/0146167213500149

Cameron, L. & Rutland, A. (2016). Researcher–practitioner partnerships in the development of intervention to reduce prejudice among children. In K. Durkin, R. Schaffer (Eds.), *The Wiley handbook of developmental psychology in practice.* Chichester, UK: John Wiley & Sons, Ltd. doi: 10.1002/9781119095699.ch14DOI: 10.1002/9781119095699.ch14.

Cameron, L., Rutland, A., Brown, R., & Douch, R. (2006). Changing children's intergroup attitudes towards refugees: Testing different models of extended contact. *Child Development, 77,* 1208–19. doi: 10.1111/j.1467-8624.2006.00929.x

Cameron, L., Rutland, A., Hossain, R., & Petley, R. (2011). When and why does extended contact work? The role of high quality direct contact and group norms in the development of positive ethnic intergroup attitudes amongst children. *Group Processes and Intergroup Relations, 14,* 193–206. doi: 10.1177/1368430210390535

Cameron, L., & Turner, R.N. (2010). The applications of diversity-based interventions to reduce prejudice. In R.J. Crisp (Ed.), *The psychology of social and cultural diversity* (pp. 322–52). Malden, MA: Blackwell.

Crisp, R., & Turner, R. (2009). Can imagined interactions produce positive perceptions? Reducing prejudice through simulated contact. *American Psychologist, 64,* 231–40. doi: 10.1037/a0014718

Crystal, D., Killen, M., & Ruck, M. (2008). It's who you know that counts: Intergroup contact and judgments about race-based exclusion. *British Journal of Developmental Psychology*, *26*, 51–70. doi: 10.1348/026151007X198910

Cummings, S.M., Williams, M.M., & Ellis, R.A. (2002). Impact of an intergenerational program on 4th Graders' attitudes toward elders and school behaviors. *Journal of Human Behavior*, *6*, 91–107. doi: 10.1300/J137v06n03-06

Davies, K., Tropp, L.R., Aron, A., Pettigrew, T., & Wright, S.C. (2011). Cross-group friendships and intergroup attitudes: A meta-analytic review. *Personality and Social Psychology Review*, *15*, 332–51. doi: 10.1177/1088868311411103

De Tezanos-Pinto, P., Bratt, C., & Brown, R. (2010). What will the others think? Ingroup norms as a mediator of the effects of intergroup contact. *British Journal of Social Psychology*, *49*, 507–23. doi: 10.1348/014466609X471020

Dunham, Y., Baron, A.S., & Banaji, M.R. (2008). The development of implicit intergroup cognition. *Trends in Cognitive Sciences*, *12*, 248–53. doi: 10.1016/j.tics.2008.04.006

Esses, V.M., & Dovidio, J.F. (2002). The role of emotions in determining willingness to engage in intergroup contact. *Personality and Social Psychological Bulletin*, *28*, 1202–14. doi: 10.1177/01461672022812006

Feddes, A.R., Noack, P., & Rutland, A. (2009). Direct and extended friendship effects on minority and majority children's interethnic attitudes: A longitudinal study. *Child Development*, *80*, 377–90. doi: 10.1111/j.1467-8624.2009.01266.x

Fletcher, A.C., Rollins, A., & Nickerson, P. (2004). The extension of school-based inter- and intraracial children's friendships: Influences on psychosocial well-being. *American Journal of Orthopsychiatry*, *74*, 272–85. doi: 10.1037/0002-9432.74.3.272

Gieling, M., Thijs, J., & Verkuyten, M. (2014). Dutch adolescents' tolerance of Muslim immigrants: The role of assimilation ideology, intergroup contact, and national identification. *Journal of Applied Social Psychology*, *44*, 155–65. doi: 10.1111/jasp.12220

Grütter, J., & Meyer, B. (2014). Intergroup friendship and children's intensions for social exclusion in integrative classrooms: The moderating role of teachers' diversity beliefs. *Journal of Applied Social Psychology*, *44*, 481–94. doi: 10.1111/jasp.12240

Guerra, R., Rebelo, M., Monteiro, M.B., & Gaertner, S.L. (2013). Translating recategorization strategies into an antibias educational intervention. *Journal of Applied Social Psychology*, *43*, 14–23. doi: 10.1111/j.1559-1816.2012.00976.x

Guerra, R., Rebelo, M., Monteiro, M.B., Riek, B.M., Mania, E.W., Gaertner, S.L., & Dovidio, J.F. (2010). How should intergroup contact be structured to reduce bias among majority and minority group children? *Group Processes and Intergroup Relations*, *13*, 445–60. doi: 10.1177/1368430209355651

Hughes, J. (2014). Contact and context: Sharing education and building relationships in a divided society. *Research papers in Education*, *29*, 193–210. doi: 10.1080/02671522.2012.754928

Jasinskaja-Lahti, I., Mahonen, T.A., & Liebkind, K. (2011). Ingroup norms, intergroup contact and intergroup anxiety as predictors of the outgroup attitudes of majority and minority youth. *International Journal of Intercultural Relations*, *35*, 346–55. doi: 10.1016/j.ijintrel.2010.06.001

Jugert, P., Noack, P., & Rutland, A. (2011). Friendship preferences among German and Turkish preadolescents. *Child Development*, *82*, 812–29. doi: 10.1111/j.1467-8624.2010.01528.x

Kawabata, Y., & Crick, N.R. (2008). The role of cross-racial/ethnic friendships in social adjustment. *Developmental Psychology*, *44*, 1177–83. doi: 10.1037/0012-1649.44.4.1177

Lease, A.M., & Blake, J.J. (2005). A comparison of majority-race children with and without a minority-race friend. *Social Development*, *14*, 20–41. doi: 10.1111/j.1467-9507.2005.00289.x

Leman, P.J., & Lam, V.L. (2008). The influence of race and gender on children's conversations and playmate choices. *Child Development, 79*, 1329–43. doi: 10.1111/j.1467-8624.2008. 01191.x

Lemmer, G., & Wagner, U. (2015). Can we really reduce prejudice outside the lab? A meta-analysis of direct and indirect contact interventions. *European Journal of Social Psychology, 45*, 152–68. doi: 10.1002/ejsp.2079

Liebkind, K., Mahonen, T.A., Solares, E., Solheim, E., & Jasinskaja-Lahti, I. (2014). Prejudice-reduction in culturally mixed classrooms: The development and assessment of a theory-driven intervention among majority and minority youth in Finland. *Journal of Community and Applied Social Psychology, 24*, 325–39. doi: 10.1002/casp.2168

Liebkind, K., & McAlister, A. (1999). Extended contact through peer modelling to promote tolerance in Finland. *European Journal of Social Psychology, 29*, 765–80. doi: 10.1002/ (SICI)1099-0992(199908/09)29:5/6<765::AID-EJSP958>3.0.CO;2-J

Mares, M.L., & Pan, Z. (2013). Effects of Sesame Street: A meta-analysis of children's learning in 15 countries. *Journal of Applied Developmental Psychology, 34*, 140–51. doi: 10.1016/ j.appdev.2013.01.001

McDonald, K.L., Dashiell-Aje, E., Menzer, M.M., Rubin, K.H., Oh, W., & Bowker, J.C. (2013). Contributions of racial and sociobehavioral homophily to friendship stability and quality among same-race and cross-race friends. *Journal of Early Adolescence, 33*, 897–919. doi: 10.1177/0272431612472259

McKeown, S. (2015). *Identity, segregation and Peace-building in Northern Ireland: A social psychological perspective.* New York: Palgrave Macmillan.

McKeown, S., Stringer, M., & Cairns, E. (2015). European-American children's intergroup attitudes about peer relationships. *British Journal of Developmental Psychology, 23*, 227–50. doi: 10.1348/026151005x26101

Miles, E., & Crisp, R.J. (2014). A meta-analytic test of the imagined contact hypothesis. *Group Processes and Intergroup Relations, 17*, 3–26. doi: 10.1177/1368430213510573

Page-Gould, E., Mendoza-Denton, R., & Tropp, L.R. (2008). With a little help from my cross-group friend: Reducing anxiety in intergroup contexts through cross-group friendship. *Journal of Personality and Social Psychology, 95*, 1080–94. doi: 10.1037/0022-3514.95.5.1080

Paluck, E.L., & Green, D.P. (2009). Prejudice reduction: What works? A review and assessment of research and practice. *Annual Review of Psychology, 60*, 339–67. doi: 10.1146/annurev.psych.60.110707.163607

Paolini, S., Hewstone, M., Cairns, E., & Voci, A. (2004). Effects of direct and indirect cross-group friendships on judgments of Catholics and Protestants in Northern Ireland: The mediating role of an anxiety-reduction mechanism. *Personality and Social Psychology Bulletin, 30*, 770–86. doi: 10.1177/0146167203262848

Pettigrew, T.F., & Tropp, L.R. (2008). How does intergroup contact reduce prejudice? Meta-analytic tests of three mediators. *European Journal of Social Psychology, 38*, 922–34. doi: 10.1002/ejsp.504

Pfeifer, J.H., Brown, C.S., & Juvonen, J. (2007). Teaching tolerance in schools: lessons learned since Brown vs Board of Education about development and reduction of children's prejudice. *Social Policy Report: Giving child and youth development knowledge away, 21*, 3–23.

Ruck, M.D., Park, H., Killen, M., & Crystal, D.S. (2011). Intergroup contact and evaluations of race-based exclusion in urban minority children and adolescents. *Journal of Youth and Adolescence, 40*, 633–43. doi: 10.1007/s10964–010–9600-z

Rutland, A., Cameron, L., Milne, A., & McGeorge, P. (2005). Social norms and self-presentation: Children's implicit and explicit intergroup attitudes. *Child Development, 76*, 451–66. doi: 10.1111/j.1467-8624.2005.00856.x

Rutland, A., & Killen, M. (2015). A developmental science approach to reducing prejudice and social exclusion: Intergroup processes, social-cognitive development, and moral reasoning. *Social Issues and Policy Review, 9*, 121–54. doi: 10.1111/sipr.12012

Rutland, A., Killen, M., & Abrams, D. (2010). A new social-cognitive developmental perspective on prejudice: The interplay between morality and group identity. *Perspectives on Psychological Science, 5*, 279–91. doi: 10.1177/1745691610369468

Schachner, M.K., Brenick, A., Noack, P., van de Vijver, A.J.R., & Heizmann, B. (2015). Structural and normative conditions for interethnic friendships in multiethnic classrooms. *International Journal of Intercultural Relations, 47*, 1–12. doi: 10.1016/j.ijintrel.2015.02.003

Stathi, S., Cameron, L., Hartley, B., & Bradford, S. (2014). Imagined contact as a prejudice-reduction intervention in schools: The underlying role of similarity and attitudes. *Journal of Applied Social Psychology, 44*, 536–46. doi: 10.1111/jasp.12245

Stefanek, E., Strohmeier, D., & van de Schoot, R. (2015). Individual and classroom predictors of same cultural friendship preferences in multicultural schools. *International Journal of Behavioral Development, 39*, 255–65. doi: 10.1177/0165025414538556

Stephan, W.G., & Stephan, C.W. (1985). Intergroup anxiety. *Journal of Social Issues, 41*, 157–75. doi: 10.1111/j.1540–4560.1985.tb01134.x

Stringer, M., Irwing, P., Giles, M., McClenahan, C., Wilson, R., & Hunter, J.A. (2009). Intergroup contact, friendship quality and political attitudes in integrated and segregated schools in Northern Ireland. *British Journal of Educational Psychology, 79*, 239–57. doi: 10.1348/978185408X368878

Swart, H., Hewstone, M., Christ, O., & Voci, A. (2011). Affective mediators of intergroup contact: a three-wave longitudinal study in South Africa. *Journal of Personality and Social Psychology, 101*, 1221–38. doi: 10.1037/a0024450

Thijs, J., & Verkuyten, M. (2014). School ethnic diversity and students' interethnic relations. *British Journal of Educational Psychology, 83*, 1–21. doi: 10.1111/bjep.12032

Titzmann, P.F., Brenick, A., & Silbereisen, R.K. (2015). Friendships fighting prejudice: A longitudinal perspective on adolescents' cross-group friendships with immigrants. *Journal of Youth and Adolescence, 44*, 1318–31. doi: 10.1007/s10964-015-0256-6

Tropp, L.R., O'Brien, T.C., & Migacheva, K. (2014). How peer norms of inclusion and exclusion predict children's interest in cross-group friendship. *Journal of Social Issues, 70*, 151–66. doi: 10.1111/josi.12052

Tropp, L.R., & Pettigrew, T.F. (2005). Relationships between intergroup contact and prejudice among minority and majority status groups. *Psychological Science, 16*, 951–7. doi: 10.1111/j.1467-9280.2005.01643.x

Turner, R.N., & Cameron, L. (2016). Confidence in contact: A new perspective on promoting cross-group friendship among children and adolescents. *Social Issues and Policy Review, 10*, 212–46. doi: 10.1111/sipr.12023

Turner, R.N., & Feddes, A. (2011). How intergroup friendship works: A longitudinal study of friendship effects on outgroup attitudes. *European Journal of Social Psychology, 41*, 914–23. doi: 10.1002/ejsp.843

Turner, R.N., Hewstone, M., & Voci, A. (2007). Reducing explicit and implicit prejudice via direct and extended contact: The mediating role of self-disclosure and intergroup anxiety. *Journal of Personality and Social Psychology, 93*, 369–88. doi: 10.1037/0022-3514.93.3.369

Turner, R.N., Hewstone, M., Voci, A., Paolini, S., & Christ, O. (2007). Reducing prejudice via direct and extended cross-group friendship. *European Review of Social Psychology, 18*, 212–55. doi: 10.1080/10463280701680297

Turner, R.N., Tam, T., Hewstone, M., Kenworthy, J., & Cairns, E. (2013). Contact between Catholic and Protestant schoolchildren in Northern Ireland. *Journal of Applied Social Psychology, 43* (Suppl. 2), E216–E228. doi: 10.1111/jasp.12018

Turner, R.N., West, K., & Christie, Z. (2013). Outgroup trust, intergroup anxiety, and outgroup attitude as mediators of the effect of imagined intergroup contact on intergroup behavioural tendencies. *Journal of Applied Social Psychology, 43* (Suppl. 2), E196–E205. doi: 10.1111/jasp.12019

Verkuyten, M., & Kinket, B. (2000). Social distances in a multi ethnic society: The ethnic hierarchy among Dutch preadolescents. *Social Psychology Quarterly, 63,* 75–85. doi: 10.2307/2695882

Verkuyten, M., Thijs, J., & Bekhuis, H. (2010). Intergroup contact and ingroup reappraisal: Examining the deprovincialisation thesis. *Social Psychology Quarterly, 73,* 398–416. doi: 10.1177/0190272510389015

Vezzali, L., & Giovannini, D. (2012). Secondary transfer effect of intergroup contact: The role of intergroup attitudes, intergroup anxiety and perspective taking. *Journal of Community and Applied Social Psychology, 22,* 125–44. doi: 10.1002/casp.1103

Vezzali, L., Stathi, S., Crisp, R.J., & Capozza, D. (2015). Comparing direct and imagined intergroup contact among children: Effects on outgroup stereotypes and helping intentions. *International Journal of Intercultural Relations, 49,* 46–53. doi: 10.1016/j.ijintrel.2015.06.009

Vezzali, L., Stathi, S., Crisp, R.J., Giovannini, D., Capozza, D., & Gaertner, S.L. (2015). Imagined intergroup contact and common ingroup identity: An integrative approach. *Social Psychology, 46,* 265–76. doi: 10.1027/1864-9335/a000242

Vezzali, L., Stathi, S., & Giovannini, D. (2012). Indirect contact through book reading: Improving adolescents' attitudes and behavioral intentions toward immigrants. *Psychology in the Schools, 49,* 148–62. doi: 10.1002/pits.20621

Vezzali, L., Stathi, S., Giovannini, D., Capozza, D., & Visintin, E.P. (2015). "And the best essay is . . .": Extended contact and cross-group friendships at school. *British Journal of Social Psychology, 54,* 601–15. doi: 10.1111/bjso.12110

Wagner, U., van Dick, R., Pettigrew, T.F., & Christ, O. (2003). Ethnic prejudice in East and West Germany: The explanatory power of intergroup contact. *Group Processes and Intergroup Relations, 6,* 22–36. doi: 10.1177/1368430203006001010

West, K., & Turner, R.N. (2014). Using extended contact to improve physiological responses and behavior toward people with schizophrenia. *Journal of Experimental Social Psychology, 50,* 57–64. doi: 10.1016/j.jesp.2013.06.009

Wilson, T.M., Rodkin, P.C., & Ryan, A.M. (2014). The company they keep and avoid: Social goal orientation as a predictor of children's ethnic segregation. *Developmental Psychology, 50,* 1116–24. doi: 10.1037/a0035040

Wright, S.C., Aron, A., McLaughlin-Volpe, T., & Ropp, S.A. (1997). The extended contact effect: Knowledge of cross-group friendships and prejudice. *Journal of Personality and Social Psychology, 73,* 73–90. doi: 10.1037/0022-3514.73.1.73

Žeželj, I., Jakšic, I., & Jošic, S. (2015). How contact shapes implicit and explicit preferences: Attitudes towards Roma children in exclusive and non-inclusive environment. *Journal of Applied Social Psychology, 45,* 263–73. doi: 10.1111/jasp.12293

10

CONCLUDING THOUGHTS

The past, present and future of research on the contact hypothesis

John Dixon

Key words: contact hypothesis, intergroup contact, intergroup relations, prejudice reduction, social change

> Prejudice (unless deeply rooted in the character structure of the individual) may be reduced by *equal status* contact between majority and minority groups in the pursuit of *common goals*. The effect is greatly enhanced if this contact is sanctioned by *institutional supports* (i.e. by law, custom or local atmosphere), and provided it is of a sort that leads to the *perception of common interests and common humanity* of the two groups.
>
> (Allport, 1954, p. 281, my emphasis)

Having read the previous chapters of this book, the reader will appreciate how far contact research has progressed since this classic formulation of the "contact hypothesis". Nowadays, our ideas about what counts as "contact", the conditions under which it is successful, and how and why it promotes psychological change have all developed well beyond the simple formulation proposed by Gordon Allport more than half a century ago. Indeed, as Hewstone and Swart (2011) observe, knowledge has grown to the extent that contact *hypothesis* is perhaps now better described as a fully-fledged *theory*. It is a theory that is widely acknowledged as one of social psychology's most important and enduring contributions to the project of improving relations between groups.

This concluding chapter has three interrelated aims. First, it discusses how the work presented in earlier chapters has advanced the field. Second, it discusses some conceptual, methodological and applied limits of current research on the contact hypothesis. Third, moving beyond summary and critique, it discusses some directions for future research, which both build on and extend contributions made in earlier chapters. The chapter begins with a historical footnote on the emergence of contact research, which contextualizes some later arguments.

The historical emergence and political significance of research on the contact hypothesis

In the quotation on which this chapter opened, Allport (1954, p. 281) underlined the need for interaction between groups to be " . . . sanctioned by *institutional supports* (i.e. by law, custom or local atmosphere)". In making this point, he revealed something important about the wider context in which early contact research emerged and took shape. That context was marked by a struggle to overcome the legacy of racial segregation in the US and to transform related practices of institutional racism—often in the face of staunch political resistance. This socio-historical context at once impelled and delimited the emerging social psychology of intergroup contact and desegregation.

On the one hand, early contact research was often designed to understand the effects of changes that were already unfolding in the US. The desegregation of parts of the Armed Forces during World War 2—enacted more as a matter of military expediency than as an attempt to promote racial equality—raised concerns about the likely effects of contact on the racial attitudes, behaviors and morale of mixed platoons and battalions. Similarly, as urbanization and urban diversification gathered pace, the prospect of ever more "mixed" residential areas in American cities raised concerns about how members of different communities would respond to sharing local facilities and meeting one another as neighbours. Then there was the vexed question of what would happen to workplace relations and productivity when Black and White Americans had to work together in close quarters. The spectre of Black bosses managing White workers loomed as among the most combustible of potential transformations of extant relations of racial status and privilege.

In many—though by no means all—early studies, the results of desegregation turned out to be more positive than expected (Amir, 1969). In the armed forces, for example, infantrymen serving in mixed platoons generally became more accepting of racial integration than those serving in segregated platoons (Star, Williams, & Stouffer, 1958). In newly formed public housing projects, neighbourly contacts seemed to promote positive interracial attitudes (Deutsch & Collins, 1958), at least some of the time. Likewise, in mixed workplaces, the battle-ground that some had feared did not emerge. Minard's (1952/2008) well-known study of workplace relations in the Pocahontas coal fields, for instance, found that Black and White miners got along well under ground, forming collegial and often friendly relationships, even if established patterns of racial division resumed "above ground".

On the other hand, early contact research attempted not merely to *describe* the social psychological consequences of desegregation, but also to *promote and guide* social change. It provided a scientific foundation that underwrote the promise of institutional desegregation. Clark's (1953) monumental review of the early evidence on desegregation, for instance, demonstrated that: (a) segregation was a form of social injustice that impacted negatively on the well-being of Black Americans,

(b) immediate, strongly enforced, institutionally sanctioned desegregation tended to be more effective than gradual, piecemeal or weakly enforced changes in transforming racial inequality—ironically, it also seemed to produce less resistance—and, (c) contradicting the received wisdom that ". . . one must change men's hearts before one changes their minds" (p. 72), desegregation was typically associated with an improvement in interracial attitudes, even among initially prejudiced Whites.

This improvement, Clark felt, could be partly explained by the normative shift that is captured by the old adage "stateways can change folkways". If we can create environments in which individuals' behavior is required to change, he argued, then their hearts and minds will follow suit, an idea later developed within theories of cognitive dissonance. Improved attitudes could also be explained by the new forms of interaction and exchange that institutional desegregation made possible. The latter were explicitly highlighted within the social science statement that shaped the outcome of the famous "Brown versus the Board of Education ruling" of 1954, initiating a process that brought to an end legalized racial segregation in the US (see the special issue assembled by Pickren, 2004, published on the 50-year anniversary of Brown). Presenting their judgements about the legality of "separate but equal" education, the Justices based their ruling partly on the evidence presented in a statement prepared by a team of social scientists and psychologists, including Kenneth Clark. Among other factors, this statement warned that segregation ". . . leads to a blockage in the communication and interaction between the two groups. Such blockages tend to increase mutual suspicion, distrust, and hostility" (Clark, Chein, & Cook, 1952/2004, p. 497).

My reason for making this introductory detour into the early history of research on contact and desegregation is twofold. First, I want to highlight that contact research originated in an attempt to understand *wider processes of institutional transformation*, notably the erosion of de jure racial segregation in the US and the associated "problem" of predicting the likely consequences of processes of desegregation across institutions of residence, education, employment and civic life. Second, I want to highlight that contact research provided a scientific basis for political advocacy for desegregation. Early work in the field sought not only to *describe* but also to *impel and guide* social change in order to overcome the legacy of institutional racism and to advocate for social conditions under which desegregation would "work". In its most progressive guises, early contact research thus formed part of a wider movement towards racial equality in the US and elsewhere; and it is thus justifiably now praised as one of the most progressive ideas in the history of social psychology (e.g. Dovidio, Gaertner, & Kawakami, 2003).

As will be highlighted later in the chapter, these historical roots are worth remembering, respecting and reaffirming. Whatever its other strengths, recent research on the contact has often detached the dynamics of contact and desegregation from the broader political project that inspired earlier researchers. Contact research now risks being reduced to a handy psychological toolkit whose primary contribution is to help members of different groups to hold more positive thoughts and feelings about one another (cf. Durrheim & Dixon, 2014).

Developments in contact research

What do we mean by contact?

The original contact hypothesis was based on the idea that positive, face-to-face interactions between members of different groups have the potential to erode all but the most deeply embedded forms of intergroup prejudice. As earlier chapters have demonstrated, recent research has moved beyond a focus on face-to-face interaction to identify a broader range of mechanisms through which "contact" can occur and come to shape the nature of intergroup attitudes.

Meleady and Crisp (Chapter 8) review the growing literature on the effects of *imagined contact*, focusing on interventions that encourage individuals to "make believe" that they are interacting with members of another group. An advantage of this kind of contact is that it is far easier to manufacture than the direct forms of interaction proposed within the original contact hypothesis; yet, as Meleady and Crisp's review shows, it is often effective in itself in transforming intergroup attitudes. Certainly, the concept of imagined contact has yielded a rapidly accumulating body of supportive evidence and has offered the field simple but effective methodological paradigms through which to study such contact experimentally (normally, a laborious and time-consuming business). Although its proponents are rightly cautious about overstating its significance, they also emphasize its valuable role in "first step" interventions to break down barriers between communities. As Meleady and Crisp note, this may be particularly important in historically divided societies where opportunities for face-to-face exchanges are difficult to create or sustain.

Another way in which contact research has moved beyond its focus on face-to-face interaction is via research on so-called *extended* forms of contact. Vezzali and Stathi (Chapter 7) review the relevant literature, which focuses on how *indirect* experiences of interactions with others may shape intergroup attitudes, either because participants are in a position to witness others experiencing exchanges across intergroup boundaries (so-called *vicarious contact*) or because they are themselves embedded in social relationships in which such interactions are known to occur (e.g. they have friends who have friends belonging to another group).

Again, the effects of such contact are important not least because in historically divided societies indirect exchanges may occur far more frequently than direct exchanges. Moreover, they may have important, cumulative effects on relations between groups. As Vezzali and Stathi discuss in some detail, for example, direct and indirect forms of contact are often closely related, with the latter creating the conditions under which the former can emerge (see also Chapter 3, González & Brown). In this respect, it is perhaps worth emphasizing that indirect forms of contact, though they may appear less tangible, are no less "real" than their direct counterparts. Indeed, Vezzali and Stathi's chapter ends by identifying a promising future line of research, which concerns the role of *social networks* in shaping both the nature and the consequences of direct and indirect forms of contact. Such networks represent the primary sociological system of relations through which individuals' experiences of contact are organized. As such, network analysis might enable us to understand better how network properties such as density, diversity and tie strength and network processes such as bonding, bridging and brokering impact upon social interactions, attitudes and relationships.

What researchers mean by "contact" has recently developed in another direction, that is, via a renewed emphasis on the effects of *negative contact* experiences. Early contact researchers were acutely aware that participants' experiences of interacting with members of other groups were not necessarily positive either in quality or in outcome. Allport (1954, p. 264), for example, cautioned that contact has the potential to ". . . strengthen the adverse mental associations" that we hold about others. However, subsequent research in the field has focused overwhelmingly on forms of social interaction that are cooperative, pleasant or supportive, thereby downplaying the less desirable experiences that mark intergroup relations in some societies.

Graf and Paolini (Chapter 6) review emerging work that has attempted to rectify this imbalance, with some revealing results. To simplify their more nuanced discussion, it turns out that negative contact experiences, though reported less frequently than positive contact experiences, tend to exert a more powerful effect on intergroup attitudes. This is partly because such experiences increase category salience, encouraging us to treat others as representatives of their social groups rather than as discrete individuals. For this reason, their psychological effects tend to generalize more readily, shaping not only our feelings about the individuals with whom we are interacting, but also our feelings about the social groups of which they are exemplars (cf. Wilder, 1984). Of course, as Graf and Paolini point out, what counts as "negative" and "positive" contact may be "in the eye of the beholder". What a high status participant experiences as a friendly exchange, for example, may be perceived as condescending or even demeaning by a lower status participant. This highlights the relativity and context dependence of "contact". It highlights too the necessity of investigating how participants themselves construct its meanings and implications, a point to which I will return later in the chapter.

When, why, how and with whom does contact work (over time)?

Allport (1954) was clear that not any form of interaction would reduce prejudice and indeed argued that the wrong kind of contact under the wrong conditions would probably make matters worse. As captured in the quotation on which this chapter opened, he felt that contact should occur between cooperating groups of equal status and should be sufficiently intimate to establish common ground. In addition, the surrounding institutional context should create an environment where interaction across intergroup boundaries is normatively and legally sanctioned. In this classic formulation, the mechanisms through which contact succeeds were under specified and did not amount to a coherent theory. However, the idea that interaction reduces our ignorance of others—and thus our prejudice towards them—was a widespread assumption that fitted well with Allport's (1954) definition of prejudice as "thinking ill of others without sufficient warrant".

Recent work in the field has refined our understanding of when, why, how and with whom contact "works". First, after a long and ultimately fruitless period in which the boundary conditions for positive contact multiplied into an unworkable "laundry list" (Pettigrew, 1998), Pettigrew and Tropp's (2006) meta-analysis brought a much needed clarification to the field, showing that: (1) positive contact generally reduces prejudice, (2) it does so even when Allport's optimal conditions are not present, but (3) when present, those conditions augment its beneficial effects. Second, this broadly optimistic message has been accompanied by advances in our understanding of how and why contact improves intergroup relations. Although knowledge transfer and a reduction in "ignorance" about others plays a role (cf. Stephan & Stephan, 1984), recent theoretical models of contact have emphasized the role of emotional shifts in intergroup empathy and anxiety as important mediators of its effects on intergroup attitudes (e.g. Pettigrew & Tropp, 2008). They have also elaborated Allport's idea that contact should foster a sense of "common humanity", notably by building upon the common in-group identity model proposed by Gaertner and Dovidio (2000).

Several earlier chapters in this book have extended these advances in contact theory and research. Cameron and Turner (Chapter 9) assess the (social) developmental literature on intergroup contact, a surprisingly neglected area. Much of the most important work on contact has explored relations in childhood contexts such as schools (e.g. Schofield & Hausmann, 2004), often seeking to understand and inform processes of educational desegregation. This work has placed faith in the power of early contact experiences to shape future relations and has sometimes used longitudinal methods to track shifts in such experience—and associated psychological consequences—across time (see Abrams & Eller, Chapter 5, for further discussion of the importance of studying contact over time). However, the *developmental trajectory* of contact dynamics across the full human lifespan—from cradle to grave—remains largely underspecified. As in most areas of social psychology, research has tended to focus on the responses of already formed adults, frozen at a particular moment in time. The idea that such adults are embedded in a *life course trajectory* that might benefit from broader advances in (social)developmental psychology has only barely begun to be recognized (though for an exception see the work of Melanie Killen and colleagues, e.g. Killen, Hitti, & Mulvey, 2014; Ruck, Park, Crystal, & Killen, 2015). Cameron and Turner's chapter demonstrates the promise of such work, patiently integrating a disparate range of conceptual and empirical resources that cross the usual sub-disciplinary boundaries of this field.

Recent research has also advanced our understanding of individual differences in the contact–prejudice relationship. Early work was not much interested in this topic. It was simply presumed that certain personality types might harbor prejudices so extreme as to be relatively impervious to intervention. Hodson, Turner and Choma's chapter (Chapter 2) brings together a small but suggestive literature that shows, for example, how personality traits such as openness, agreeableness and extraversion can shape participants' contact experiences, which in turn can influence their levels of prejudice. Rather intriguingly, they also report several recent studies that have found that the prejudice-reducing effects of contact are sometimes *stronger* for participants' scoring higher in traits generally associated with prejudice (e.g. authoritarianism). Such findings qualify the received wisdom that contact cannot change the attitudes of those who arguably require such change the most, namely the highly prejudiced. As Hodson, Turner and Choma emphasize, whatever its methodological limitations, this emerging tradition of research attests to the power of intergroup contact to overcome deep seated antipathies at an individual level, even if, of course, such antipathies also powerfully shape individuals' willingness to engage in contact in the first place.

The present book presents another advance on the traditional contact literature, which is at once methodological and conceptual. This concerns the potential value of longitudinal work in developing the field. Most of what we know about contact has been derived from two kinds of methods: (1) the cross-sectional survey and (2) the laboratory experiment. Both approaches offer a relatively static snapshot of processes of intergroup contact that are far more dynamic, fluid and temporally structured. In Chapter 5, Abrams and Eller present a compelling case for moving beyond these methodological mainstays of the contact tradition to conduct work that is able to explore the complex relations between contact, prejudice and various mediating variables *over time* (see also the special section of the British Journal of Social Psychology edited by Christ, Hewstone, Tropp, & Wagner, 2012).

More specifically, they propose a temporally integrated model of intergroup contact and threat (TIMICAT), which challenges the idea that intergroup threat is simply a mediator of the contact–prejudice relationship. In so doing, they seek to broaden and complicate the terms of debate about the relationship between direct and indirect forms of contact, threat in its various forms (e.g. symbolic, realistic and anxious), and indicators of prejudice such as negative feelings and stereotypes. When these variables are viewed as representing processes that dynamically unfold across different social and temporal contexts, the complexity of their interrelations becomes apparent (see Table 5.1, pp. 80–81).

A final contribution to current knowledge is offered by González and Brown in Chapter 3, which explores how contact affects the dynamics of acculturation, focusing particularly on the factors that predict positive acculturation preferences among majority groups (e.g. members of host communities "receiving" immigrants). Capitalizing on a series of longitudinal studies conducted in a Chilean–Peruvian immigration context, their work shows how both direct (e.g. friendship relations) and extended contact may shape majority members' acceptance of minority group cultural maintenance, as well as increasing their desire for further intergroup contact. It shows, too, that these effects may be mediated over time by increased intergroup trust and the adoption of in-group norms of tolerance. On a broader level, Gonzales and Brown's work represents a valuable attempt to integrate two areas of psychology—on intergroup contact and acculturation—that have developed largely in isolation (though see Bochner, 1982). In so doing, they explicitly link research on the contact hypothesis to the broader dynamics of social change in societies facing the opportunities and challenges of immigration.

What do we mean by social change?

Research on contact generally takes changes in intergroup prejudice—or close proxies such as intergroup forgiveness, empathy and reconciliation—as its primary outcome measure. Indeed, over the past 50 or so years, the contact hypothesis has become arguably the most influential social psychological theory of *prejudice reduction*. A vast accumulation of evidence has confirmed that contact is inversely related to prejudice across diverse contexts and types of intergroup relations. The relationship is not of course uniform. Contact seems to be more effective in improving, for example, attitudes towards gay people than attitudes towards the elderly (Pettigrew & Tropp, 2006). Yet few would dispute the existence of generalized contact–prejudice relationship that, though comparatively weak in strength (Pettigrew & Tropp, 2006), emerges reliably in many situations.

The prejudice reduction model on which contact research has been based is built around a series of assumptions about social change. The point of prejudice reduction, for example, is not merely to get individuals to hold nicer thoughts and feelings about one another. By targeting in particular the responses of members of historically advantaged groups, prejudice reduction sets in motion a series of social and psychological changes that, in theory at least, culminate in the reduction of wider practices of discrimination that sustain social inequality. As noted earlier in the chapter, this link between contact, attitude change and social justice was emphasized by early researchers such as Kenneth Clark (1953). For Clark and others, educational desegregation was not only about getting Black kids to sit next to White kids in the classroom so that they could come to like one another more. To the contrary, the process of getting kids to like one another more was framed as part of a broader process of institutional change and was important not only in itself, but also because of its implications for promoting racial justice (e.g. for creating a stable, racially integrated education system in which Black kids could have equal access to resources and opportunities).

Recent work in the field, however, has raised a number of questions about the limitations of the prejudice reduction model of change on which the contact hypothesis is founded (e.g. Dixon, Levine, Reicher, & Durrheim, 2012; Wright & Lubensky, 2009). Chapter 4, written by Tamar Saguy and colleagues, provides an overview of such work, focusing particularly on the idea that the creation of harmonious relations between historically advantaged and disadvantaged communities may have "ironic" effects on participants' social change orientation. Specifically, they review recent work showing how, when and why contact reduces perceptions of injustice among disadvantaged groups, decreasing their support for policies designed to redress inequality or willingness to participate in collective action to achieve social change.

I want to lift three themes from this chapter, simplifying a richer set of arguments. First, evidence of the ironic effects of contact—and similar prejudice reduction techniques—has now achieved critical mass, with such effects being documented across a wide range of societies (e.g. South Africa, Israel and the US) and using a variety of methodological frameworks and outcome measures. It seems that we are dealing with a comparatively robust and widespread phenomenon here. Second, although this line of research is in its infancy and several key questions remain unanswered, there is some consensus about the theoretical mechanisms that underpin such effects. Ironically, it seems as though the very mechanisms through which contact improves intergroup attitudes are also the mechanisms through which it undermines political activism. That is, by fostering positive feelings towards the advantaged, by diminishing a sense of group boundaries between "us" and "them", and by reducing perceptions of fraternal discrimination and inequality, intergroup contact with the advantaged has a so-called "sedative effect" (Cakal, Hewstone, Schwar, & Heath, 2011) on the collective action orientation of the disadvantaged.

Finally, Saguy et al. not only review but also extend recent arguments in the field, elaborating two original lines of research. The first shows how so-called "harmony based hope"—ostensibly a positive intergroup emotion—reduces the collective action intentions of the disadvantaged, particularly among individuals with comparative low levels of identification with their social group. The second explores the effects of contact within a domain that has seen remarkably little research. Intimate relations between men and women fulfil many of the optimal conditions proposed by Allport (1954) and elaborated by later researchers: they are intimate, cooperative and involve the formation of deep friendships with a lot of mutual self-disclosure. Yet they are also a site for the reproduction and maintenance of power relations based around acceptance of paternalistic ideologies that wrap inequalities in the "coercive embrace" of warm feelings (cf. Jackman, 1994). As Saguy et al.'s unpublished study reveals, for instance, women whose contact in romantic relationships more closely approximates the optimal conditions laid out by Allport (1954) are also more satisfied with gender relations in general and more willing to buy into the idea that such relations are legitimate. Romantic intimacy, it turns out, has a darker side.

Critical reflections and future directions

In the final section, I want to end on some broader critical reflections, both building on and extending the contributions of earlier chapters in this book.

Re-contextualizing contact

Several previous chapters have made a case for moving beyond the study of contact under relatively benign conditions, an approach that arguably neglects the harsher realities of intergroup exchanges in historically divided societies. Manufacturing the ideal conditions of contact in the laboratory or investigating relations in settings that broadly conform to Allport's (1954) "optimal conditions" is inherently limited as a long-term strategy for the field. For one thing, as we have seen, this strategy has led to a neglect of several key features of contact in "real" world settings: it may be associated with negative emotions, thoughts and behaviors; it may both express and reproduce relations of intergroup power and status; and it may be curtailed by ongoing practices of segregation operating at both institutional and interpersonal levels of analysis (cf. Dixon, Durrheim, & Tredoux, 2005). For another thing, this approach to studying contact has arguably fostered a somewhat idealistic and at times self-congratulatory narrative in the recent literature. The benefits of contact interventions in specific circumstances—as evidenced by modest negative correlations with prejudice in questionnaire surveys or by small shifts in intergroup attitudes in "one shot" experimental analogs of real-world interactions— are presumed to carry important implications for the broader patterning of intergroup relations in divided societies. The dangers of such an extrapolation are captured wittily by Abrams and Eller in Chapter 5, p. 76, who observe that in reality:

> . . . the aspiring social psychological interventionist is likely to be in the situation of a chef who is expected to produce a gourmet dish but whose Michelin star capabilities remain thwarted by being unsure of which or how many guests are coming for dinner, being equipped only with a single camping gas, a small aluminium pan and a maximum of three ingredients.

In my view, the antidote to this kind of decontextualized idealism is to prioritize the study of contact "in the wild", using methods that are able to capture its nature and consequences across:

- a range of everyday settings, including the mundane spaces of interaction in which most contact occurs
- circumstances where relations may be hierarchical, threatening or conflictual and where contact may be "negatively" experienced
- institutional settings where desegregation is being resisted as well as promoted in order to better understand the obstacles to social change

This kind of work, admittedly, presents numerous challenges. It takes social psychologists outside the comfort zone of studying relatively nonthreatening exchanges, using standard questionnaires and laboratory methods. It involves recovering a broader range of everyday situations where contact is unfolding, including situations that do not normally feature within the literature (for an instructive example, see Blackwood, Hopkins, & Reicher, 2015). It requires us to understand the institutional and political processes that pre-empt or restrict as well as facilitate the forms of positive interaction prioritized in much of the contact literature. In this respect, for example, the concept of "institutional support" may need to be further unpacked. What exactly does it mean, for example, to create organizational structures, norms and values that support intergroup contact and, correspondingly, what institutional processes may, either directly or indirectly, undermine the possibility for meaningful, equal status interaction across group lines?

Recovering participants' own constructions of the meaning of contact

My second point revisits the theme of how researchers define, measure and analyze "contact". What is meant by contact, as we have seen, has been greatly enriched by recent work in the field, which now explores the role of imagined contact, vicarious contact, extended contact and negative contact. We could add to this list equally important work on virtual contact, which explores how our communications with others are increasingly occurring not only in situations of physical co-presence, but also via the mass mediation of cell phone technology, social media sites, blogs, twitter messages and so on (e.g. Amichai-Hamburger & McKenna, 2006). The significance of this kind of contact, both positive and negative in quality, is only beginning to be understood and will doubtlessly form an important line of research in the future.

In some ways, however, these expansions of the field continue to be dwarfed by a more important restriction. In most contact research, the measurement, analysis and interpretation of contact serve to reduce a complex, context-specific set of experiences to a few generic dimensions. Typically, for example, questionnaire-based research on the nature of interactions in a given context begins by filtering participants' own understandings into simple and abstract categories, e.g. quantifying the self-reported degree of "intimacy", "cooperativeness" and "friendliness" of their encounters with others. Whatever other advantages it confers, this approach effectively shoehorns disparate kinds of experiences into a set of common categories that may ultimately hide as much as they reveal. Contact between, say, men and women involved in interactions within romantic relationships (Chapter 4) is framed (and operationalized) in the same terms as contact between immigrants and host communities (Chapter 3). Moreover, the possibility that the same event of contact is experienced in *qualitatively different* terms by different participants (e.g. located in different positions within an unequal power relationship) is effectively masked.

I would argue that this process of abstraction, involving the top down imposition of (measurement) categories created by psychologists, needs to be counterbalanced by bottom up exploration of how and with what consequences participants' themselves make sense of their day-to-day interactions with others. A similar point is made by Graf and Paolini in Chapter 6. As part of an argument calling for greater attention to the "subjective" nature of everyday constructions of "positive" and "negative" contact, they argue that:

> Although experimentation using *objective* operationalizations of contact valence still has its place (see Paolini & McIntyre, 2016) and was important

in instigating an interest in positive-negative contact comparisons (e.g. Paolini, Harwood, & Rubin, 2010), we have grown into believing that when it comes to defining what is positive and what is negative contact, "beauty is in the eye of the beholder" and "there are many shades of grey": contact valence is a fundamentally *subjective* experience, which is exposed to a host of modulating influences impacting on its downstream consequences.

(p. 107)

I would simply add that in order to explore such "subjective experiences", and to unravel their "downstream consequences", contact researchers need to make greater use of methodological resources beyond their "go to" tools of the laboratory experiment and the questionnaire survey. The small, rather scattered, qualitative literature on intergroup contact exemplifies an approach that has not, to date, had sufficient influence on the field (e.g. Durrheim, Jacobs, & Dixon, 2014; Hopkins & Kahani-Hopkins, 2006).

Intergroup contact and social change revisited

As the opening section of this chapter argued, the contact hypothesis emerged as a way of improving intergroup relations in the context of a wider struggle for racial justice in the US. Yet how we define "improving" is increasingly a subject of debate in the field. Is a society improved by interventions that encourage citizens to like one another more but leave intact fundamental inequalities? Is it enough to change the hearts and minds of the historically advantaged or should we be aiming to get them to endorse interventions that aim to redress inequality? What if, in some circumstances, positive intergroup contact enables paternalistic forms of exploitation and disadvantage to flourish, becoming part of the ideological apparatus that maintains the status quo? Conversely, are there contexts in which the drive for social justice needs to be subordinated to the need for social harmony?

These are clearly complex questions and they defy simple or "once and for all" answers. They arguably point to a deeper set of underlying tensions between two models of social change in psychology: a prejudice reduction model, based around the creation of warmer intergroup feelings and beliefs, and a collective action model, based around mass mobilization and political activism to challenge social inequality (Dixon et al., 2012; Wright & Lubensky, 2009). Evidence that interventions to promote prejudice reduction set in motion social psychological processes that undermine participants' collective action orientation has recently fuelled speculation that these two forms of social change may ultimately be irreconcilable (see Chapter 4).

Complicating this idea, however, some researchers have identified conditions under which interventions to reduce prejudice—such as the promotion of positive intergroup contact or common identification—do *not* exercise a "sedative effect" on the collective action orientation of disadvantaged communities. Becker, Wright, Lubensky and Zhou (2013), for example, have shown that this sedative effect only emerges under specific conditions of intergroup contact. When dominant group members either defend the legitimacy of the status quo or keep their political opinions private, then it occurs, but when they openly acknowledge the illegitimacy of the status quo it does not occur. In other words, the nature and content of intergroup communication during events of contact shapes its relationship to collective action.

Dixon and colleagues (2015) propose that the sedative effects of intergroup contact primarily occur when members of lower status groups interact with members of higher status groups. By contrast, when groups who share a common history of disadvantage within a given society are given the opportunity to interact, then this may actually foster a sense of common grievance and empowerment, thereby increasing rather than decreasing the likelihood that they will act collectively to challenge the status quo.

In their case study of residential relations in the city of Pietermartizburg in KwaZulu-Natal, for example, Dixon et al. (2015) investigated relations between an established Indian community and a newer community of Black African residents. In line with other research on the contact hypothesis, they reported that positive neighbourly interactions were associated with positive intergroup attitudes. Perhaps more important, however, they also found that such interactions laid the foundations for political solidarity between the communities, who shared a history of disadvantage during the apartheid era. Indian residents who had experienced positive contact with their Black neighbours, for example, were more willing to participate in collective action to improve conditions in the local settlement where the majority of Black residents lived. In other words, this form of contact had "mobilizing" rather than "sedating" effects on participants" political attitudes.

Closing remarks

I want to end on a broader point about the relationship between contact and social change, which again emphasizes the importance of *contextualization*. In my view, the question of which model of social change is likely to be most effective in reducing social inequality and discrimination cannot ultimately be answered in the abstract. To the contrary, it demands a close analysis of the historical and socio-political organization of intergroup relations within a given context at a given point in time. In societies where social inequalities are limited and social justice has been largely achieved, for instance, prejudice reduction and the creation of intergroup harmony may be vitally important goals in their own right. By contrast, in societies marked by inequality and injustice, prejudice reduction interventions may be of more limited importance or, more dangerous, they may become part of the ideological process through which the status quo is maintained (Maoz, 2011).

Ultimately, perhaps the most important contribution of recent debates about the "irony of harmony" has been to return to center stage fundamental questions about the relationship between contact, political change and social justice. As we have noted, such questions impelled some of the best early work in the field, which sought both to understand the social psychological consequences of racial desegregation and to guide the dismantling of institutionalized segregation in the US. Pettigrew (1969, p. 66) captured the political spirit of this project when he wrote: "Racially separate or together? Our social psychological examination of separatist assumptions leads to one imperative: the attainment of a democratic America, free from personal and institutional racism, requires extensive integration in all realms of life".

References

Allport, G.W. (1954). *The nature of prejudice*. New York, NY: Addison-Wesley.

Amichai-Hamburger, Y., & McKenna, K.Y.A. (2006). The contact hypothesis reconsidered: Interacting via the Internet. *Journal of Computer-Mediated Communication, 11*, 825–43. doi: 10.1111/j.1083–6101.2006.00037.x

Amir, Y. (1969). Contact hypothesis in ethnic relations. *Psychological Bulletin, 71*, 319–42. doi: 10.1037/h0027352

Becker, J.C., Wright, S.C., Lubensky, M.E., & Zhou, S. (2013). Friend or ally: Whether cross-group contact undermines collective action depends on what advantaged group members say (or don't say). *Personality and Social Psychology Bulletin, 39*, 442–55. doi: 10.1177/1368430208095400

Blackwood, L., Hopkins, N., & Reicher, S. (2015). "Flying while Muslim": Citizenship and Misrecognition in the Airport. *Journal of Social and Political Psychology, 3*, 148–70. doi: 10.5964/jspp.v3i2.375

Bochner, S. (1982). The social psychology of cross-cultural relations. In S. Bochner (Ed.), *Cultures in contact: Studies in cross-cultural interaction* (pp. 5–44). Oxford, UK: Pergamon.

Cakal, H., Hewstone, M., Schwar, G., & Heath, A. (2011). An investigation of the social identity model of collective action and the "sedative" effect of intergroup contact amongst Black and White students in South Africa. *British Journal of Social Psychology, 50*, 606–27. doi: 10.1111/j.2044-8309.2011.02075.x

Christ, O., Hewstone, M., Tropp, L., & Wagner, U. (2012). Dynamic processes in intergroup contact. *British Journal of Social Psychology, 51*, 219–20. doi: 10.1111/j.2044-8309.2012.02104.x

Clark, K.B. (1953). Desegregation: An appraisal of the evidence. *Journal of Social Issues, 9*, 1–77.

Clark, K.B., Chein, I., & Cook, S.W. (1952/2004). The effects of segregation and the consequences of desegregation: A (September 1952) social science statement in the Brown v. Board of Education of Topeka Supreme Court case. *American Psychologist, 59*, 495–501. doi: 10.1037/0003-066X.59.6.495

Deutsch, M., & Collins, M.E. (1958). The effect of public policy in housing projects upon interracial attitudes. In E.E. Maccoby, T.M. Newcomb, & E.L. Hartley (Eds.), *Readings in social psychology* (pp. 612–36). New York, NY: Holt, Rinehart and Winston.

Dixon, J., Durrheim, K., Thomae, M., Tredoux, C., Kerr, P., & Quayle, M. (2015). Divide and rule, unite and resist: Contact, collective action and political solidarity amongst historically disadvantaged groups. *Journal of Social Issues, 71*, 576–96. doi: 10.1111/josi.12129

Dixon, J., Durrheim, K., & Tredoux, C. (2005). Beyond the optimal contact strategy: A "reality check" for the contact hypothesis. *American Psychologist, 60*, 697–711. doi: 10.1037/0003-066X.60.7.697

Dixon, J., Levine, M., Reicher, S., & Durrheim, K. (2012). Beyond prejudice: Are negative evaluations the problem and is getting us to like one another more the solution? *Behavioral and Brain Sciences, 35,* 411–25. doi: 10.1017/S0140525X11002214

Dovidio, J.F., Gaertner, S.L., & Kawakami, K. (2003). Intergroup contact: The past, present, and the future. *Group Processes and Intergroup Relations, 6,* 5–21. doi: 10.1177/1368430203006001009

Durrheim, K., & Dixon, J. (2014). Intergroup contact and the struggle for social justice. In P.L. Hammock (Ed.), Oxford handbook of social psychology and social justice. Oxford, UK: Oxford University Press.

Durrheim, K., Jacobs, N., & Dixon, J. (2014). Explaining the paradoxical effects of intergroup contact: Paternalistic relations and systems justification in domestic labour in South Africa. *International Journal of Intercultural Relations, 41,* 150–64. doi: 10.1016/j.ijintrel.2013.11.006

Gaertner, S.L., & Dovidio, J.F. (2000). *Reducing intergroup bias: The common ingroup identity model.* Philadelphia, PA: Psychology Press.

Hewstone, M., & Swart, H. (2011). Fifty-odd years of intergroup contact: From hypothesis to integrated theory. *British Journal of Social Psychology, 50,* 374–86. doi: 10.1111/j.2044-8309.2011.02047.x

Hopkins, N., & Kahani-Hopkins, V. (2006). Minority group members' theories of intergroup contact: A case study of British Muslims' conceptualizations of Islamophobia and social change. *British Journal of Social Psychology, 45,* 245–64. doi: 10.1348/014466605X48583

Jackman, M.R. (1994). *The velvet glove: Paternalism and conflict in gender, class, and race relations.* Berkeley, CA: University of California Press.

Killen, M., Hitti, A., & Mulvey, K.L. (2014). Social development and intergroup relations. In J. Simpson & J.F. Dovidio (Eds.), *APA Handbook of personality and social psychology, Vol. 2, Interpersonal relations and group processes* (pp. 177–201). Washington, DC: American Psychological Association Press.

Maoz, I. (2011). Does contact work in protracted asymmetrical conflict? Appraising 20 years of reconciliation-aimed encounters between Israeli Arabs and Palestinians. *Journal of Peace Research, 48,* 115–25. doi: 10.1177/0022343310389506

Minard, R.D. (1952/2008). Race relations in the Pocahontas coal field. *Journal of Social Issues, 8,* 29–44. doi: 10.1111/j.1540-4560.1952.tb01592.x

Paolini, S., Harwood, J., & Rubin, M. (2010). Negative intergroup contact makes group memberships salient: Explaining why intergroup conflict endures. *Personality and Social Psychology Bulletin, 36,* 1723–38. doi: 10.1177/0146167210388667

Paolini, S., & McIntyre, K. (2016). Several reasons why evil is stronger than good in intergroup relations: Taking tests of negative valence asymmetry from the field back to the laboratory. *Under review.*

Pettigrew, T.F. (1969). Racially separate or together? *Journal of Social Issues, 25,* 43–69. doi: 10.1111/j.1540-4560.1969.tb02577.x

Pettigrew, T.F. (1998). Intergroup contact theory. *Annual Review of Psychology, 49,* 65–85. doi: 10.1146/annurev.psych.49.1.65

Pettigrew, T.F., & Tropp, L.R. (2006). A meta-analytical test of the intergroup contact theory. *Journal of Personality and Social Psychology, 90,* 751–83. doi: 10.1037/0022-3514.90.5.751

Pettigrew, T.F., & Tropp, L.R. (2008). How does intergroup contact reduce prejudice? Meta-analytic tests of three mediators. *European Journal of Social Psychology, 38,* 922–34. doi: 10.1002/ejsp.504

Pickren, W.E. (Ed.) (2004). *Fifty years on: Brown v. Board of Education and Psychology, 1954–2004* (Vol.. 59). Washington, DC: American Psychologist.

Ruck, M., Park, H., Crystal, D., & Killen, M. (2015). Intergroup contact is related to evaluations of interracial peer exclusion in suburban and urban Africa American youth. *Journal of Youth and Adolescence, 44*, 1226–40. doi: 10.1007/s10964-014-0227-3

Schofield, J.W., & Hausmann, L.R.M. (2004). School desegregation and social science research. *American Psychologist, 59*, 538–46. doi: 10.1037/0003-066X.59.6.538

Star, S.A., Williams, R.M., & Stouffer, S.A. (1958). Negro infantry platoons in white companies. In E.E. Maccoby, T. Newcomb, & E.L. Hartley (Eds.), *Readings in social psychology*, (pp. 596–601). New York, NY: Holt, Rhinehart and Winston.

Stephan, W.G., & Stephan, C.W. (1984). The role of ignorance in intergroup relations. In N. Miller & M.B. Brewer (Eds.), *Groups in contact: A psychology of desegregation* (pp. 229–57). Orlando, FL: Academic Press.

Wilder, D.A. (1984). Intergroup contact: The typical member and the exception to the rule. *Journal of Experimental Social Psychology, 20*, 177–94. doi: 10.1016/0022-1031 (84)90019-2.

Wright, S.C. & Lubensky, M. (2009). The struggle for social equality: Collective action vs. prejudice reduction. In S. Demoulin, J.P. Leyens, & J.F. Dovidio (Eds.), *Intergroup misunderstandings: Impact of divergent social realities* (pp. 291–310). New York, NY: Psychology Press.

INDEX